# GAZING AT NEIGHBOURS

**Bishwanath Ghosh**, born in Kanpur on 26 December 1970, is the author of the hugely popular *Chai, Chai: Travels in Places Where You Stop but Never Get Off*. He's also a Hindi poet, who has two well-received compilations—*Jiyo Banaras* and *Tedhi-Medhi Lakeeren*—to his credit. His other books include *Tamarind City: Where Modern India Began*; *Longing, Belonging: An Outsider at Home in Calcutta* and *Aimless in Banaras: Wanderings in India's Holiest City*. He is an Associate Editor with *The Hindu* newspaper and lives in Calcutta.

BISHWANATH GHOSH

# GAZING AT NEIGHBOURS

## Travels Along the Line That Partitioned India

First published by Tranquebar, an imprint of Westland Publications Pvt ltd, in 2017

Published by Westland Non-Fiction, an imprint of Westland Books, a division of Nasadiya Technologies Private Limited, in 2024

No. 269/2B, First Floor, 'Irai Arul', Vimalraj Street, Nethaji Nagar, Alapakkam Main Road, Maduravoyal, Chennai 600095

Westland, the Westland logo, Westland Non-Fiction and the Westland Non-Fiction logo are the trademarks of Nasadiya Technologies Private Limited, or its affiliates.



ISBN: 9789360458980

10 9 8 7 6 5 4 3 2 1



Typeset by SÜRYA, New Delhi

Printed at Manipal Technologies Limited, Manipal

*For*
*Tarun Gautam*
*Q. Rumman Dastgir*
*Lakshya Mehta*
*in friendship*

# Contents

# Prologue

No other seemingly benign exercise has such far-reaching consequences as drawing a line on a map. On the face of it, you merely put pencil to paper, but the line actually runs through towns, villages, valleys, farmlands, forests, rivers, ponds—and people.

Sometimes those assigned to run the pencil do so, without realising the impact their line is going to have on humankind. Sir Cyril Radcliffe was one of them.

Sir Cyril had built a formidable reputation in Britain as a barrister before he went down in history as probably the world's most infamous cartographer. In July 1947, he was summoned to New Delhi and given five weeks to partition India. Accordingly, he drew two lines on its map. One of the lines, 553 kilometres long, created the province of West Punjab; the other, 4,096 kilometres long, carved out a province called East Bengal. They both joined the newborn nation of Pakistan—an event that saw fifteen million people displaced and over one million dead.

An equally horrifying number of people were killed and many hundreds of thousands of women raped in 1971 when East Bengal, rechristened East Pakistan in 1956, fought to free itself from Pakistan and became an independent nation called Bangladesh—but that's a different story.

By the time I was born—a day after the Christmas of 1970, in the city of Kanpur—India had already been partitioned for nearly a quarter of a century. But in spite of being comfortably insulated from the event by time and distance, I grew up amidst constant reminders that something terrible called Partition had happened.

I grew up in a neighbourhood not very far from the banks of the Ganga, and in the market nearest to our home nearly all the shops were owned by Punjabis who had been uprooted from what had become Pakistan. They were seen as trespassers and not one of us: 'us' being the people who, unlike them, had willingly migrated (as opposed to being driven away) to Kanpur, from other parts of India (as opposed to Pakistan) in search of a living. To be driven out of your home was a matter of shame.

One evening—I must have been around sixteen then—a classmate and I were out on a stroll in that market when he drew my attention to a popular electronics shop: 'You see that old man at the cash counter? He came penniless from Pakistan and used to repair punctures for a living. Today he owns that bloody shop!'

Looking back, I understand the resentment. A penniless refugee, who once fixed punctures in bicycle tyres, had become prosperous, whereas our fathers, who were never penniless, still earned only a fraction of what he now made every month.

Today if I were to walk through the same market—I

still do once in a while when I visit home—I would look at the old man with respect, bearing in mind the years of humiliation and hardship he must have endured before coming to own a large electronics shop. But he is no more.

Most refugees who went through the horrors of Partition as adults have passed on. The succeeding generations have long grown roots in India. They are now old-timers in cities where their forefathers had arrived homeless and penniless, and someday their grandchildren will grow up reading about Partition with the same detachment of someone never affected by it.

The surgical scars, however, remain—and will remain as long as India, Pakistan, and Bangladesh exist as separate countries. The scars, considered together, are called the Radcliffe Line. In the places it runs through, the line is referred to variously as zero line, boundary line, international border, or simply, border. Here, barbed wires have split families; concrete pillars have turned neighbours into foreigners; people follow restrictions which their countrymen elsewhere don't, and wish sometimes silently, and sometimes aloud, that the line did not exist.

The following pages describe my travels along the scars. I had read and watched enough about the horrors inflicted on humankind by the creation of the Radcliffe Line to be curious to take a look at the line itself. It turned out to be an imaginary line though.

# West

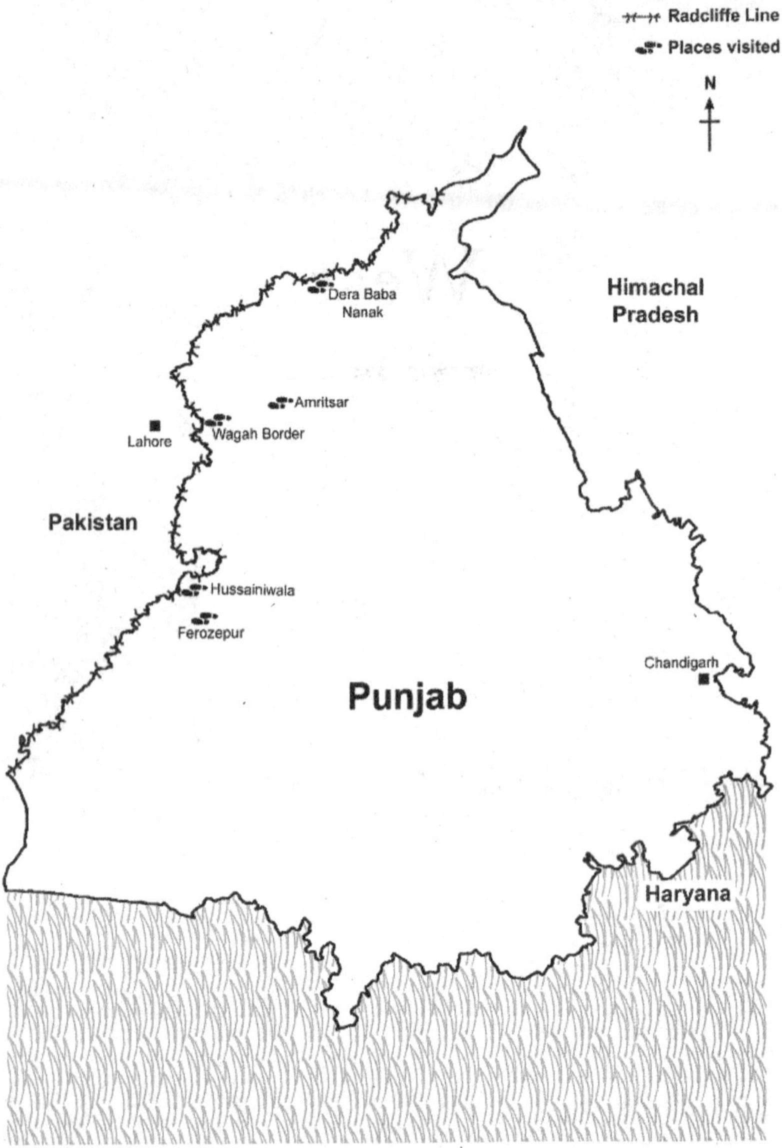


This map is not to scale and its borders have not been verified or authenticated independently.

# 1

Amritsar turned out to be grey—not sunbathed green, as I had always imagined Punjab to be—when the plane touched down that August morning. Through raindrops trickling down the aircraft window, I tried to recognise the land I had known only from books and films. But an airfield hardly lets on anything about the city it lets you into.

I had not been sure if Amritsar even had an airport, though common sense suggested that the home to the holiest shrine of the Sikhs was unlikely to be without one. It turned out that the airport, barely ten years old and named after Guru Ram Das, the fourth Sikh guru, was already a pulse point on the international aviation circuit.

I was sitting in a 787 Dreamliner, a luxury that domestic fliers stumble upon only rarely. It had come to Amritsar from Birmingham via Delhi, where I had boarded. And now as the plane came to a halt and I stood up to claim my bag from the overhead bin, I noticed that the three women in the row behind whose non-stop chattering had given me company—and a mild headache—during the hour-long journey were not British but Punjabis. I should have known. The British almost never get into an animated conversation in public. Perhaps the women were returning home after a long gap and could not contain their excitement.

The Dreamliner had played host to Indian excitement all along its flight, and now, when stationary, it was hostage to Indian impatience. Passengers in India rise from their seats the moment the aircraft comes to a halt, and they continue to stand, often uncomfortably, until the doors open. Perhaps they believe that they can hasten their exit by standing up rather than staying seated.

Only one family clung to its seats while the rest stood. It was evidently a Pakistani family: two large men clad in salwar-kameez and three women wearing burqas but with their faces uncovered. Since one of the men wore a surgical mask, I could safely assume that they were headed home after his treatment in an Indian hospital. Their presence in the aircraft reminded me that Amritsar bordered Pakistan, and that I had come to the city only because it sat on the border.

What caught my eye, as soon as I walked into the arrival hall, was a large advertisement for Aeroplane brand of basmati rice. I had always thought of Punjab as a proud producer—and consumer—of wheat. While it is true that Punjab also grows some of the finest rice available in India, I didn't quite expect a rice billboard welcoming me into the state. Producers of Aeroplane obviously wanted to strike a chord with those arriving in Amritsar in an aeroplane.

The clouds had cleared, exposing a rather ruthless sun, by the time I booked a cab and stepped out of the airport. The driver, who looked just out of college and could have been a hero in Punjabi films—stubble-wearing, slim and handsome—cheerfully held open the door for me, as if I was a familiar face.

Since the driver was young and friendly, not elderly or indifferent, I asked him if we could stop by the road for a few minutes once we were out of the airport so that I could have a quick smoke. I had had my last cigarette several hours ago, and since Sikhism strictly prohibits smoking, I wasn't sure when I would get the opportunity to light up again.

'Why, you can smoke inside the car,' he said.

'Are you sure?'

'Yes, just roll down the window.'

Even though deeply gratified, I realised I still had a problem: I had no matchbox or lighter.

'Not to worry,' he assured me, 'we will find a shop.'

Soon we approached a group of labourers gathered by the road. The driver stopped next to them and I asked for a matchbox. 'Who has a matchbox,' they asked one another. They were all from Bihar. The one who eventually produced a matchbox asked, 'Will I get a cigarette in return?'

I thought he was being cheeky, but my driver gave me a look that said, 'You were desperate for a smoke and he is helping you light your cigarette. Will you be any poorer if you parted with one?' So I handed the labourer a cigarette and, with the window rolled down, sped in the direction of the city.

Amritsar: pool of nectar. Every Indian who has been to school is familiar with the name. The more informed will also know that if you stir the pool with a little force, the nectar will be stained red, for there is a lot of blood settled at the bottom.

Nearly 400 killed in 1919 when, on the day of Baisakhi, Brigadier-General Reginald Dyer led his troops through a narrow lane into Jallianwala Bagh, near the Golden Temple, and opened fire on a peaceful congregation.

Nearly 600 killed in 1984 when, in June that year, the then prime minister, Indira Gandhi, ordered the storming of the Golden Temple by the Indian Army to flush out Sikh separatists entrenched there. The army action, codenamed Operation Blue Star, angered Sikhs across the world and became the cause of her assassination by her two Sikh bodyguards later that year. Her killing, in turn, led to thousands of Sikhs being murdered by hoodlums across north India.

Almost midway between the two bloody smudges on the calendar, sticks out an indelible blot: the year 1947, when about a million people got butchered across Punjab as the prosperous province was split between India and Pakistan, shifting Amritsar's location from the heart of the state to the border.

The border crossing with Pakistan, the driver said, lay 32 kilometres from downtown Amritsar. He was referring to what is popularly known as the 'Wagah border,' where every evening, shortly before sunset, exceptionally tall sentries from both countries take part in a choreographed confrontation before lowering their respective flags. It's a spectacle watched by thousands of Indians and Pakistanis from their respective soils.

'I have relatives living in villages on the border,' he said. 'You know, they live on the Indian side but their fields are across the barbed-wire fence.'

'Will you take me there?'

'Where? Wagah border?'

'Yes, and to the villages where your relatives live.'

'But I will be off duty as soon as I drop you. I will have to hand over the vehicle.'

'Can't you find me another taxi and come along with me?'

'Good idea! I haven't seen my sister in three months. So I will drop you and come back to the hotel in, say, about two hours?'

'That would be perfect. What's your name?'

'Husanjeet. Husanjeet Singh.'

At the hotel, the young petite receptionist with blue eyelids informed me that I had been upgraded to the 'executive suite'—at no extra cost.

But the room boy who was to show me into the suite was nowhere to be seen. When he finally appeared, after about ten minutes, Ms Blue Eyelids scolded him under her breath, without changing the polite expression on her face: 'Where the hell were you lying dead? The guest has been standing on my head forever.'

That was the literal translation of the scolding, meted out in Hindi. The English equivalent of the rebuke would have sounded something like this: 'Where the hell had you disappeared? The guest has been breathing down my neck forever.'

I was neither standing on her head nor breathing down her neck. I was merely looking around, at the various certificates the hotel had earned, at the decorations, at the idol of Ganesha, and sometimes, yes, at her blue eyeshadow. 'Enjoy your stay, sir,' she smiled as the room boy led me to the elevator. I actually liked her.

I also instantly liked the room: nothing fancy, but large and well-lit, welcoming enough to a first-timer in the city. The centre table had a clean ashtray, and the toilet seat was secured by the sanitised-for-your-protection paper band.

The menu-book on the dresser had an entire page devoted to paneer dishes, apart from the standard fare offered by nearly every hotel across the country. I ordered rice and dal, the simplest and least oily of meals, and the rice, when it came, turned out to be basmati. Was I eating Aeroplane?

I was on the Grand Trunk Road, or GT Road—'such a river of life,' as Rudyard Kipling described it, 'as nowhere else exists in the world.'

The ancient road runs almost parallel to the length of the mighty Himalayas, sweeping down from the Khyber Pass all the way to Chittagong. After Partition, its extremities in India came to lie at the Wagah border in the west and Petrapole in the east.

Wagah itself lies in Pakistan. It's the village located just across the iron gates where the choreographed confrontation takes place every evening. The last village on the Indian side happens to be Attari, better known for the railway station that saw the arrival and departure of corpse-laden trains during Partition and that today connects India and Pakistan by rail.

The car Husanjeet had hired for me belonged to his friend Sunny, another young man with a stubble, who wore a coloured tattoo—a rose—on his neck. Until three months ago, he too had worked for the same taxi company as Husanjeet, when he met with an accident.

'Today I am driving after a long time,' Sunny said. 'Until the other day I could barely walk, so badly injured I was.'

'How did the accident happen?' I asked him, suddenly wondering whether it was a good idea to be in his car.

'I was sitting on a bike parked outside my house. A tractor was passing by, driven by a chap who clearly didn't know how to drive a tractor, and he rammed straight into me,' he said.

The wall between passenger and driver had come tumbling down. The trip was more like an outing of friends. Punjabi songs played on the car speakers, the volume too loud for my comfort, but still a perfect background sound for the terrain we drove through.

On one occasion I asked Sunny to slow down for a moment so that I could take pictures of a terracotta-coloured building we were passing by. So grand was it architecturally—a blend of Sikh and Mughal styles, to my untrained eye—that it stood like a mirage in the rustic landscape. It looked like a palace, grander than many palaces I had seen, and such was its expanse that it remained in the frame of my phone camera almost forever. It turned out to be the Khalsa College.

In a setting so Punjabi, I found something amiss. Not many men wore turbans. One would have spotted more turbans in Delhi in the few hours that I had been in Amritsar. Or was I imagining the lack of turbaned men? Or maybe I had come to the spiritual home of the Sikhs, with the unfair expectation that all men in the town wore turbans.

I decided to ask Husanjeet about it.

'If you visit the area around the Golden Temple,' he said, 'you will find almost everybody wearing a turban.'

'What about the rest of Amritsar?'

'Sir, it is the question of comfort, and sometimes style,' he replied.

'Is it stylish not to wear a turban?'

'Boys of my generation think so,' he laughed. 'My father wears a turban though.'

'So you are a Sikh who doesn't like to wear a turban?'

'Why only me, even him'—Husanjeet pointed at Sunny—'he is also a Sikh who gave up wearing a turban long ago.'

Sunny grinned. He turned out to be a good driver: calm, steady, confident. Unlike Husanjeet, who had discarded his uniform for a black T-shirt and jeans, Sunny was dressed like the quintessential Punjabi villager, wearing a long-sleeved, collared kurta and salwar.

If I were to make a Punjabi film, I would show the girl romancing the bubbly Husanjeet in the first half and falling in love with Sunny—and eventually marrying him—in the second. But right now, they were the scriptwriters of my trip to the border.

# 2

I have an emotional attachment with the GT Road.

I grew up by this 'river of life', in the city of Kanpur, and also set foot on it countless times during my early years as a journalist in Delhi, and during childhood visits to relatives living around Calcutta.

Then there was this time when, emerging from Mughal Sarai station on a cycle-rickshaw, I found myself to be the sole commuter on it, searching for a hotel at four in the morning—I had gone there to collect material for my first book and practically lived on the GT Road for three days.

But never had I imagined that someday, while travelling on this road, I would approach a signboard that would place Lahore only 24 kilometres away and the India-Pakistan border a mere two. Reaching the border-crossing at Wagah was going to be like the end of a lifelong quest: I was going to see for myself the spot where the road terminated or, should we say, entered India.

Shortly afterwards came a signboard that announced the village of Attari.

'This is the way to the Attari station,' said Husanjeet, pointing left to a road branching off the 'river of life'.

'Can we visit the station on our way back?'

'If we are not too late,' he said. 'It's only a station, there's nothing to see.'

'I would like to see it.'

Minutes later Sunny brought the car to a halt. We found ourselves parked outside a thoughtfully-constructed red-brick building that belonged more to a fashionable street in a city rather than the rural landscape of a border crossing. But it clearly intended to be there and nowhere else, for it was named Sarhad, the Urdu word for border.

It turned out to be a restaurant-cum-boutique—it called itself 'the food and culture park'—and a banner on the glass door of the boutique advertised women's ethnic wear: 'Exclusive Pakistani dresses only at Sarhad.' All three of us used its restroom—no one questioned us—and then took pictures against a mural, depicting the horrors of Partition, in its forecourt.

We got into the car again and just when we were about to be waved down by a party of policemen—Independence Day was three days away and every vehicle headed for the border crossing was being checked—Sunny calmly turned right, into the fields of ripening paddy, where a winding path led to the homes of Husanjeet's relatives who lived along the barbed-wire fence.

'The harvest will begin exactly a month from now,' Husanjeet said. I didn't rule out some of the produce being packaged as Aeroplane.

The monotony of the green landscape was broken occasionally by clusters of houses, grocery shops, and modest school buildings. A picture-postcard Punjab countryside one saw in Hindi films, a picture of prosperity and not poverty.

Eventually we came across a canal and Sunny stopped the car. Husanjeet and I got off. We were now in the village of Udhar Dhaliwal and from the canal, I was told, the house of Husanjeet's aunt was just about a minute's drive away.

By now the barbed-wire fence had come into view, barely 200 metres away, standing as a partition between the green paddies. And so, for the first time in my life I set eyes on the physical border between any two countries.

Since the two countries happened to be India and Pakistan, the fence not only represented the border but an emotion, a symbol of heartbreak as well as hostility: heartbreak for those who see Pakistan as the land of their ancestors, hostility for those who consider it an evil neighbour.

The truth is that the fence, visible even from outer space when the floodlights come on after sunset, is not the actual border between India and Pakistan. The real boundary, as drawn by Sir Cyril Radcliffe, remains an imaginary line that connects the demarcating pillars implanted on the fertile soil of Punjab (and also Bengal) after Partition.

Since an agreement between the two countries prohibits all construction within 150 yards on either side of the Radcliffe Line, the fence, erected by the Border Security Force or BSF, stands well within the Indian side. So there's still an Indian strip of land across the fence, seamlessly joining Pakistani territory—it's on this strip that Indian farmers, like Husanjeet's relatives, grow their crops.

'We stopped here because I wanted to show you the *nullah*,' Husanjeet said, referring to the canal. 'It connects to Pakistan and is used for smuggling heroin packets. That's what we have heard, none of us has ever seen anything.'

A brick path ran parallel to the canal, and the two were separated by a bushy strip of land which, I found out, camouflaged bunkers. Each bunker was identified by a set of numbers painted on its concrete inlet. I thought of stepping into one but instantly decided against it. They must have been last occupied in 1971, when I had just been born, and I had no idea what I was going to find inside. They might have been occupied even during the Kargil War in 1999, but I wasn't very sure of that because the three-month conflict had remained confined to Kashmir.

'Go in, nothing to worry,' Husanjeet urged me. 'Soldiers come here every now and then to take a look.'

'Do they look into the bunkers?'

'I am sure they do.'

'Why don't you come along with me?'

'No, I think we must get going.'

What prevented me from stepping into a bunker was the fear of snakes. Soldiers coming this way on periodic inspection would not consider a snake, if at all they found one, to be an unwelcome guest. For me, however, the prospect of bumping into an angry cobra was far more terrifying than facing an enemy soldier. I could at least talk to the enemy, perhaps even talk my way out of a situation, but how would I explain myself to an alarmed snake?

I also understood why Husanjeet did not want to accompany me into the bunker. He wasn't a journalist like me, only a taxi-driver visiting his elder sister, who happened to live in a sensitive area where civilians are generally under watch. He did not wish to bring any trouble to his sister's family.

We got back into the car and in a minute arrived at his sister's place. Hugs were exchanged, kisses planted on foreheads, pairs of feet touched. I watched the family reunion from a distance. And then everyone's attention turned on me. I felt like a groom as I was led in.

The house was large. A similar construction in the heart of a city would be called palatial. I walked into a hall where, in an alcove, children sat around a TV set watching a Shah Rukh Khan film. The hall, adorned with pictures of Guru Nanak, opened into several rooms. I was shown into the drawing room.

I had barely taken my seat when the refreshments arrived, brought in by Husanjeet's sister. Sweets, savouries, and coffee. I had expected *lassi*.

Husanjeet respectfully introduced me to the sister's turbaned husband who sat in front me on a bed, 'He is Sardar Ranjit Singhji.'

Ranjit Singh, born in 1976, turned out to be the eldest male member in that house. Next to him sat his younger brother, Daljit Singh, born in 1979. They had a sister, younger to both, who was married and lived in Amritsar. Their father died two years ago at the age of seventy—he must have been about four at the time of Partition. Their mother, who lived with them, was sixty-five, born three years after Partition.

It was their grandfather who had settled in this village after leaving behind their ancestral home, in a village near Lahore, during Partition. The grandfather had five sons, and over time each of the five sons built a house of his own. The five families formed a village within a village, and that's how it remains even today. Between them they own seven tractors, eighty buffaloes and 200 *killa* of agricultural land, about 600 acres in my calculation, across the barbed fence.

'So there is nobody in the family who can recall Partition?' I asked Ranjit Singh.

'*Nahin ji*, there is nobody,' he said. 'My father, had he been alive, would have given you more information. He was only a child during Partition, but later on he travelled a lot in Pakistan. He even spent five years in a prison there.'

'Five years in a Pakistani prison? Why?'

'Somebody got him falsely implicated. We don't know what really happened.'

Ranjit Singh need not have parted with that information. I could have done without it. But he was a simple villager, telling me all that he knew.

'Why did your father keep going to Pakistan?'

'To travel, to visit family friends. He loved travelling.'

'Was it that easy to travel to Pakistan?'

'During my father's time, yes. You could just walk across the border. Who was there to stop us villagers? The barbed wires came up only in 1986.'

'Do you have memories of the time before the fence was erected?'

'Nothing that stands out, except that it was all open. My father and my uncles could freely go to the fields. Today we need to show identity cards to cross the fence, and are permitted to work there only between eight in the morning and five in the evening. We need to be home by six, because the whole area along the fence comes under curfew at six.'

His brother Daljit said, 'Anybody going near the fence after six can be shot.'

'Does that mean you can't venture out of home after six?' I asked.

'We can,' Ranjit Singh replied, 'but we need to stick to the main road. As long as we don't behave in a manner that arouses suspicion, there is no problem. The border is notorious for smuggling of heroin,' he said.

'How does it get smuggled?'

'From what I have heard, sometimes it is pushed across the fence through pipes, sometimes thrown over the fence. Who knows what's true. We deliberately don't show curiosity in these matters because we need access to our fields and don't want to get on the wrong side of the BSF.'

Ranjit Singh, even though he did not hesitate to tell me that his father had spent five years in a Pakistani prison, was clearly uncomfortable talking about the smuggling. A farmer like him, working across the fence and coming into direct contact with the Pakistani soil (Pakistan has no fence of its own) on a daily basis, was likely to have at least some knowledge about the manner in which heroin is pushed through the border. But he sought to insulate himself from the whole smuggling business with the 'see no evil, hear no evil, speak no evil' policy. He seemed to me the quintessential Sikh farmer: honest, good-natured and proud to live by his labour. Even the salwar-kameez he wore was sweat-soaked and soiled. In all likelihood, he had hurried back from the field because he had been told of our arrival.

I asked him to take me to the terrace for a glimpse of Pakistan. It was highly unlikely that I would ever set foot on its soil, unless I got lucky someday. For an Indian, it can be easier getting into Panama than Pakistan.

The terrace turned out to be a furnace. The sun, even though it had begun its downward climb, was brutal—but it bounced happiness off the carpet of crops: hardly the place that was soaked in blood seventy years ago. I could even visualise a dance sequence being filmed, the hero and heroine surrounded by dozens of extras dressed as village belles, garnishing the green with their colourful costumes. As for the barbed wires, they could have been guarding the property of a rich farmer.

But no, the fence had an official look about it.

'So all that is our land, from there to there,' Ranjit Singh's index finger moved to cover a long stretch of green across the fence. And you see that small tree? Beyond that tree is all Pakistan.'

My eyes, however, couldn't tell the merger, rather the separation, between India and Pakistan. The land leading up to the small tree as well as the portion beyond it looked the same. But then, Partition is about drawing a line across sameness.

'How are your fields separated from theirs?' I asked him.

'There are two paths running between our fields, one belongs to us and the other to them. Sometimes, when the path on our side is waterlogged, we use theirs to reach our fields.'

'And they allow you?'

'Why not? There is no hostility between villagers. People imagine there is hostility because of what they see in Wagah'—he was referring to the flag-lowering ceremony—'but here we live peacefully.'

'You are friends with Pakistani farmers, then?'

'Not friends, but not enemies either. I greet them whenever I run into them and enquire about their well-being. They also greet me, "*Sardarji, ki haal chaal*?" Since the BSF tells us to keep the interactions to a minimum, we mostly mind our business.'

I was about to ask him how the village had fared during the wars in 1965 and 71 but realized that he wasn't even born then. 'How was it during the Kargil War?' I asked.

'This entire place was mined,' Ranjit Singh turned around to indicate a long stretch behind his house. 'But no fighting happened here. We continued going to the fields as usual. Not a day's work missed.'

As I followed his finger I noticed the golden dome of a gurdwara adjacent to the house. We walked across the terrace to take a look. It seemed like a new construction.

'We built it just three years ago,' Ranjit Singh said.

'It used to be a mosque before Partition and was lying abandoned.'

'No one objected when you converted it into a gurudwara?'

'Who will object? There are no Muslims living here.'

I suddenly found my question silly. The whole idea behind Partition was that people leave everything behind—including their places of worship—and start life from scratch across the newly-drawn border.

'You will hardly find Muslims in Punjab,' Husanjeet stepped in, 'they all went to the other side.'

It occurred to me that in some corner of Pakistan, a Muslim family must be telling their children, 'Our ancestral village is Udhar Dhaliwal, near Amritsar. Your great-grandfather had a big house there, next to a mosque. One day he had to leave everything behind.'

# 3

Today when you imagine pre-Partition India, you most likely picture the combined maps of India, Pakistan and Bangladesh.

But British India was much smaller, about half the size of what the three countries put together on the map would look like. The remaining half of the subcontinent was made up of princely states—more than 560 of them—whose rulers had accepted the British as their masters and in return had been allowed to remain the masters of their respective states. These included Kashmir and Hyderabad, each almost as large as Great Britain. Then there was Goa, which belonged to Portugal, and the tiny French pockets in Bengal and in south India.

What was partitioned, therefore, was British India, more specifically two of its most fertile provinces, Punjab and Bengal. But what led India to be partitioned?

The question has been answered countless times before and, needlessly to say, will be answered countless times in the future. Partition, as a subject for research, is far from dead, even though most people with distinct memories of it are.

But in spite of countless books and films on Partition, the question still hasn't found an answer that can be considered satisfactory and acceptable by one and all, without further questions being raised. That's because Partition wasn't as simple as two units of hydrogen combining with one unit of oxygen to form water, but the result of a far more complex chemical reaction.

It truly was about chemistry, more than anything else—the chemistry between Hindus and Muslims; the chemistry between Mahatma Gandhi and Jawaharlal Nehru; the chemistry between Nehru and Muhammad Ali Jinnah; the chemistry between Lord Mountbatten and Jinnah; the chemistry between Mountbatten and Nehru; and so forth. The more you read about it the more you realize that you cannot hold one particular leader responsible for the way things turned out once it became certain that Britain, too bankrupt after the Second World War, to hold onto its colonies, was going to pull out of India.

Many in India, even today, thoughtlessly blame Gandhi for Partition, the charge against him being that he did not stop it. The truth is that Gandhi had very little say in the months leading to Partition, when the political landscape was dominated by Nehru and Jinnah, the public faces, respectively, of the Congress and the Muslim League.

There was a time when Jinnah strongly advocated Hindu-Muslim unity, which he believed held the key to *swaraj*, or self-rule. All he wanted was the Hindu-dominated Congress to acknowledge the Muslim League as the sole representative of India's Muslims. But Nehru considered the Congress to be the sole voice of India, its Muslims included. He saw the fight for independence as a direct contest between the British and the Congress—a duel in which Jinnah or the Muslim League had no significant role to play.

Jinnah, slighted and eager to be counted, worked on expanding the base of his party, and there finally came a time when he became politically strong enough to declare that the 90 million Muslims in India were not a minority but a nation, and that no way would he allow them to be dominated by the 220 million Hindus when the British left. To demonstrate his strength, he called for a general strike on 16 August 1946, naming it Direct Action Day. Bengal, at the time, was ruled by the Muslim League and tens of thousands of its supporters gathered at the Maidan in Calcutta to listen to their leaders speak in support of the creation of Pakistan.

Even before the rally could end, the thuggish lot in the audience began grouping into mobs and descended on Hindu neighbourhoods with iron bars and other crude weapons. Retaliation by the Hindus was swift, and the manslaughter lasted three days. At least 5,000 were butchered in what came to be known as the Great Calcutta Killings. Vultures came to be the best-fed guests of famine-stricken Calcutta during the carnage.

The bloodbath in Calcutta, and the riots it set off in other parts of Bengal and Bihar, drove home Jinnah's point to the British: that leaving behind Hindus and Muslims together in an undivided India could result in a civil war.

On 3 June 1947, Britain formally declared that a new country called Pakistan would be carved out of India. The hands of the clock moved swiftly thereafter.

While most of the eleven British India provinces were either predominantly-Hindu or predominantly-Muslim and therefore not contested, Punjab and Bengal had almost equal number of Muslims and non-Muslims, with the former outnumbering the latter by a slender margin in both. The legislative assemblies of these two provinces were asked to vote on Partition, and the majority in both voted in favour. A referendum was also held in Sylhet, a predominantly-Muslim district in predominantly non-Muslim Assam, and there too a majority of its citizens voted to merge with Pakistan's side of Bengal.

Finally, on July 4, Britain introduced the Indian Independence Bill in its parliament and fixed August 15 as the date of independence. On the same day it entrusted Sir Cyril Radcliffe, an eminent barrister, with the task of drawing boundaries across Punjab and Bengal.

Radcliffe, who had never travelled east of Paris, arrived in New Delhi on July 8, with precisely five weeks at his disposal to split one people into two nationalities. By then violence had already begun in Punjab, with Muslims raiding Sikh villages and subsequently Sikhs organising themselves to carry out retaliatory attacks, and it wasn't long before riots broke out in its cities, especially the holy Amritsar and beautiful Lahore.

Radcliffe completed his assignment on August 12 and within three days an Independent India—without Kashmir,

Hyderabad and over 500 other princely states in its fold—came into being. At the time of its birth, it had no idea where its borders with Pakistan lay.

Mountbatten, fearing that the violence in Punjab would explode into a civil war, had chosen not to publicise Radcliffe's maps until power had been handed over to the two countries so that Britain would no longer be responsible for maintaining law and order in the subcontinent. He made them public only on August 17.

By then Radcliffe was back in London. He refused to accept his fee for the assignment, so disgusted was he by the violence caused due to Partition, and went on to burn all papers related to it. The creation of the two countries resulted in the death of one million and displacement of another 12 million.

Gandhi, who was away in Bengal on the day of Independence, trying to broker peace between the Muslims and Hindus of Noakhali, was quoted by newspapers as saying, 'Partition is bad, but whatever is past is past. We have only to look to the future.'

India, today, has nearly as many Muslims as Pakistan does. Problems erupt from time to time, peace returns soon after, and India goes on. Could an undivided India also have gone on?

Imagine Nehru, a secular Hindu, as the prime minister, and Jinnah, a secular Muslim, as the deputy prime minister—or even the other way round. And imagine the size of such an India and the richness of its culture and the clout it would have wielded in the world. But individual ambitions and egos often stand in the way of what can be an ideal arrangement. The price of Partition was eventually paid by millions of commoners, who overnight became outsiders in their own country.

But while independent India was born a secular nation, on the cradle of anti-British sentiments, Pakistan turned out to be a product of anti-India sentiments. Because of this inherent animosity towards its Hindu-majority neighbour, it was only a matter of time before the army became the most powerful institution in that country.

Pakistan had another inherent flaw, a geographical one. A part of it lay northwest of India and another on the eastern extremity of India. Religion was supposed to keep the two united, but culturally they were too disparate to be together for long.

East Pakistan—where the majority of the combined Pakistan's population lived, most of them being poetry-loving Bengalis—deeply resented its subjugation by West Pakistan, where the political power was centred, resting mainly in the hands of martial races dominated by the Punjabis and Pathans.

When the East finally revolted in 1971, the West sent in the army, which went about killing men and raping women with impunity. With help from India, East Pakistan broke away from West Pakistan to become Bangladesh.

Today's Pakistan is only West Pakistan: a fragile democracy squeezed between the all-powerful army and

Islamic fundamentalists, something the anglicised, cigar-smoking Muhammad Ali Jinnah wouldn't have dreamt of.

While Pakistan may have been a creation of Jinnah, the idea did not originate in his head. A separate province for Muslims in northwest India was first proposed in 1930 by his friend, the poet-politician Muhammad Iqbal, who many years earlier had composed a poem that continues to be India's most popular patriotic song:

*'Saare jahaan se achha, Hindostan hamara hamara'*—In the entire world our Hindustan is the best.

# 4

On the way back to GT Road from Ranjit Singh's home, we stopped at another village, Bachiwind, where Husanjeet's aunt lived.

Once again hugs were exchanged and the feet of the elderly touched. These reunions radiated such pure joy that I felt a bit left out. I have felt such joy only as a child; as a grown-up I usually kept aloof from demonstrative relatives and now it is too late in the day for noisy reunions.

We sat in the well-furnished drawing room along with Vijender, the aunt's son, who must have been in his early thirties. He, like Husanjeet, kept his hair short and sported a groomed stubble. He eyed me with curious amusement and kept his gaze fixed on me. His son, about four years old, fiddled with the father's mobile phone.

'So what is it like to be living right on the border?' I asked Vijender.

The child picked up the word and started chanting, 'Border! Border! Border! Border!'

'It is the same as living anywhere else,' Vijender replied after the child had quietened down. 'Only that we are never short of light because the fence is lit up.'

Refreshments were placed on the table: samosas, laddoos, potato wafers, peanuts and milky tea.

'So what do you do?' I asked him.

Husanjeet spoke instead, 'His family also owns land across the fence. They are all into agriculture.'

Vijender had very little to say on his own. Wearing a faint smile, he kept eyeing me, as if he had met me before and was now trying to recall where.

'Have you ever seen smugglers at work?' I asked him.

Once again, Husanjeet spoke on his behalf, 'See, as my brother-in-law just told you, these people must vacate their fields by five. They don't know what goes on in their fields after five. If smugglers come at night, it is not their problem. It is the BSF's problem.'

We soon slipped into an uncomfortable silence. I suddenly didn't know what to ask my host, even though he lived right along the fence that is visible at nights from outer space. The fence, a source of excitement for me, was a fact of life for him. He seemed to have no feelings towards it; if anything, he might wish it didn't exist, sparing him the trouble of showing his identity card to the BSF men each time he walked across to his fields and back. Even that process—showing his ID and sticking to timings—must be a way of life for him.

Vijender might have been more forthcoming had I asked him about seeds and fertilisers. But I have almost no knowledge about agriculture. I thought it was best to leave as soon as we had finished tea—but not before I had taken one more look at Pakistan from his terrace.

By now the sun had sunk much lower and it hung over the trees of Pakistan, making the terrace a far more agreeable place to stand and stare. If there was no fence, I would have probably walked up to the nearest boundary pillar and maybe placed one foot on Pakistani soil, just for kicks. It wouldn't have been the same as stepping into, say, Burma or even China. The long enmity between India and Pakistan makes the imaginary line separating them seem insurmountable.

Come to think of it, in spite of the long history of military conflict, the fence was erected only in 1986, when the separatist movement in Punjab was at its peak, to prevent terrorists from sneaking in or just striding across.

Today the fence seeks to check smugglers and suicide bombers, but in spite of its reputation of being impregnable, the smuggling of narcotics continues to flourish and heavily-armed suicide bombers sneak in every once in a while to wreak havoc at heavily-guarded installations.

The fence or the BSF cannot check every single transgression. There are terrains, such as riverine stretches, which are impossible to fence or guard round the clock with an eagle's eye. Moreover, nothing is impossible for a man who is desperate, or who has made up his mind to die.

A man who does not earn even sixty rupees a day but is promised Rs 60,000 to get a few packets of heroin across the border, or a man who is determined to copulate with seventy-two virgins in paradise—how can a manmade border prevent him?

These thoughts were crossing my mind when Husanjeet

reminded me that we should leave right away if I intended to catch the flag-lowering ceremony at the Wagah border.

'Why are you dragging him to Wagah?' Vijender admonished Husanjeet, 'It's not even an hour that you guys came. Let him relax a bit.'

'But he has come all the way from Chennai only to watch the parade,' Husanjeet said.

Vijender ignored him and asked me, '*Drink-shrink to karte hoge*?'—You drink, don't you?

'Yes, I do.'

'Then let's have some drinks now, right here.' Vijender was now talking. So far he had been speaking only when spoken to.

'But I must get to Wagah now, hopefully we will meet again,' I shook his hand.

Vijender looked disappointed as we left. As soon as we left his house, once again driving across the green paddies to reach GT Road, I realized that I had just made one of the stupidest decisions of my life by turning down his offer for drinks.

I could have always returned for the Wagah ceremony the following evening, whereas if I had taken up Vijender's offer, I would have been celebrating the magical hour of dusk by nursing a drink on a terrace overlooking Pakistan. How often does one get to do that? And Vijender, who was just about beginning to talk, would have talked more after a drink or two, and perhaps told me stories about life on the border. At some point the floodlights would have come on, bright enough to light up the whole village, and eventually Vijender's mother would have brought us dinner—the most authentic Punjabi dinner.

Of course, I also had the choice of returning the next afternoon to take up his offer, but spontaneity has no replacement.

Back on the GT Road, Sunny parked the car in an open space adjacent to the Integrated Check Post, or ICP, a new domed building that opened in 2012 to regulate road trade between the two countries. From here it was about a kilometre's walk to the gates where the flag-lowering took place.

Sunny, who still walked with a limp because of the accident, suggested that Husanjeet and I hurry ahead and that he would follow us at his own pace. From here on, the road wore the festive air of a village fair. Hawkers sold snacks and fruits, and a song from the Hindi film *Border* blared from a BSF booth. It was a while before the song faded away and live patriotic sounds came within my hearing range: *Bharat Mata Ki Jai*! *Hindustan Zindabad*! *Vande Mataram*!

As we hurried in the direction of the jingoistic cries we ran into a barricade. The BSF sentry manning it said, 'But the parade has already begun, I can't let you proceed.'

'But I have come all the way from Chennai,' I pleaded with him, 'I am a journalist.'

'Ok, show me your ID.'

When I produced my ID, he exclaimed with delight, 'Oh, Bengali! Where from?'

'Chennai.'

'I know, but native place?'

'Murshidabad.'

'Really? Even I am from Murshidabad! Which village?'

'Panchthupi, even though I have never been there.'

'Really? My village is right next to Panchthupi!'

'That makes us neighbours.'

'Of course! Nice to meet you!'

He gladly let us walk through the doorframe metal detector, but only after frisking us and taking away my packet of cigarettes and a new lighter. 'I will keep them safe for you, don't worry,' he assured me.

From the metal detector the two arches were clearly visible—the nearer arch belonging, obviously, to India and the farther arch, adorned with a portrait of Jinnah, belonging, obviously, to Pakistan. It is on the stretch between these two arches that all the high kicking and the stamping takes place.

Since the ceremony had already begun, we weren't allowed beyond the Indian arch and had to watch it standing, often on our toes, from behind a crowd of latecomers already gathered there. I had watched videos of it on numerous occasions; but videos, even though they capture the action, don't always faithfully convey the atmosphere, and the atmosphere, at this moment, was electrifying.

I felt like a wannabe spectator who, for the want of a ticket, was stranded outside a stadium hosting a cricket match between India and Pakistan. I could hear the crowds bursting into applause from time to time but couldn't figure why exactly they were cheering. Did the Indian batsman hit the ball for a six or narrowly escape a run out?

All I could see, from under the arch, was the silhouettes of two BSF women, marching in a pair in the direction of the gates, their male counterparts following suit. I had absolutely no idea what was going on at the Radcliffe Line for the crowds to go ecstatic. Perhaps the Indian sentries were raising their legs higher or kicking the ground harder than their Pakistani opposites?

In the end it turned out to be a cricket match that both sides pretended to win. The crowds, as they slowly dispersed, were euphoric, faces flushed with triumph. Many lingered on to take pictures with the BSF sentries, the stars of the evening, who were clearly used to posing for the camera.

As I elbowed my way to the gates, for a closer look at Pakistan, I did not feel overcome by a rush of patriotism. If anything, I wished the gates didn't exist so that I could ask Sunny to continue our journey on the GT Road into Pakistan.

We could have had dinner in Lahore.

# 5

The railway station sat wrapped in silence when I got there after sunset. The yellow signboard that gave its name in four scripts—Hindi, English, Gurmukhi and Urdu—was bathed in light, but hardly a soul was around to be informed that this was Attari, the last Indian station before the railway tracks entered Pakistan.

Husanjeet and Sunny, sulking because I had insisted that they bring me here (they wanted to return to Amritsar), decided to stay in the parking lot as I walked into the station. A pair of turbaned policemen, carrying rifles, walked ahead of me. Another pair strode past on the platform.

Had it not been for its location, Attari would have been one of those countless wayside stations you find sprinkled throughout India: a small charming building, invariably British-built, sitting in the remote countryside, where it would be hard to find people, leave alone policemen.

Attari used to be one such station until August 1947, when the Radcliffe Line placed it right on the border. Trains entering it from the west carried bodies of Hindus and Sikhs murdered on their way to India. Trains entering it from the east carried bodies of Muslims butchered on their way to the newly-created Pakistan. Those who crossed Attari alive, lived.

Silence aids imagination, but I found it horrifying to even imagine trains packed with just-murdered passengers pulling into the station. The ones still alive in those trains—had they still been screaming or were they shocked into silence? How did those at the station react to the arrival of such trains? Was it with horrified disbelief? Fear? How did the drivers of these trains feel?

If I were to walk into such a sight now, I would probably not be able to sleep the rest of my life: the open eyes of the dead would haunt me each time I shut mine.

One of the turbaned policemen walking ahead of me happened to turn around. Noticing me he stopped. The other cop stopped too.

'Who are you?' he asked me. He was menacing. 'What brings you here?'

I introduced myself, but they regarded me with suspicion. Then I pulled out my wallet and handed each of them my business card. I hoped the gesture would make them feel important.

'During Partition,' I said, 'trains filled with bodies pulled into Attari station. Soon India will mark seventy years of Partition, so I have come to see how the station looks today. Partition was such a horrible thing, the politicians decided on it but it was the common man who got butchered. What was the fault of the common man? He was content going about his life, until Partition was thrust on him.'

The policeman who had questioned my presence nodded thoughtfully and said, '*Baat toh aapki theek hai*'—'You are right.'

It was now his turn to explain why he had to ask me to prove my identity: 'Independence Day is close, you see, and there are troublemakers all around. You know this is a sensitive station, we cannot trust anyone. I suggest you meet the station superintendent, he will give you all the information you want.'

We shook hands like old buddies.

The station superintendent was off duty. In his place now sat the assistant station manager, a thirty-something man called Roop, surrounded by apparatuses that looked as antiquated as the office.

'This building dates back to 1863,' he informed me. 'You see the ceiling?' he pointed upwards, 'I just got it renovated. It was about to fall.'

'How does it feel to be posted at Attari?'

'Attari station is the only international railway station in the country,' he replied with a touch of pride.

International railway station—the description would bring to mind images of a busy station, swarming with Westerners, because we tend to associate everything international with them. But at seven-thirty in the evening Attari looked more deserted than a remote station. I soon gathered why.

Two passenger trains make a return trip each between

Amritsar and Attari every day, and the last of those trains was long gone. And the train that runs between India and Pakistan—Samjhauta Express, whose compulsory halt at Attari for the purpose of immigration and customs checks earned this wayside station its 'international' status—arrived only on Mondays and Thursdays. Today was Wednesday.

'I realized I had been posted in an important station,' Roop went on, 'when my teacher at the railway training institute called me excitedly to find out how differently Attari functioned from other stations in India.'

The only difference apparent to me was that unlike other station masters in India, Roop had the privilege of communicating with counterparts in a foreign country. But considering that the foreign country happened to be Pakistan, his job did make a difference: he was a part of the machinery that conducted twice-a-week emotional reunions between citizens of the two hostile nations.

'We communicate with our Pakistani counterparts through this magneto phone,' Roop patted a time-worn box that was connected to an old-fashioned handset. He wasn't sure how old the equipment was: he had inherited it.

Roop's counterparts sit in Wagah, the nearest Pakistani station, barely three kilometres west of Attari. Passengers travelling across the border must also stop at Wagah for clearance by Pakistani immigration and customs.

The Samjhauta Express—*samjhauta* means agreement—began running in July 1976, a result of the Simla Agreement signed by Indira Gandhi and Zulfikar Ali Bhutto in 1972.

It has been running ever since, connecting Old Delhi and Lahore railway stations, except for brief periods of interruption.

Delhi and Lahore are barely 530 km apart. That's almost the distance between Delhi and Lucknow, covered by the Shatabdi Express in seven hours. But passengers travelling in Samjhauta Express spend more than a day to reach their destination, only because of the interminable halts at Attari and Wagah.

Since it is mostly the poor who now take the train, the fare being very cheap, no one considers shortening the travel time, even though the air-conditioned bus between New Delhi and Lahore, which began running in 1999, completes the journey in twelve hours. More buses now cross the border than before, plying not just between New Delhi and Lahore but also between Amritsar and Lahore, and between Amritsar and Nankana Sahib, the birthplace of Guru Nanak.

Listening to Roop, sitting in his timeless office, it occurred to me that India and Pakistan were far better connected than I had imagined. When you live hundreds of miles away from the border, reading and hearing, day in and day out, only about hostilities, you imagine only birds, and not people, crossing it.

The Samjhauta Express not only reunites relatives but is also a vehicle of trade. India sends, among other things, textiles, agricultural machinery and machine parts, seeds, and chemicals across the border. Pakistan sends, among other things, textiles, cement, spices, and dry fruits.

Strictly speaking, Samjhauta Express is the train that runs between Lahore and Attari. It arrives at Attari station on Mondays and Thursdays at about half past noon, and returns with passengers bound for Pakistan. The train that goes up to Old Delhi station—the carriages are sealed and there are no halts in between—is called the Attari-Delhi Express.

But that's a small technicality, often overlooked. When in February 2007, explosions ripped through two carriages of the Delhi-Attari Express, killing close to seventy people, mostly Pakistanis, the media referred to it as 'Samjhauta Express blasts.'

'So who runs the train?' I asked Roop.

'Both countries do. For six months we give power to them, for the next six months they give power to us.'

'What do you mean by power?'

He explained: for six months an Indian engine pulled the train and for the next six months a Pakistani one.

'Wait, let me show you something interesting,' Roop said, and he got busy tapping on his phone.

I looked around. A chart on the wall had recorded 'nil' accidents in Attari's jurisdiction over the last many years. Hardly surprising.

'Here, this is what I was looking for,' he handed me his phone. It was an hour-long BBC documentary on the Samjhauta Express, available on YouTube. I told him I would watch it once I got back to the hotel.

'So tomorrow is Thursday,' I said. 'If I come here by noon, would I be able to watch the train coming in?'

'Sure, you can. But I won't be here. My senior will be on duty, Mr Shashikant Madan. He is on the verge of retirement and knows a lot more about the station than I do.'

Seeing me approach the car, Sunny switched on the ignition. As we got moving, Husanjeet turned around and asked, 'Happy?'

So they were still sulking.

'Happy for what?' I feigned ignorance.

'Happy that you got to see Attari station?'

'Oh yes,' I said, 'I am very happy.'

# 6

Partition, even though it tore Punjab into two and scarred its people, succeeded in popularising Punjabi food throughout India. Refugees, as they left their kitchens behind, took family recipes along.

No one, any longer, thinks of daal makhni or paneer butter masala as uniquely Punjabi food—they are available all over India now. So much so that my eyes failed to locate an exclusively Punjabi dish as I scanned the menu to order dinner. Everything I saw on the list was available, easily, in any part of the country.

Finally I ordered daal makhni, in the hope that it would taste more Punjabi in Amritsar than anywhere else. Then I sent the room boy to get me a bottle of whisky. Dinner and drinks taken care of, I called up a friend who heads the Chennai plant of a Punjab-based automobile-manufacturing company.

'Treat Punjab as your home,' he had told me before I left for Amritsar, 'if you need any help, call me.' Now I needed help: a car, to take me to Attari the next morning.

Husanjeet and Sunny, even though they almost became friends, had finally charged me a bomb for the trip, not to mention the sulking. It was partly my fault because I had not discussed money with them before setting out for the border.

I asked my friend if he could find me a driver whose rates were reasonable and not whimsical. He called me back to say that a driver would report at the hotel at eleven. Meanwhile, the room boy was back. I poured myself a drink and switched on my laptop.

I ended up watching three documentaries back to back, starting with the one on Samjhauta Express, recommended by Roop. Then I watched one on Partition, followed by another one on Jinnah. In four hours I learnt more about Partition than I did in forty-five years. The dinner had gone cold, my heart heavy.

As I tore the leathery tandoori roti, I felt sad at the transformation of Jinnah: from an upright and honest man, committed to Hindu-Muslim unity and to a united India, to the wrecker-in-chief of united India.

I also felt sad for the old wrestler from Lahore, who recalled how Hindus would not let Muslims drink water directly from their taps and, even worse, would attach a long pipe to the tap if at all they allowed a Muslim to drink their water.

I felt equally sad for the elderly Hindu man who, in spite of being driven away from Lahore by Muslim mobs during Partition, blamed orthodox Hindus for creating a social wall that kept the two communities apart. His mother, for example, would not allow Muslim women into the kitchen and had separate crockery for them.

The writer Khushwant Singh was quoted in one of the

documentaries as saying that the mixing of Hindus and Muslims was only superficial, with no intimate friendship, except a certain amount of wining and dining that took place in the upper class.

Was Jinnah, then, right in demanding Partition? Yes, if you are in a Pakistani classroom. No, if you are in an Indian classroom. But people interviewed in these documentaries were not from the pages of history, but people who were alive to see the making of history.

The interview of an elderly Sikh called Bir Bahadur Singh was particularly heart-wrenching, even gut-wrenching. He recalled the time when, right in front of his eyes, his father beheaded all the girls in the house, including his sister, to save their honour from a Muslim mob. The sturdy old Sikh broke down in front of the camera as he replayed in his mind those moments when his father brought down the sword on the girls and the sound it made while severing their heads.

In the documentary about Samjhauta Express, I watched Shashikant Madan, the station superintendent of Attari whom I was to meet the next day, saying that he saw no difference between the people of India and Pakistan: 'My parents are also from Pakistan, and after Partition they came to India.' Another railway employee interviewed in the documentary—a young woman who sat at the ticket counter at Attari—said: 'Common man wants only food, clothing, and shelter, he doesn't want boundaries.'

The very last line from the documentary played in my ears as I went to sleep that night: 'While the border divides, the train unites.'

# 7

The ringing of the phone woke me up. It took me a few moments to gather where I was: home or elsewhere, if elsewhere, where?

'Good morning, sir,' Ms Blue Eyelids was on the line. 'You have a visitor.'

It turned out that my friend from Chennai had not only arranged for a car but also assigned a junior colleague posted in Amritsar to escort me. The colleague was now waiting at the reception. It was eleven o'clock. I could keep him waiting, but the Samjhauta Express was not going to wait for me.

I sprang out of bed. My dream of waking up in Punjab to a hearty breakfast of alu parathas went out of the window.

Attari, the international railway station, wore a deserted look even at noon. No waiting passengers, no hurrying porters, no shouting vendors, and the sun exceptionally cruel.

On Platform No. 1, a lone emaciated dog slept under a

bench. Platform No. 2—separated from No. 1 by a wire-mesh wall—was equally empty, save the occasional pair of gun-toting sentries strolling past. The building on that platform looked fairly new, with large glass panels, but the glass was tinted and it was not possible to see what was going on inside—it was the immigration hall.

I walked into the ancient office where I had met Roop the evening before and introduced myself to his boss, Shashikant Madan, who seemed to be hurrying through some paperwork.

'The train will be coming in any moment now. Please come back after two o' clock,' he said and promptly returned to the sheet of paper awaiting his attention.

'Can I watch the train coming in?'

'But it will come on Platform No. 2,' he said without looking up, 'You are not allowed to go there.'

'Can't I watch it from here?'

'Sure, that you can.'

Not only was the heat killing, even the humidity was ferocious. Only those driven by absolute necessity would be out in the sun at this hour. For someone like me, who had read *Train to Pakistan*, being in Attari station at this hour was more than a necessity: this was a golden opportunity to watch a train *from* Pakistan.

I was more concerned about my friend's colleague—his name was Ramesh—who was following me like a shadow. Why should he be subjected to the hardship? But if he was unhappy being with me here, he didn't show it.

His presence helped because he was not only a local but

also looked one. As we waited in the shade of a tree in a corner of the platform, we were asked, from time to time, by policemen in uniform, as well as in plainclothes, who we were and what we were doing there. Ramesh dealt with them and they went away.

But there were times when cops singled me out for questioning. I wanted to tell them that I was waiting to watch the train come in, but they wouldn't believe me because no sane man would get drenched in sweat just to watch a train arriving. So I told them I had an appointment with the station superintendent, which was equally true.

Soon we got talking to a friendly plainclothes cop with a blue turban. He told us he was from the intelligence department of the police. For a long time we exchanged personal information—where each of us was born, which college we went to, who all comprised our immediate families, how thankless and poorly-paying our jobs were and how we still stuck to them because we were not cut out for anything else.

Presently he went back into the small red-brick guardroom where he had emerged from. The ancient structure was marked 'Abandoned' in white paint, which meant it was no longer in use for the purpose it had originally been built for. He re-emerged with a cup of tea and asked us, '*Chai-shai logey*?'—Would you like some tea?

Sipping hot tea standing under an incredibly hot sun? 'No, thank you,' I politely declined his offer. He sipped his tea and told me that I was only wasting my time waiting for the Samjhauta Express.

'Don't expect any drama,' he said, 'the train brings only poor people who are eager to meet their relatives in India. They come mainly from Sindh and Pakistani Punjab, and are usually headed to places in the Indian Punjab, Uttar Pradesh, Rajasthan and Madhya Pradesh, apart from Delhi.'

He went on: 'It is the responsibility of their hosts in India to ensure that they do not overstay or stray from the place they are meant to visit.'

Even as we talked, an old Maruti 800 pulled into the parking lot. From it emerged a sunburned Sikh in a bright yellow turban. He hesitantly approached the plainclothesman. His name was Dalbir Singh and he had driven all the way from Majitha, a town 50 kilometres away, to receive his *maasi da munda*—maternal aunt's son—who was travelling in the Samjhauta Express along with his wife. Dalbir Singh wanted to confirm whether they were indeed on the train and whether they would be alighting at Attari.

'How am I to know, brother?' the plainclothesman said, 'It all depends on the destination printed on their visa. There have been cases when passengers meaning to get down at Attari had to travel all the way to Delhi just because the destination mentioned happened to be Delhi. And then they had to come back to Attari on their own.'

This wasn't true at all, as far as I knew. It wasn't the same train that proceeded to Delhi. The train for Delhi departed only around nine in the night. But Dalbir Singh looked nervous. It had taken him a year of paperwork and repeated police verifications to facilitate the travel of the cousin and his wife. He had no choice but to wait till the train arrived and the passengers began to emerge after clearing immigration.

The train appeared on the horizon. It moved very slowly, as if an inch at a time. 'Now all the passengers will be checked thoroughly by all agencies, including the intelligence department,' said the plainclothesman as he prepared to cross over to Platform No. 2.

'Can I come with you?' I asked him.

'Of course not,' he said.

Dalbir Singh, eager and anxious, kept standing with me. He was fifty and had never met his cousin before. I would have loved to witness the union of the two middle-aged cousins taking place on Platform No. 2. But both of us were forbidden from going there.

The train finally began rolling into the station. We watched it from Platform No. 1. The engine was green and bore the letters 'PR': Pakistan Railways. Immediately behind it were half-a-dozen goods wagons, painted red and belonging to NR, or India's Northern Railway. Behind them were the passenger coaches, painted in the Indian blue. The signboard on the train identified it as Samjh*ou*ta Express, and not Samjhauta Express, perhaps in keeping with the Punjabi pronunciation.

A thought crossed my mind. If a Pakistani engine could pull Indian coaches and an Indian engine could pull Pakistani coaches, couldn't Nehru and Jinnah have settled for a similar power-sharing? Had that happened,

I wouldn't be braving the sun to watch the arrival of an otherwise nondescript train and consider it a momentous event. I would have simply hopped on when it returned to Lahore and spent the entire day there before finding my way back to Amritsar in the evening. Thousands of people, I am sure, did that on a daily basis before the Radcliffe Line separated Amritsar from Lahore. In the olden days Punjabis believed that if you haven't seen Lahore, you are not born yet: *'Jinne Lahore nai vekhya, woh jamiya ee nai.'*

There weren't too many passengers in the Samjhauta Express that afternoon. My experience as a rail traveller told me that each coach—there were seven coaches—would not have held more than twenty passengers. That worked out to 140 passengers at the most. Most of them were women and young girls, who nervously looked out of the window, their faces not showing any of the joy associated with train travel or with arrival at destination. Perhaps they were nervous about coming to India, aware that the two countries weren't the best of friends. Or perhaps they knew that in Attari, arrival at destination only meant the beginning of a long wait to clear formalities.

The arrival of the Samjhauta Express saw the station suddenly being invaded by turbaned police guards. Some of them seemed to have walked alongside the train from the border, and they looked angry and impatient. One of them, a tall menacing Sikh who had his finger on the trigger, spotted me from a distance and came charging, 'Who are you? Why are you standing here?'

I told him I was waiting to meet the station superintendent.

'Then wait for him in his office, not on the platform!' he yelled. He looked so angry that he could have shot me. Perhaps it was the heat.

The superintendent had asked me to come at two. I still had about forty-five minutes to kill. The three of us—Dalbir Singh, Ramesh, and I—stepped out of the platform and sat under a tree in the parking lot. Dalbir Singh ran a grocery store in Majitha and his cousin, who lived in a *kasba*—hamlet—about 20 kilometres from Lahore, earned his living as a driver. The cousin's wife had come to India once before, and this time she was accompanying her husband for a month-long stay.

Soon Ramesh got talking to Dalbir Singh, and I excused myself and went outside the station compound to smoke a cigarette. There I noticed two shops with their shutters down. Each had a fading signboard. One announced, 'Pakistan currency exchanged here.' The other advertised Cash brand of whisky: 'Enjoy Cash with friends.'

The shutters did not seem to have been raised in many years, but the signboards told you that they functioned once upon a time for the sole benefit of passengers from legally-dry Pakistan. In all probability the two shops had the same owner, who, of course, understood the value of cash.

At two o'clock I presented myself at the station superintendent's office. Mr Madan looked busier than before. He said, 'I am sorry I am going to take much longer. Why don't you come back, say'—he looked at his watch—'at four?'

'Sure,' I said, even though I had decided to leave.

I shook Dalbir Singh's hand and said goodbye. The short time we had spent waiting together had made us friends.

'Wait, why don't you take his number?' Ramesh suggested to me. 'You can visit him later and meet his cousin.'

I felt ashamed that the idea had not struck me. Perhaps it was the heat.

# 8

For people living along the border of Punjab, the Radcliffe Line is what it is: an imaginary line. They harbour no hostility towards Pakistan because they have a good look at Pakistan every day and what they see is another Punjab, where many of their ancestors lived before Partition.

Which should explain why the shrillest anti-Pakistan cries are always heard in places far from the border—such as Mumbai, which is about 1,000 miles from Wagah—and never on the border. The border, nothing but a string of villages, is the quietest of places.

So while the railway station transformed into a scene of activity and excitement with the arrival of Samjhauta Express, Attari itself remained lifeless as we drove out of the station. That's when I realised I was hungry. I hadn't eaten anything in more than twelve hours. More than feeding myself, I felt duty-bound to treat Ramesh to a lavish lunch, the least I could do. He was probably used to the heat, because his job was to go around Amritsar, particularly its villages, selling the ten-tyre truck his company manufactured, but this thankless assignment was not going to help him get closer to his monthly target.

I suggested we have lunch at Sarhad, the red-brick 'food and culture park' closer to the border whose restroom I had used the day before. Ramesh agreed.

'But before that,' he said, 'I would like you to meet someone who might give you more information about the border.'

As soon as we emerged on the GT Road he asked the driver to park outside a two-storied building whose signboard read: 'Attari Border Truck Operators' Association.' He led me through a hall on the ground floor, where groups of turbaned men sat chatting, to the first floor and showed me into a rather plush office that was fitted with air-conditioners and CCTV-monitors. There, behind the screen of a Toshiba laptop, sat an elderly and affable Sikh who was introduced to me as Kulwinder Singh, an office-bearer of the association.

The elderly man lowered the laptop screen as a courtesy and gestured us to take our seats. Glasses of chilled water arrived—what a welcome sight, the moisture-coated glasses—followed by coffee and cookies.

'He has come from Chennai,' Ramesh introduced me, 'to write about the border.'

'Ah border,' Kulwinder smiled, 'you know, when we grazed cattle as kids, we would often stray into Pakistan because we did not know were exactly the border lay. So we would be grazing our cattle in Pakistan without even realising we were in Pakistan.'

'Once, shortly after the 1971 war,' he continued, 'a boy from my village—he was about my age—lost a leg because he happened to step on a mine while grazing cattle. Poor fellow, how was he to know that the grassy patch he was stepping on was hiding a mine?'

'What's the name of the village?'

'It is called Roranwala Khurd, quite close from here, maybe 600 metres.'

'And how old were you in 1971?' I asked.

'I was born in 1964. So I must have been seven or eight.'

It was my mistake to have regarded him as elderly. He was born only six years before me. But how was I to know? Perhaps six years from now I too will look elderly. Who knows if I already do: the mirror can flatter you if you look at it every day

'Do you have any memories of the war?' I asked him.

'The villagers were asked to vacate their homes and move away. So we packed essential items and shifted to a relative's house that was farther away from the border. But my father returned after a day or two because he did not want our house to be left unguarded.'

Presently we were joined by another affable Sikh: this man was way younger, muscular and smartly turned out in a white shirt and jeans. He gave his name as Harpal Singh, also an office-bearer of the truckers' association. He shook my hand with so much warmth that for a moment I wondered if we knew each other from before. His effervescence, I realised, was not put on: true-blue Punjabis are like that, gregarious and eager to make a guest feel at home. His arrival had transformed this information-gathering meeting into a chat between old friends.

As the conversation livened up, it struck me that even though India and Pakistan are considered long-standing enemies by their own people, there is always a bit of India present in Pakistani homes and vice-versa: each day, truckloads of tomatoes and other vegetables go to Pakistan just as truckloads of cement bags come into India.

'Pakistani cement is very popular in Punjab,' Harpal Singh said, 'there are so many brands coming in. They are cheaper than Indian cement, costing about a hundred rupees less per bag.'

'Can you name some of the brands?' I asked him.

'Elephant, Maple Leaf, Bestway.'

I found it ironical that in Punjab, where homes were once destroyed because of the creation of Pakistan, homes were now built with cement from Pakistan—and I mentioned this to the people in the room.

Kulwinder Singh smiled and, adopting the expression of a sage, said, 'End of the day, we are the same people, only the religion is different. Pakistanis—I am talking about the common man—are nice people. I am sure they think the same about Indians. It is only the debates on TV that make you believe that India and Pakistan are constantly at each other's throats.'

Harpal Singh, smiling all along, suddenly turned sombre and said, 'Common man wants peace, and as far as the common man is concerned, there is peace.'

Time to break one more myth, besides the one that the Radcliffe Line is a highly volatile zone where soldiers from both countries stand with guns pointed at each other—in reality you only see farmers, bent over their crops. This myth is about food.

Since I live in Chennai, I have noticed friends coming from the north sometimes expressing surprise at how non-vegetarian food is so commonly available in a Tamil city. A Tamilian, to them, is usually the god-fearing, castemark-wearing Brahmin who would prefer suicide over sausage. But Brahmins constitute hardly four per cent of Tamil Nadu's population: the remaining 96 heartily enjoy non-vegetarian fare.

Compare the figures with Punjab, famous for butter chicken: only 33 per cent are non-vegetarians and the remaining 67 vegetarians. I wasn't surprised, therefore, when Ramesh ordered a vegetarian thhali at Sarhad.

I, the reluctant meat-eater, lingered over the menu for a while. When it comes to non-vegetarian food, I am like the man standing on the beach and watching the surfers: tempted to join them but lacking courage. Mutton is the only thing I can eat with some relish, because I grew up eating it and developed some taste for it. As I became old enough to start drinking I realised I enjoyed mutton best after a drink or three, otherwise I remained acutely aware of the fact that I was eating the flesh of a goat.

So I ordered a bottle of Kingfisher beer and Lahori thhali, described in the menu as 'Sarhad special'. The thhali, costing Rs 390, was to consist of 'chapli kebab, nihari gosht, Lahori biryani, Lahori naan, panchmahal dal, salad and gulab jamun.'

But what was Ramesh, a teetotaller, going to drink? For him I chose a can of Peach Malt, a non-alcoholic beer manufactured at the Murree Brewery, 'Estd. 1860'.

Murree is to Pakistan what Shimla is, or was, to India—the premier hill station. Several generations of pre-Partition Indians swore by alcoholic drinks produced by the brewery at Murree, which began producing non-alcoholic drinks as well once Pakistan declared itself as an Islamic republic in 1956.

As I handed over the can to Ramesh after examining it, I wondered whether the Muri Express, a train I was familiar with because it stopped at Kanpur, owed its name to Murree. It is not uncommon for trains in India to be named after hill stations and it was quite likely that Murree, over the decades, had morphed to Muri. To confirm I searched the internet on my phone, and found that I was wrong: there is indeed a station called Muri, in existence since 1907, in present-day Jharkhand.

During the search, I also came across a website that had a facsimile reproduction of the *Report by the Railway Board on Indian Railways for 1938-39*. It contained, among other things, photographs to show how efficient Indian Railways was. A set of two pictures, reproduced side by side, caught my eye: both pictures were of the Lucknow railway station—one showed the Mohammedan Refreshment Room and the other, the Hindu Refreshment Room. Patrons in both the refreshment rooms could be seen dining happily, served by liveried waiters.

So, Indian society was quite neatly partitioned well before Partition. What was partitioned in 1947 was merely the map.

'The man sitting at that table in the corner,' Ramesh told me, 'he is the owner of this place. I have met him once before, but I don't think he will remember me.'

The man Ramesh was referring to was a distinguished-looking Sikh who was presently being served by a waiter. I had no idea what he was having for lunch but I could see steam erupting from his plate. I too wanted to order whatever he was eating—obviously the safest and the best item to order—but it was too late. I flagged down the waiter who had just served him.

'Is he the owner of this place?' I asked.

'Yes, he is the one.'

'Ok, here is my card. Give it to him and tell him that I would like to have a word with him after lunch.'

I could see the waiter carry my business card to the gent, who kept it in his breast pocket and continued eating without even looking up to see who among the patrons was eager to meet him.

Our food arrived, looking delicious. Everything that I ate tasted special, and I knew why: the location. We were only 22 kilometres from Lahore, and this was as authentic as Lahori thhali could get in India. It was painful for me to leave one Lahori naan untouched, but my stomach had no place for it.

'I have an emotional connection with Lahore,' said Damanbir Singh Jaspal, the owner of Sarhad, when I met him after lunch. 'My father was born there, he studied at the Government College there, my grandfather also studied there.'

His grandfather was the ADC to the Maharaja of Kapurthala, while his father joined the Indian Railways shortly before Partition. Damanbir, who was born in Lucknow when his father was posted there, went on to join the Indian Administrative Service. He retired in 2011 and two years later opened Sarhad to—in his words—celebrate the culinary heritage of undivided Punjab.

'Culturally Lahore and Amritsar are the same, just like West Bengal and Bangladesh. The spices we use in our kitchen all come from Lahore. We are, in fact, closer to Lahore than to Amritsar. Lahore is only 22 kilometres from here, Amritsar is 40,' he said.

Damanbir showed me around the boutique—'Exclusive Pakistani dresses only at Sarhad'—which showcased the creations of a Pakistani designer called Sania Iqbal, who grew up in Singapore and is now settled in Karachi. According to him, Sania—whose mother was a Sikh—was eager to have a connection with India, especially with Punjab, so he gave her the space and does not charge her.

Damanbir said, 'You see, there are fringe elements that do not want India and Pakistan to have good relations, but if you take the common people in Lahore, they are very fond of us. They get very nostalgic when they meet someone from this side of Punjab.

'I remember, in 2002 or 2003, when Capt Amarinder Singh was the chief minister of Punjab, he paid an official visit to Lahore. I was a part of the delegation. A day before we were supposed to return to India, the chief minister of Pakistani Punjab told Capt Singh, "How can you go back without visiting Nankana Sahib (the birthplace of Guru Nanak)?" Capt Singh replied that his visa did not permit that. So their chief minister said, "Don't worry, I will arrange all that." And so we went to Nankana Sahib.

'And on the day we were leaving Lahore, Capt Singh held a press conference at the Circuit House there. As you know he comes from the royal family of Patiala, and there were a number of Muslims in the service of the Patiala State before they migrated during Partition. One journalist whose ancestors worked for the Patiala State—and journalists usually don't show their emotions at a press conference—was so overwhelmed by his interaction with Capt Singh that he broke down. He was sobbing uncontrollably. It is a sight I will never forget. Our phones didn't have cameras back then or else I would have recorded it, as an evidence of how emotionally close the people of the two Punjabs are.

'You know, when people from Pakistan come to India, they say they feel 100 per cent at home when in Punjab, seventy per cent at home in Delhi, and only when they go beyond Delhi do they feel they have come to a different land.

'We Indians also don't know much about Pakistan, our opinion is mainly formed on the basis of what we see on

TV. You must go to Lahore—you will find more women in burqas in Old Delhi or Meerut than in Lahore. Its restaurants are classy, several notches above our restaurants.'

Damanbir took me to the first floor of his restaurant, which had the bar. On its walls, in a corner, was displayed information—including newspaper clippings—related to Partition. From the 5 July 1947 edition of *The Tribune*:

> NEW DELHI, July 4—Sir Cyril Radcliffe, a well-known British lawyer, has been appointed Chairman of both the Boundary Commissions for the Punjab and Bengal.
>
> LAHORE, July 4—It is learnt that the Punjab Boundary Commission will commence its work from Saturday (today).
>
> The office of the Boundary Commission will be situated in the Punjab Assembly buildings where rooms have been allotted to the four members of the Commission, where they are sitting from to-morrow.
>
> It is understood that pending the arrival of the Chairman of the Boundary Commission, the four members will continue their work in his absence and try to settle the details on which there is no difference of opinion.

So the spadework was done by local members of the commission. Radcliffe's job was mainly to decide on lands claimed by both parties—and there were many such lands, more in Bengal than in Punjab—and finally draw the boundaries.

And then, from a poster that showed the picture of a brass plaque:

> Immediately after Partition, since there was no pillar or marker to demarcate where the Grand Trunk Road left India and became Pakistan, a joint check post was established on October 11, 1947 by Brigadier Mohinder Singh Chopra. A few hastily whitewashed drums and a rubble of stones were put along the berms of the GT Road, making the new international border between the separate dominions of India and Pakistan.
>
> Some tents were pitched to house the few troops on duty (1 Dogra from the Indian Army and 4 Baluch of the Pakistani Army), with two sentry boxes painted in the national colours of each country, along with a small swing gate to regulate traffic.
>
> Two flag masts completed the picture, with a small brass plaque commemorating the historic event of October 1947.

To me this was news: that the check post was set up on 11th October 1947. There was something else I had learnt only a few days ago: that the passport and visa system for travel between India and Pakistan came into effect only on 15th October 1952. Which meant that for five long years from the time of Partition, Indians and Pakistanis could freely walk into each other's countries—something so difficult to believe today.

When I mentioned this to Damanbir, he said: 'The atmosphere was pretty relaxed even after 1952. Things really changed only after the 1965 war. Until then army officers from Pakistan would cycle across the border to watch Hindi films.'

The war had a bigger impact in the east. Until 1965,

river trade was thriving between Calcutta and Assam, with boats crossing what was then East Pakistan to reach their destination. When the war broke out, boats that happened to be in East Pakistani waters were seized, while those stranded in Assam and Calcutta eventually began ferrying passengers locally. That's how the ferry service began between Calcutta and Howrah.

Damanbir said, 'The common man never wants war. He has enough problems to deal with in his day-to-day life. He only wants peace. Soon you will find Sarhad housing a Museum of Peace, we are working on it. It will celebrate Punjab—the undivided Punjab.'

As I shook his hand and walked back to the parking lot with Ramesh, I wondered: if Indian Punjab and Pakistani Punjab were given the choice, would they reunite? If you ponder over the question sentimentally—perhaps over a drink under a starlit sky, sitting on a charpoy in the fields, dreaming of being served with delectable kebabs in a classy Lahore restaurant—then you might hear a yes.

Reality, however, is as harsh as the scorching sun. No one had forcibly split Punjab: its people had voted to separate, Muslims on one side and Hindus and Sikhs on the other. Such was the animosity prevailing at the time. But once Partition was achieved, the animosity got blunted and anger was replaced with nostalgia. When you get nostalgic, you sometimes want to go back in time—only that barbed wires will now block your way.

# 9

In late July 1947, a two-member Sikh delegation travelled all the way to London in the hope they could persuade Prime Minister Clement Attlee to use his influence to prevent Sir Cyril Radcliffe from giving the three holiest shrines of Sikhs to Pakistan.

The Punjab Boundary Commission consisted of two Muslims, one Hindu and one Sikh. Since Radcliffe, as its chairman, had the casting vote, the Sikh delegation wanted Attlee to impress upon him to act in favour of the Sikhs.

There are no subsequent reports to suggest whether the two Sikhs got to meet Attlee, and if yes, what transpired in the meeting, but Radcliffe eventually placed two of the shrines—both related to the first Sikh Guru—in Pakistan: Nankana Sahib, where Guru Nanak was born, and Kartarpur Sahib, where he died. With Amritsar remaining in India, staying clear of Radcliffe's pen by about 40 kilometres, the Sikhs got to keep Harmandir Sahib, or the Golden Temple, the holiest of all gurdwaras.

I did not find Amritsar to be a pretty city, and I can't be blamed for thinking that way. Even the website of the government of India does not wish to mislead potential tourists: 'First-time visitors to Amritsar could be forgiven for the impression that Amritsar is like any other small town in northern India. But Amritsar stands head and shoulders above any other city, its status elevated and sanctified by the presence of the venerable Golden Temple.'

Fair enough, and true too, as I was to find out.

Amritsar—pool of nectar—which grew around the tank from which it derives its name, dates back to the 1570s when the fourth Sikh Guru, Guru Ram Das, ordered the construction of the tank. That makes Amritsar older than Shah Jahan's Delhi, Francis Day's Madras and Job Charnock's Calcutta. A city that old—clothed in layers of lapsed centuries, each having its own share of turbulent times—cannot exactly be pretty.

But I am talking about core Amritsar. There is another Amritsar that encircles the old Amritsar, and the circle is gradually expanding to include new areas within the magnetic field of the Golden Temple. Many of these new areas resemble the planned sectors of Chandigarh, my hotel being located in one such. Driving around the city, you will come across some of the most creative names for establishments: I spotted a restaurant that called itself Tummy Full Food Villa, a modest hotel that declared itself as Hotel Seven Star, and a hospital named Dukhnivaran, or Sorrow-Curing Hospital.

At the moment, however, I was in old Amritsar. I wanted to see the Golden Temple. Luckily for me, Ramesh too had to meet a prospective client who ran a shop not far from the shrine. We got down at an intersection, under a flyover, and walked in different directions, deciding to meet at the same spot in about an hour. The driver said he was going to find space to park and asked me to note down his number. He also cautioned me: 'Take care of your wallet, and if someone offers you anything to eat, *do not* accept it.'

And so, somewhat nervously, I began my walk on what would perhaps be the oldest and busiest road of Amritsar, where four-wheelers are no longer allowed. I walked past shops and hawkers, sometimes stepping aside to make way for a cycle-rickshaw and all the while feeling my wallet.

Finally I was in Sikh country. Probably there were more turbaned men here than in the rest of Amritsar put together. Walking on this road, even if you were a non-Sikh, you would want to sport a turban, or pagri, and wear a steel bangle, or kada, in order to fit into the surroundings. I wasn't sure about the turban, but I stopped at a shop and bought myself a bangle—brass and not steel—that would forever remind me of my maiden visit to the Golden Temple, apart from serving as a fashion accessory.

I resumed my walk, and right where the road ended to form a T-junction, I stood face-to-face with a two-storey red-brick building with grey windows, that looked old enough to belong to an era bygone and yet was well-preserved. Right outside the boundary wall of the building, five pani-puri sellers—all young men, probably from Bihar—stood with tripods that held their wares. Only one of them attracted all the customers, and the rest looked at him with envy. Directly above the wall hung a large red banner: 'Punjabi Dhaba: 100% pure desi ghee preparation. Breakfast. Lunch. Dinner. Indian & Chinese food.'

I wondered if the red-brick building served as the Punjabi Dhaba, but as I walked closer I discovered that the advertisement was for a restaurant located elsewhere, whereas what I stood facing was the facade of the Jallianwala Bagh.

It was my fault that I had imagined Jallianwala Bagh to be located somewhere on the outskirts, and not hidden in the congested lanes, of Amritsar. And so I had chanced upon this all-important piece of history all by myself: neither Ramesh nor the driver had mentioned its presence there. Probably they had assumed that I wouldn't miss it.

I walked into Jallianwala Bagh through a passage wide enough for three adults to walk shoulder to shoulder. A plaque informed visitors: 'General Dyer conducted soldiers for firing on an innocent crowd of Indians through this passage.'

It turned out to be a well-kept garden, hemmed in by tall buildings that looked too modern to mesh with the era it represented. One cannot blame the owners of these buildings for moving with times just because thc garden needed to be preserved the way it was in 1919. For that matter, the garden itself was not a garden when troops led by Brigadier-General Reginald Edward Harry Dyer fired on the people gathered there: it was just an empty piece of land, purchased by the Indian National Congress shortly after the massacre and developed into a garden—and a memorial—only after Independence.

I couldn't help thinking of the cruelty that Dyer, at the time a colonel serving as temporary brigadier-general, had shown himself to be capable of. It is one thing to have a terrorist or a bunch of terrorists randomly shooting at people, but quite another to have highly efficient soldiers opening fire, without a word of warning, on a crowd of 10,000 unarmed and ordinary Punjabis who had nowhere to hide or escape. Many people jumped into a well to save themselves from bullets but ended up meeting death at its bottom: 120 bodies were retrieved from it. The well remains intact, with a rather gaudy memorial constructed over it.

As many as 1,650 rounds were fired that evening, leaving 379 dead—that was the official figure—even though other sources put the toll between 1,000 and 1,500. Many of the dead happened to be villagers who had visited the Golden Temple on Baisakhi and were on their way home when they, out of curiosity, stopped by at the ground to listen to the speeches being made against the Rowlatt Act, which basically allowed the authorities to throw anyone they thought was a troublemaker into prison without trial.

In all probability, these villagers did not even know who Justice S.A.T. Rowlatt was or what the Act, based on his recommendations, was all about. They were merely out to celebrate Baisakhi and were expecting to be home for dinner. But Dyer—unrepentant till his dying day—had sent them to the cremation ground instead.

Even though Dyer was censured by the British Parliament and forced to resign from the army, his sympathisers—which included Rudyard Kipling—contributed generously for the fund that was raised for him by the public. And so Dyer, born in Murree in 1864—his father was employed by the brewery there—died a patriot in a town near Bristol in 1927.

The massacre saw the birth of Indian revolutionaries who weren't scared of embracing death. India's best-known poet, Rabindranath Tagore, also revolted against the massacre by renouncing his knighthood. This was when the British still believed they would rule India forever.

Holes punched by the bullets of Dyer's men remain visible on the walls of a solitary red-brick structure that stands in the garden, which was probably a temple and is now cordoned off by glass panels. There are also bullet marks on the rear wall of one particular building: it is perhaps the only building abutting the garden that remains untouched by time, and that is because the bullet marks had to be preserved.

I exited Jallianwala Bagh thinking people with guns often decide the destiny of people without guns, people with money often decide the destiny of people without money, and people having both, money and the best guns, often decide the destiny of an entire nation—even nations. Though once in a while, there comes a time when such people are put in their place by those who may not have the money or the best guns but who have something else: courage.

It takes a lot of courage to be happy all the time and Sikhs are perennially happy, even though in the short time that the community has been in existence it has had more than its share of adversities.

First the persecution by the Mughals: two of the ten Sikh Gurus—Guru Arjan and Guru Tegh Bahadur—were executed during the regimes of Jahangir and Aurangzeb respectively for not embracing Islam. The tenth guru, Gobind Singh, who was Guru Tegh Bahadur's son and is most revered after Guru Nanak, died soon after being stabbed by a Muslim assailant. Exactly forty years after his death began a series of raids—seven in all—by the Afghan king Ahmed Shah Abdali, whose army routinely butchered Sikhs. After that came the massacre at Jallianwala Bagh, followed by Partition in which countless Sikhs were killed.

Their troubles did not end with Independence.

After Partition, the Punjab that fell in India's share also included what is today Haryana and Himachal Pradesh. Sikhs, protesting against the imposition of Hindi in schools, demanded a separate state for themselves. It was only in 1966 that Hindi-speaking areas—in the form of Haryana and Himachal Pradesh—were separated from the Sikh-majority Punjab.

Then in 1977 began a chain of events that was to stretch for about a decade and a half, a period as painful as Partition. That year when Prime Minister Indira Gandhi lifted the Emergency and called for elections, her Congress party was routed in almost all the states including Punjab, where the coalition of Akali Dal and Janata Party formed the government. The defeat did not go down well with the Congress, and it propped up a thirty-year-old spiritual teacher called Sant Jarnail Singh Bhindranwale to weaken the Akali Dal.

But the steely-eyed Bhindranwale was clearly marked for a permanent place in history. He rapidly rose to be a prominent leader of the Sikhs, earning widespread admiration for not only preaching the purest form of the faith but also championing their cause: he believed that Sikhs were discriminated against in India and that the fruits of their labour were actually enjoyed by people living outside Punjab. He also asked Sikhs to be armed so that they could fight for their honour.

His rise saw the growth of insurgency in Punjab, and once again its fertile soil was soaked in blood as killings began to take place on a daily basis. Young men on motorbikes, carrying Sten guns, would murder anyone they saw as enemies of Sikh pride. Their victims often included Sikhs themselves.

By 1984 Bhindranwale had become law unto himself. Entrenched in the Golden Temple, he became the mascot for the separate Sikh nation of Khalistan that was being demanded by many of his followers, even though Bhindranwale himself never specifically called for a separate homeland. For him, the fight was between Sikhs and the Indian government, which he saw as pro-Hindu. The government, irony of ironies, was led by Mrs Gandhi, whose son Sanjay had handpicked Bhindranwale in 1977, to be a thorn in the flesh of the Akali Dal.

The thorn was now embedded in her skin and she decided to remove it. As the Golden Temple turned into a fortress and the call for Khalistan grew louder, she sent in the army in June 1984 to flush out the extremist elements holed up there. Some 1,000 people died, including about a hundred soldiers.

The move, apart from angering even moderate Sikhs, turned out to be fatal for her.

Five months later, she was gunned down by her two Sikh bodyguards. Her killing triggered the mass murder of Sikhs across north India. In most places, policemen sat back as hoodlums went about hunting down Sikhs and burning their shops. Over three days, anywhere between 3,000 and 8,000 Sikhs were butchered across India.

I may not have seen Partition, but I was witness to the aftermath of Mrs Gandhi's assassination. I was fourteen then, studying in the ninth standard, when on the afternoon of October 31 the principal walked into the classroom and told the teacher to let us all go home.

'It seems the prime minister has been assassinated,' we overheard the principal—a nun—telling the teacher. *It seems.* I still remember those words. Back then, there was no way of confirming a piece of news immediately: you either had to wait for the evening bulletin on Doordarshan or for the next morning's newspaper.

So that afternoon I got back home, had lunch, did my homework and went to the playground outside my house to play cricket. By the evening, the entire nation had learned, from Doordarshan, that Indira Gandhi had been assassinated.

At the time, at least in the part of the world where I lived, people went to sleep as soon Doordarshan or All India Radio ended its transmission for the night. The night of October 31 wasn't any different, except that people had still not digested the news. The next morning the same playground was milling with grown-ups. They stood in small circles, each formed around a person holding the morning's paper. And then I saw the mob marching past my home, twenty to thirty people, many of them familiar faces—the 'loafers' of the neighbourhood.

They went to each Sikh home and demanded that the male members surrender their turbans. While most Sikhs did as asked, one man made the fatal mistake of challenging the mob, and his body lay on the street for two days. I didn't witness the killing because he lived a few streets away, but I did get to see the body some hours later—from a distance.

I would now say that this mob was made of angels, considering what went on at the time in other parts of Kanpur and the rest of north India, particularly in Delhi, where Sikhs were killed in the most savage manner. My maternal grandfather, who lived in Delhi and who happened to visit us soon after, told us about one killing that he had witnessed himself: that of a young Sikh who lived opposite his house. I remembered him quite well—his nickname was Bittu—because I would spend my summer vacations in Delhi.

According to my grandfather, when the mob banged at his gates, Bittu came out smiling, pleading for mercy with joined hands. But the mob felled him instantly with iron rods, and once he was nearly dead, set him on fire. He lay there half-burnt for a day, or perhaps two, until his sister flagged down an Army jeep and begged for a dignified cremation for her brother. The soldiers, sympathetic but helpless, asked her for a mattress and, carrying the half-burnt body on the mattress to a nearby ditch, set it on fire once again.

Fortunately, our neighbourhood in Kanpur had been spared such brutality. We enjoyed the holidays thrust upon us by the curfew and would play cricket until policemen chased us away. When the curfew was lifted, several of our neighbours came to own TV sets overnight. Many of the electronics shops were owned by Sikhs.

Until the end of that decade, Sikhs were viewed with suspicion. Sometime in 1989 or 90, a friend was taking the train from Kanpur to New Delhi, and one of his fellow passengers happened to be a Sikh who carried a briefcase. Each time the train stopped at a station the Sikh would get down to stretch his legs, and each time he did that, another fellow passenger would tell my friend, 'Look, he has left his briefcase behind again. What if it has a bomb?' Finally that man could not contain himself and told the Sikh, 'Sardarji, I have no problem with you getting down at every station, but please take your briefcase along.'

The Sikh, according to my friend, had responded only with a smile and chosen not to get down at subsequent stations. One couldn't entirely blame the man for being anxious: briefcase bombs were indeed killing people at the time. But it must have been quite humiliating for Sikhs back then to be seen as possible terrorists just because a few hundred among them happened to be so.

And yet, as I stepped into the Golden Temple, it felt as though nothing had ever happened. No trace of anger, not a hint of bitterness, no sign of sadness—only the smile, the default setting of a Sikh face.

Just about any human on this planet—no matter what religion, race, or nationality—can freely enter the Golden Temple: to pray, eat or just to have a look. There are only two requirements: you will need to leave your footwear at one of the many shoe counters, and cover your head with a cloth. Few places of worship in the entire universe leave their doors so wide open—in fact the Golden Temple has four entrances, one in each direction, to signify that all are welcome. The gold-plated temple itself—located in the middle of the square tank, pool of nectar, and accessed by a marble causeway—sits on a level slightly lower than the surrounding land, to signify humility.

I sat on the marble floor by the tank, watching the shrine glitter in the last rays of the sun, and its reflection on the water. There was a long queue on the causeway, so instead of joining it, I had decided to watch the spectacle from a distance, as had many others. There were hundreds of people around at that hour—devotees and tourists alike, taking pictures, taking selfies, some excited, some meditating—but the noise generated by their presence seemed to be absorbed by the water. All you heard was the strains of gurbani, words of the gurus, wafting out of the sanctum sanctorum. I never felt calmer.

When I walked out of the temple to reclaim my leather

chappals, I found they had been polished. I couldn't help but marvel at Sikhism: the most practical, pragmatic, and progressive of religions, built on selfless service and sacrifice. And yet, being a Sikh has never been easy.

# 10

Names, like looks, can be deceiving. I smiled over this thought as I set out for Ferozepur in the morning.

Ramesh, who had taken me to the Attari station and Golden Temple, had not allowed me to pay for the travel. 'Let's not discuss money, sir,' he had said, 'it was my privilege I could show you around.'

While on the one hand I did not mind not paying, on the other hand I did not want to be seen as a freeloader. So this morning I did what I should have done in the first place: asked Ms Blue Eyelids to arrange a car for me.

I had barely finished my breakfast of alu paratha and curd when she had called to inform me that the driver had arrived. 'He is waiting in the parking lot. His name is Balbir Singh.'

The distance between Amritsar and Ferozepur is about 150 kilometres, which can be covered, I was told, in about three hours. Would Mr Balbir Singh take it kindly if I were to ask him to stop the car occasionally so that I could step out for a smoke?

The question weighed heavily on my mind—wouldn't

it be so much easier to kick the habit?—as I walked to the parking lot, looking for a turbaned driver with angry eyes and a flowing black beard. But only one car turned out to be parked there, and in that a soft-faced, non-Sikh man dozed in the driver's seat.

I tapped his shoulder and asked, 'By any chance are you Balbir Singh?'

'*Haan ji, haan ji,*' he woke up with a start. 'It is so hot that I dozed off.'

'You might want to splash some water on your face,' I suggested.

'I am all right,' he assured me. He rolled up the windows, turned on the AC, and soon we hit the highway. 'Where are you from?'

'I am a Bengali, but I live in Chennai.'

'Chennai? I see. Isn't Tamil Nadu somewhere in Chennai?'

'It's the other way round. Where are you from?'

'Bihar, but settled in Amritsar. More than thirty years now.'

I suddenly felt bold enough to tell him that he might have to stop the car occasionally to let me satisfy my nicotine cravings.

'What's the need to stop,' he said, 'just roll down the window whenever you want to smoke.'

I relaxed. I could now sit back and enjoy the drive.

'You are from Bihar, but your name is very Punjabi. Were you always called Balbir Singh?'

'My real name is Babu. You can call me Babu.'

'How did Babu become Balbir Singh?'

'It's a long story,' he smiled.

It is essential to have a good driver when you are setting out on a long journey in a strange place. When I say good I don't just mean driving skills, but talkativeness. A driver who minds his business is a blessing only when you are driving from, say, home to office, when you have a million things on your mind and the last thing you want is a nosey driver. But when you have hundreds of kilometres ahead of you, that too in an unfamiliar land, the last thing you want is a driver who keeps to himself.

A good driver is someone who first presses for your personal details—where are you from? Where do you work? What brings you here? Are you married? How many members are there in your family?—and then volunteers his own personal details. Before long, you become friends—two lonely souls together in one car due to circumstances. You begin to care for each other. For example, he will make sure you eat at the right place when you stop for lunch on the highway, while you will make sure that he eats too.

There is something else as well, apart from the camaraderie. The driver, since he knows the route like the back of his hand, is often familiar with the history and culture of the land he takes you through. He is capable of diagnosing the pulse of a place better than its elected representatives, for the simple reason that he is always on the road and has an ear to the ground. He is invaluable if you are writing about a place.

'Why are you going to Ferozepur?' Babu asked me, 'Business or personal work?'

'We are actually going to a place called Hussainiwala, heard of it?'

'Sounds familiar, is it in Ferozepur?'

'Not exactly, it is about 10 kilometres from Ferozepur, right on the border.'

'Not a problem, we will find our way. Finding a place is never a problem. I have been driving for god knows how many years, fifteen or maybe twenty? I don't even remember.'

'But I am sure you remember how you became Balbir Singh. Tell me that story.'

Babu laughed. 'It was just a matter of destiny, sir. God has been kind to me, what else can I say?' Then he told me the story.

Babu was born in a village near Chhapra city in Bihar. His parents, farm labourers, migrated to Amritsar in 1978 in the hope that they would earn a little more than they did back home. Babu, who was going to the village school, never went to a school again once the family moved to Punjab.

He grew up doing odd jobs to add to the family income, though there were occasions when they went without food. For a long time Babu worked as a waiter, a lowly member of the small army that assists caterers during weddings and parties, earning twelve to fourteen rupees for every event and sharing leftover food with fellow waiters.

One day he decided he had had enough of surviving on leftovers and that he wanted a better-paying job. But who was to give him that, considering that he was nearly illiterate? So he learned driving and found employment in a small taxi company.

One morning, he was assigned to a Sikh couple who had to attend a wedding. Babu drove them to the venue, waited for them until the wedding got over, and as he was driving them back home—it was a long drive—the couple began to make enquiries: '*Beta*, how old are you? How much do you earn? Who all are there in your family? Do you drink or smoke?'

Babu replied to their queries with utmost honesty. The couple, who had five sons and one daughter, were so impressed by him that they decided, while they were still on the road, that they would marry their daughter to him.

It was at his own wedding, conducted Sikh style, that Babu was rechristened Balbir Singh.

'That's why I said god has been kind to me,' Babu said, '*Jo sardarni se shaadi kar le, samjho usko swarg mil gaya*'—If you marry a Sikh woman, your life turns into paradise.

'How is that?'

'Sikhs take care of their daughters. Take my father-in-law, for example. He and his five sons are farmers, and he makes sure that my house is always well-stocked with food grains. He sends us a year's supply after every harvest. My wife is particularly pampered because she is the only daughter.

'Raksha Bandhan is round the corner, for example, and

each of her five brothers has been calling her to ask what he should gift her. My wife has been protesting, "No, no, don't bother about gifts," but I know they will all end up giving her expensive gifts. Tomorrow if I fall sick or meet with an accident, I can afford to stay without work easily for a year or two. I will be taken care of.'

Babu and his wife went on to produce three children—two sons and a daughter—in quick succession. Today one son is twenty-four and the other twenty-two—both are married—and the daughter is twenty. Neither of the sons wears the turban, and the elder one is already the father of a three-year-old child.

'So you are a grandfather now,' I remarked.

'Of course, of course,' Babu laughed. It was a laughter inspired by pride. 'When I get back home after a long day, the child comes running to me and hugs me and lies on my stomach. I forget all the tiredness.'

I could see that even though his eyes were on the road, his mind had suddenly wandered off to his bedroom, where Babu, clad in a vest and lungi, has barely rested his back on the bed after a long day when the child jumps on to him, admonishing the grandfather for being away for so long. The grandfather melts with joy and hugs the child, showering it with all kinds of names that have no meaning as such but drip with affection.

This part was easy to imagine. What was hard to digest was that the Sikh couple had chosen Babu to be their son-in-law on the spot. When I expressed my amazement to him, he said, 'Don't go by how I look today. Now I am old,

I have lost hair, put on weight. But back then I was very handsome, I had a good personality. I wish I was carrying an old picture of mine to show you.'

'How old are you now?'

'Must be around fifty, I am not sure. All I know is that I was born in the year 1970, you can do the calculation.'

'1970? We are the same age, Babu. We are both forty-five. And you are already a grandfather?'

Babu smiled sheepishly. 'But you know something,' he said, 'I don't think of myself as a grandfather when I am on the road. As they say, two things never age.'

'What are they?'

'*Ghoda aur lauda*'—The horse and a man's dick.

# 11

Amritsar was barely 20 kilometres behind us when Babu slowed down near a gurdwara that sat right on the highway.

'Do you see commuters throwing money at the gurdwara?' Babu said. 'No one goes past it without making a small donation because they want to have a safe journey.'

I noticed passing motorists pausing for a moment, directly in front of the gurdwara, bowing with utmost reverence and then flinging currency notes with their entire might so that the money landed in a designated enclosure that served as the receptacle for such donations. Many missed their aim but they moved on, having done their bit. It was left to volunteers to pick up the fallen money and drop it in the enclosure.

'I think it would be a good idea to visit this gurdwara,' I told Babu, who then parked the car by the road, under a tree. As we walked to its entrance, covering our heads with handkerchiefs, a couple of hundred-rupee notes fell near my feet. I picked them up and dropped them over the pile that had already built up in the enclosure. It was strewn with coins as well—some people can be stingy—but I was sure the caretakers would consider those coins as drops that add up to become an ocean.

Very strangely, even though the gurdwara sat right on the busy highway, inside there was quiet. In the large hall sat about a dozen men and women, immersed in prayer. They were scattered around the pedestal that held the Guru Granth Sahib.

Guru Gobind Singh, the tenth guru, had willed that after his death he should have no successor and that the holy book of hymns—containing the teachings of not only his predecessors but also some non-Sikh saints including Kabir and Namdeo—should be considered the eternal guru. And so the book became Guru Granth Sahib.

It was also Guru Gobind who, after having formed a military order called the Khalsa, surnamed the Sikh men Singh and the women Kaur. He ordered them not to cut their hair and mandated that they always wear a *kada* (metal bangle) and *kachchha* (underpants), and carry a *kangha* (comb) and *kirpan* (dagger).

Babu spotted a *sevadar*—caretaker—identifiable because of his deep blue robe and the dagger, who sat cross-legged in the hall. We sat next to him and Babu, now my interpreter, introduced me and said, 'He wants to know about the history of this gurdwara.'

The *sevadar*, in chaste Punjabi, told Babu whatever little he knew, much of which was lost in translation. What I gathered was that the gurdwara was built on the spot where Baba Naudh Singh, a saint-warrior, was killed fighting the Mughal army and that his tomb was located in the gurdwara compound—I had noticed a marble tomb while walking in.

An elderly Sikh, who sat near enough to hear us, interrupted, 'His head got severed in the fighting, and the moment the head fell on the ground, a miracle happened: the soldiers of the mighty Mughal army lay scattered on the ground, wounded or dead. Baba Naudh Singh Ji then picked up his severed head and walked all the way to the Golden Temple to make an offering of his head.'

The *sevadar* was evidently relieved that the elderly man had taken over from him. But the beheaded warrior he mentioned was not Baba Naudh Singh, as far as I knew, but Baba Deep Singh, about whom I had read on a display board in the Golden Temple. Was the old man confusing one warrior-saint with another, or were there actually two saint-warriors who had walked to the Golden Temple carrying their severed heads on their own palms?

That night I read up about the two names, and also spoke to a friend who spends all his free time reading Indian history, and was able to piece together the story.

In 1757, when the Afghan ruler Ahmad Shah Abdali was returning home after raiding India for the fourth time, Sikh guerrillas waylaid his caravan and not only freed many of the captives but also relieved the invader of some of the loot. An enraged Ahmad Shah then anointed his nine-year-old son, Timur Shah, the ruler of Punjab, placing him under the care of a general called Jahan Khan, and ordered them to demolish Harmandir Sahib, which, at that time, was not known as the Golden

Temple because it hadn't been gold-plated yet. The Afghan soldiers razed the temple and desecrated the holy tank—the pool of nectar—by throwing carcasses of cows into it. At the time, Baba Deep Singh, seventy-six years old, was leading a retired life, having served as the first chief of the Damdama Taksal, the religious school several miles from Amritsar that, more than two centuries later, was headed by Jarnail Singh Bhindranwale. When Deep Singh heard of the desecration, he set out for Amritsar at once to seek revenge, collecting an army of saint-warriors along the way. One of them was Baba Naudh Singh, already over ninety years old. They were met by the Afghans in a village called Gohalwar and a fierce battle ensued. During a sword fight with Jahan Khan, Deep Singh's head got nearly severed and he collapsed. When a fellow Sikh reminded him of his vow to reach the pool of nectar as a victorious man, he got up and, keeping his head in place with one hand, went on to slaughter the enemy with the other. He swung his sword through the enemy until he reached Harmandir Sahib, where he finally dropped dead. Baba Naudh Singh, on the other hand, died on the battleground.

But that morning, as I sat in the gurdwara, I had no idea that I was actually on the site of the Battle of Gohalwar, which took place in 1757, the same year that Robert Clive fought the Battle of Plassey against the Nawab of Bengal. My ignorance was greater than that of the elderly Sikh—I shall call him Hoshiyar Singh—who had merely confused the Afghans with the Mughals and Baba Deep Singh with Baba Naudh Singh.

Hoshiyar Singh looked like an aged saint-warrior himself: he wore a white salwar-kameez and a flowing silver beard, the black sling of his dagger case running conspicuously across his chest. I asked him to tell me about himself: his own story wouldn't need cross-checking. Moreover, he spoke fluent Hindi and also, from time to time, broke into English. His English wasn't very fluent, but the accent was that of an Englishman.

Hoshiyar Singh said he was born in Lyallpur, now in Pakistan and renamed Faisalabad, and was five years old when India was partitioned. His family packed its belongings and left on a bullock-cart for Amritsar, where his maternal grandfather lived. On the way, they were nearly butchered by a mob of Muslims when soldiers from the Dogra regiment came to their rescue.

The government allotted the family a piece of land in Rajasthan, in lieu of the land they had lost in Pakistan, and, while his two elder brothers became farmers, Hoshiyar Singh grew up to join the Rajasthan State Transport Corporation as a mechanic.

'I studied up to the eighth standard in Rajasthan. After that I went to Jalandhar to complete my schooling. I came back to Rajasthan and joined the roadways as a helper on a monthly salary of 120 rupees. But I worked very hard and went on to become a supervisor. When I retired, in 2008, I was earning Rs 17,000 a month. By then I had built a house of my own and educated my children. Today the children are doing well, by god's grace. My daughter is happily married and lives in Haryana. My son is settled in Adelaide, he is married to a doctor. My wife and I spend a few months with him every year (that explained the accent). Our life is set.'

'What about the land the government gave you?' I asked.

'My brothers look after it. I have nothing to do with them.'

'Why so?'

'They are both *naalayak* (good for nothing). They have become slaves of their wives who come from *ghatiya* (lowly) families. They are quarrelsome women, it is best to keep away from them.'

The *sevadar*, who had been listening quietly until now, suddenly spoke up. 'Look at me, I am such a fool,' he admonished himself loudly. 'You people have come all the way and I have not even offered you anything to eat or drink.'

He looked around and called a volunteer, who handed steel bowls to Babu and me and poured *badam* milk from a kettle. As soon as we drank it up, the bowls were filled up again on the insistence of Hoshiyar Singh.

Babu looked most gratified. He said, 'This is a wholesome drink, it gives you strength. Sometimes it can also make you drowsy.' I wasn't very pleased to hear that: we had to cover hundred kilometres.

The *sevadar* had successfully deflected the conversation away from the personal life of Hoshiyar Singh, who now ranted about what politicians had done to the country: 'Why is the Gandhi family given so much importance? What did Gandhi do for the country anyway? Why do currency notes carry his picture—and not pictures of Maharaja Ranjit Singh, Bhagat Singh or Subhas Chandra Bose?' Since he had gathered that I was a Bengali, he added, 'Why not the picture of Jyoti Basu? He was such a great man.'

He went on and on until I ran out of my patience and he of his energy. I tried getting up but he grabbed my arm. He summoned the volunteer and asked him to pour us more badam milk, this time for him as well. Babu's face lit up. I pleaded to be spared of another helping, not sure what the potent drink was going to do to my stomach, but Hoshiyar Singh brushed aside my pleas with a wave of his hand. He drank the milk with great urgency and once he was done, he wiped his moustache and said, 'So where was I? Yes, so things will not improve in this country until the youth takes over.

'Talking of the youth,' I said, 'I find many young Sikhs without the turban. What do you have to say about that?'

'That can't be true. A true Sikh can never be without the turban.'

'But that's what I have noticed. I have been going around Amritsar.'

'It is only the children of *ghatiya* people who don't care much about the turban,' he said.

'By *ghatiya* people you mean?

'Those people who have got married to Biharis and Rajasthanis and others. *Ek sachche Sardar ka ladka sir katwa lega magar baal nahin katwayega*'—The son of a true Sikh would have his head chopped, but not his hair.

I avoided looking at Babu. I knew the old man was wrong—sons of many 'true' Sikhs don't wear the turban—but nodding vehemently in agreement seemed to be the easiest way out of Sardar Hoshiyar Singh's grip.

# 12

Punjab means the land of five rivers—Jhelum, Chenab, Ravi, Beas and Sutlej—all of which happen to be tributaries of the Indus, the river that gave the subcontinent its name: India or Hindustan.

The soul who coined the name obviously hadn't imagined that someday Pakistan would be carved out of Hindustan, and that Punjab, a homogenous land irrigated by the five rivers, would be split into two.

The Indian Punjab today is left with not even two-and-a-half of these five: there is the Sutlej; there is the Beas; and a bit of the Ravi, which runs hugging the border for a short distance before meandering into Pakistan. Its Pakistani counterpart, however, is laced with four of the five rivers, minus the Beas. But then the Beas is nothing but a tributary of the Sutlej, and the two reunite shortly before they enter Pakistan under the name of Sutlej. So in a sense, the Punjab of Pakistan is still watered by all the five rivers and therefore can be said to be living up to its name.

Babu and I now stood at the confluence of the Beas and Sutlej, in a place called Harike. The town of Ferozepur was still about an hour away. We munched on roasted corn and sipped Thums Up as we watched the furious Beas unite with the calmer Sutlej and flow under the bridge as one river, its currents washing along hyacinth. Almost perpendicular to the river ran a canal which, a heavily-armed sentry posted at the headworks told me, went straight into arid Rajasthan.

Headworks is a structure built across a river, often doubling as a bridge, to divert some of its water into canals feeding drier areas. It was easy to guess why Harike Headworks was heavily guarded. If the bridge got blown up, not only would the irrigation system go haywire but also Ferozepur would lose a vital link to the rest of Punjab, which would be a catastrophe considering that Ferozepur hugs Pakistan.

Ferozepur almost went to Pakistan during Partition. If it stayed in India, it was only because of a particular headworks on the Sutlej—no, not the one at Harike, which was built only in the early 1950s, but one built further downstream way back in the 1920s, in a village called Hussainiwala.

Sir Cyril Radcliffe was merely going by demographic congruity when he had placed the district across the new border. Since Hussainiwala sat on its western fringe, giving Ferozepur to Pakistan meant giving the headworks, which helped in the irrigation of a large part of Rajasthan, to Pakistan as well—something that was not acceptable to the top Indian leadership, which had been offered a sneak peek at the map by Mountbatten himself.

Mountbatten then nudged Sir Cyril into shifting the border slightly west. As a result, while Hussainiwala went to Pakistan, its headworks and the rest of Ferozepur remained with India.

Fourteen years later, however, Hussainiwala came back to India. The reason behind its return is connected to yet another headworks on the Sutlej—one even further downstream, also built in the 1920s, in a village called Sulemanki. During Partition, while the Sulemanki Headworks was awarded to Pakistan, its auxiliary waterworks had remained on the Indian side. This division of the apparatus became a matter of dispute, resolved only in 1961 when the two countries reached an agreement, under which the twelve Indian villages that were part of the Sulemanki waterworks were transferred to Pakistan, and in exchange, the village of Hussainiwala came to India.

Symbolically and emotionally, for India, the lone village of Hussainiwala was of far greater importance than those twelve Sulemanki villages put together.

Hussainiwala was where I was headed now.

Babu, letting out a thunderous belch after finishing the bottle of Thums Up, asked me innocently, 'By the way, why are we going to Hussainiwala?'

'Have you heard of Bhagat Singh?' I asked him.

'I know I am illiterate but even I have heard of Bhagat Singh,' he laughed.

From the bridge we flung the corncobs, which instantly got sucked into swirling waters; then, returning the soft drink bottles of Thums Up to the stall, we walked back to the car. That's when I told Babu the story.

In 1928, when the Simon Commission arrived in India to report on the working of the Indian Constitution—as enacted by the British in 1919—freedom-hungry Indians were appalled that the commission did not have a single Indian member. Protests broke out across India. In Lahore, it was Lala Lajpat Rai who led the protest, one peaceful one, only to be beaten up by the police. He died days later.

Bhagat Singh and his comrades—Rajguru and Sukhdev—decided to avenge Lajpat Rai's death by killing Lahore's superintendent of police James Scott. But they ended up assassinating Scott's deputy John Saunders instead: a case of mistaken identity. The three were eventually caught and sentenced to death in October 1930.

At 7 p.m. on 23 March 1931, they were hanged at the Lahore Central Jail. Bhagat Singh, by then, had become the poster boy of the militant nationalist movement. He was not a hot-headed Punjabi who had killed a British officer in a fit of rage, but a cold-blooded revolutionary who had evolved an ideology of his own: a blend of atheism, communism and militant nationalism. The British thought he was too dangerous to be kept alive. For them, it was even more dangerous to hand over his body to his people because that could trigger an uprising.

Once the prison doctor declared the three revolutionaries to be dead, the authorities smuggled the bodies out of the prison and transported them out of Lahore to the village of Hussainiwala, where they were hastily cremated by the Sutlej in the dead of the night.

After Radcliffe placed Hussainiwala in Pakistan, there was, of course, no question of Pakistan developing the cremation site as a memorial. Unlike independent India, which was born out of anti-Britain sentiments, Pakistan was born out of anti-India sentiments and it remained by and large indifferent to the heroes who had fought the British.

Once Hussainiwala came to India in 1961, attempts began to be made to build a memorial. From a 2007 piece written by civil servant K.S. Bains in *The Tribune*, titled *Making of a Memorial*:

> I was Deputy Commissioner, Ferozepore, in 1967. Two of my predecessors had tried to mobilise funds by donations to construct a memorial but nothing worthwhile emerged. I tried to do the same but realised that my efforts would not succeed. Lachhman Singh Gill, who belonged to Ferozepore, was the Chief Minister of Punjab at that time.
>
> One day I proposed to the CM that a proper *samadhi* be constructed in memory of Bhagat Singh, Rajguru and Sukhdev. He was shocked when I told him that no memorial had so far been set up at the site of the cremation of the three martyrs. I also mentioned to him that efforts made to mobilise donations had been of no consequence.
>
> We got to work immediately thereafter. The first step was to properly identify the site. I, along with SDM, tehsildar and elders of the area, went to the spot in Hussainiwala and marked the area for setting up the *samadhi*.
>
> The spot was roughly marked by the local people. Sometimes it would be washed away by floods.
>
> I sent the tehsildar along with a few other persons to Bhagat Singh's village, Khatkar Kalan, to see whether any

> photograph of his with a turban was available. The family had a few photographs. One of these, a group photograph of students who had performed in a drama, showed Bhagat Singh in turban. This was taken when he was in Class XII. The style of his turban could be clearly seen in the picture. These pictures were given to the sculptor for making Bhagat Singh's bust. That is how for the first time we got a picture of Bhagat Singh as he must have looked during most of his life.

The memorial was inaugurated by the chief minister in 1968—on March 23, the same day in 1931 that the three had been executed. Bains wrote that Bhagat Singh's elder brother Kultar Singh, a devoted communist, was also present at the event but declined to participate in the dedication ceremony, saying it was a 'government function'.

Less than four years later, nothing was to remain of that memorial.

During the 1971 war, Pakistani forces wrested Hussainiwala from India. The Indian forces guarding it belonged to 15 Punjab, which had a formidable reputation as a fighting force, but the commanding officer, for reasons best known to him, panicked once the Pakistanis mounted a determined attack and decided to withdraw, and in that panic also prematurely blew up the Kaiser-e-Hind, the road-cum-rail bridge that connected Hussainiwala to the rest of India, so that Pakistani tanks could not roll deeper into Indian territory.

Hussainiwala was eventually retrieved by fighter jets of the Indian Air Force, but not before the Pakistanis had destroyed the memorial and walked away with the busts of Bhagat Singh, Sukhdev and Rajguru. It, of course, hadn't mattered to them that Bhagat Singh was born in Pakistan—in Lyallpur, or Faisalabad—and that he had fought against the British as a citizen of undivided India. For them, an Indian icon was an enemy of Pakistan.

I have often wondered how Bhagat Singh, if he had lived, would have reacted to Partition: he would have been only forty at the time. What if he got to watch the events unfold from a gallery up in Heaven: to see India no longer fighting the British but a new nation carved out of it called Pakistan, and some of the pitched battles taking place on the very site of his cremation?

The memorial was rebuilt in 1973. Close to it lies the Hussainiwala border crossing where a flag-lowering ceremony, similar to the one held at Wagah, is conducted every evening.

Of course, I did not narrate this entire story to Babu. When he asked me why we were headed for Hussainiwala, all I told him was: 'To visit the spot where Bhagat Singh and his comrades were cremated and also to watch a Wagah-type parade that is held on the border there.'

Babu's eyes lit up. He now seemed to have a sense of purpose.

We drove into Ferozepur under a signboard, 'Welcome to the land of martyrs.'

I had heard of Ferozepur ever since I was a child because

there was always some classmate or the other whose father was either getting posted there or was posted from there. I always imagined it to be peopled with soldiers, ready to fire their guns at the enemy at a moment's notice. Later several of my classmates themselves went on to serve in Ferozepur, though by then my fascination for the uniform had extinguished. I had applied for the Indian Air Force twice—first at the age of seventeen and then at the age of twenty-two—and even though I cleared what is called the Pilot Aptitude Battery Test, which must be cleared at the first chance, I was found lacking in what they call Officer Like Qualities. Thankfully, they had realized I wasn't cut out for the job before I could.

Unfortunately no one I knew was presently stationed at Ferozepur, I would have not only had local support but also been assured of drinks and dinner in the evening. It is such a pleasure to be the guest of an army—or air force or navy—officer. You don't even have to walk up to his bar for a refill: he will insist on getting it for you. This is one thing that crosses my mind occasionally: the real beneficiaries of the etiquette that a uniformed officer gets inculcated with are actually slouchy civilians like me. When I entertain guests at home, I like to recline on a bolster in one corner, absorbing the chatter, only too happy if one of the guests offers to refill my glass. No wonder the air force rejected me—twice.

'We are now in Ferozepur, sir, how do we go to Hussainiwala?' Babu asked me.

'It's simple, Babu,' I said. 'Ask for directions.'

'I don't know why I thought you knew the way.'

'This is my first ever visit to Punjab.'

He stopped the car and walked up to a fruit stall. During the moments he tried to understand the roadmap from the fruit seller, I looked around. Not a soldier in sight, but then this was the main city and not the cantonment. Ferozepur predates Amritsar by about two centuries but appeared smaller and sleepy.

We drove on and shortly afterwards approached the bridge across the Sutlej. The river, as we travelled from Harike to here, had entered Pakistan and re-emerged into Indian territory and was now flowing into Pakistan once again—thanks to the zigzaggedness of the Radcliffe Line.

As soon as we had got onto the bridge, we could see, to our right, the furious waters of the river washing along the hyacinth, but the view to the left was blocked by yellow-painted tin sheets. In other words, we knew what the Sutlej looked like on the Indian side, but were only left to guess what it must be looking like on the other side.

It would have looked the same of course, just that the deliberate visual obstruction made one curious. It wouldn't have evoked such curiosity in the year, say, 1931, when there was just one Punjab, a prosperous province in British India, its capital city being Lahore, the most progressive Indian city at the time, where Bhagat Singh and his two comrades were hanged in its central prison.

Babu and I now stood at the spot where they were cremated. It was on the riverbank, but the river has since changed course and shifted south, leaving behind a vast tract of fertile land, heavily cultivated, between its present bank and the memorial.

Two more people were cremated at the site: Batukeshwar Dutt, in 1965, and Bhagat Singh's mother Vidyavati, in 1975. Bhagat Singh and his comrades, after killing Saunders, had gone into hiding, but Singh emerged soon after to throw bombs in the Central Legislative Assembly in Delhi along with Batukeshwar Dutt, knowing fully well that if caught he would be tried and hanged for the murder. Sure enough, he was arrested and shortly afterwards Rajguru and Sukhdev were picked up too. All three awarded the death sentence. Batukeshwar Dutt—since no one had died in the explosions at the Assembly—was handed life imprisonment and he died at the age of fifty-five, unsung, eighteen years after independence.

On a pedestal in a corner of the memorial park stood the life-size statues of the three revolutionaries—they are depicted walking in a resolute manner, each one with a raised fist, as if they were shouting 'Inquilab Zindabad!'—Long live the revolution! In another corner stood a red wall embedded with facial portraits of the three heroes and information about their bravery in three scripts—Gurmukhi, Hindi, and English.

Then there were several plaques certifying the bravery shown by Indian soldiers during various conflicts with Pakistan: in 1956, they are said to have thwarted an attack on the Hussainiwala Headworks; in 1965, they are said to have prevented the enemy from capturing the headworks; and in 1971, they are said to have repelled the enemy, which was in overwhelming strength, 'several times'.

There is, quite understandably, no mention of the fact that in 1971, the very spot where the plaques stood now—where I stood now—had been captured by the Pakistani forces before they were driven out by Indian Air Force bombers. The role of the air force is not acknowledged in the plaque pertaining to the 1971 war because that—quite understandably again—would amount to the army admitting to the reversal at Hussainiwala.

At the centre of the memorial park stood the imposing north-bank tower of the erstwhile Kaiser-e-Hind Bridge across the Sutlej. The bridge may have been blown up by the retreating Indians but the tower remained almost intact, except that it bore scars inflicted by Pakistani tanks. You can easily find black-and-white pictures on the internet showing a Pakistani flag atop the tower in 1971 and victorious Pakistani soldiers posing against it.

The pillars of the erstwhile bridge—all of them—stood entirely intact. The pillars that fell within the perimeter of the memorial park still had the ironworks mounted on them, now painted in the tricolour of the Indian flag. The successive pillars were all bald and sprouted like pieces of history from the crops that covered the land left behind by the shifting river.

I walked into the base of the tower and found a railway track there. History became easy to imagine. Back when the tower was built, it must have been situated right on the riverbank, receiving traffic from across the Sutlej—the train on the lower deck and all other vehicles, including the bicycle, on the upper. It also had witnessed the flames erupting from the pyres of Bhagat Singh and his comrades on the pleasantly chilly night of 23 March 1931. Today the tower stood like a warrior decapitated.

The present bridge was built as recently as in December 2013. For forty-two years Hussainiwala had remained connected to India with a makeshift wooden bridge.

Hussainiwala is named after a Muslim peer Hussaini baba, whose mausoleum stands close to the memorial park: you have to walk past it on your way to the galleries where people gather every evening to watch the flag-lowering ceremony.

A signboard outside the shrine said that Hussaini baba—long dead—is often spotted at nights, clad in white robes. It also said that travellers who prayed at his shrine on Fridays had their wishes fulfilled, and listed four categories of people who must seek the peer's favour: childless women wanting to be mothers; employees wanting promotion; students wanting good results; and businessmen eyeing profits. Unfortunately, the paint on the three digits that indicated the age of the shrine had faded, though from what my eyes could gather, the *dargah* was stated to be 'approximately 150 years old'.

Why did the signboard say travellers and not visitors? That's because for the longest time, the road on which the shrine stood was one of the arteries of the subcontinent. After Partition, until the 1971 war, the border crossing at Hussainiwala was one of the principal road links between India and Pakistan—and the sole link between them after the 1965 war when the Wagah border was shut down. Some years later, the Wagah crossing was reopened and today serves as the only road link between the two countries, whereas the Hussainiwala border remains closed and the gates are pulled apart only towards sunset for the flag-lowering ceremony.

Today was Friday, the day when Hussaini baba was said to grant your wishes. But I did not see anyone—apart from myself—stepping into the shrine. I prayed for the success of the book you are holding in your hands.

We joined the stream of people headed for the galleries. Unlike in Wagah, where visitors come from every corner of the country to witness the flag lowering, the crowd here was almost entirely Punjabi. Like others, I too wrote down my name and address on a BSF register, suffixing my name with '+1' to include Babu, and was handed a chit that was to be returned at the check-post on our way back from the ceremony.

As we sat down on the concrete steps, I found the stands on the Pakistani side—barely 100 metres away, in my estimate—packed to capacity. Today was Pakistan's Independence Day. The men swayed to the music and cheered in chorus. The women, unlike the men, sat wearing dignified expressions, while schoolchildren, mostly girls, obediently stuck to their seats, holding their country's flags.

Loudspeakers on the Indian side played bhangra numbers, while the DJ on the Pakistani side kept up a carnival-like atmosphere by playing fast numbers and frequently changing the songs. Sometimes the crowd there got so euphoric that the DJ would stop the music to tell them, 'Please calm down, *aapko apne watan ki kasam*.'

At one point, *Dama dam mast kalandar*, the highly popular Sufi song, burst out from their speakers and the man next to me exclaimed, '*Arrey yeh to Mikke ki aawaz hai*!'—This is Mika's voice! Mika Singh is a popular Indian singer, and Pakistan was playing his song now to celebrate its Independence Day.

The next song was in the unmistakable, inimitable voice of Nusrat Fateh Ali Khan, accompanied by a children's chorus: '*Pakistan Pakistan, mera imaan Pakistan, mera paigham Pakistan...*' It was a sweet, catchy song in praise of Pakistan.

The foot-stomping began at six—the sun now a benign amber ball hanging in the Pakistani sky—as sentries from the Border Security Force and Pakistan Rangers took positions on their respective sides of the Radcliffe Line.

Compared to what unfolded at Hussainiwala, the event at Wagah border seemed to be a crowd-pulling *tamasha* aimed at promoting—if I can take the liberty of coining the term—'patriotourism'.

There was high kicking and foot stamping at Hussainiwala too, but it all seemed a part of a drill than a taunt. When it was time to lower the flags, the sentry of each country entrusted with the job untied the rope from the respective posts and, holding on to the rope, marched into the soil of the opposite country and slowly brought down the flag to the sound of the bugle.

In other words, the BSF man lowered the Indian flag

while standing in Pakistan, and the Pakistan Ranger man lowered the flag of his country while standing in India. What heart-warming coordination.

On the drive back, we once again crossed the Sutlej, the yellow tin sheets blocking the view of the Pakistani side. But homebound birds flew over the metal screen. Birds don't recognize manmade borders. Neither does music, come to think of it. *Dama dam mast kalander* is as much Indian as it is Pakistani. They did not shy away from playing Mika Singh's rendition of the famous song, that too on their Independence Day, that too at an event held right on the border, even though Mika is an Indian. But then Mika is also a Punjabi. Nusrat Fateh Ali Khan, on the other hand, was a Pakistani but has probably left behind far more fans in India. For that matter, the next morning, when India celebrated its Independence Day, schools across the country would reverberate with *Saare jahaan se achchha*—composed by Muhammad Iqbal who, as the president of the Muslim League, had sowed the seed of Pakistan.

Back in the hotel, as I settled down with a glass of whisky, I switched on my laptop and opened You Tube. I had to listen to a song that had been playing in my head throughout the drive back: '*Pakistan, Pakistan, mera imaan Pakistan.*' It was easy to find and I listened to it once, and after another drink, once again. I did not feel shy or guilty. I was alone anyway.

# 13

I woke up around noon to total silence, hardly a sound—not even a voice—rising from the road below. Then I realized today was Independence Day, a holiday. On the same day, in 1947, Amritsar was bleeding because a scalpel was run against the skin of Punjab. I had finished visiting the two most important spots on that wound, so was it time now to leave? But today was Saturday, and I was booked to fly out only on Tuesday afternoon, which meant I had three days to kill. A friend I spoke to suggested I drive up to Himachal Pradesh, and I was seriously considering the idea when I remembered something.

At Attari station, I had made friends with a Sikh called Dalbir Singh. He had come to receive his *maasi da munda*—aunt's son—and his wife, who were travelling from Lahore in Samjhauta Express. When I had said goodbye to Dalbir Singh that hot afternoon, he was bracing himself for a long wait while the cousin and the cousin's wife cleared immigration and customs checks. It had been about forty-eight hours now since I took leave of Dalbir Singh—after taking down his phone number—at Attari, and his Pakistani relatives would surely be home by now.

I called him up. He was happy to hear from me. He gave me his address—a village called Nag Khurd in a town called Majitha, about fifteen kilometres from the hotel. I promptly dialled the reception to ask Ms Blue Eyelids to arrange a cab for me.

The cab driver, once again, turned out to be Babu. He even wore the same pink shirt. I was as happy to see him as he was to see me.

'The moment my *maalik* (employer) told me to report at the hotel, I knew it had to be you,' he laughed. Then, handing me a business card, he said, 'Next time call me directly. Why pay commission to the hotel?'

I examined the card. It bore the name of Balbir Singh, identified as the proprietor of Golden Travels. It had four mobile numbers listed on it.

'The Balbir Singh on the card is you?' I asked.

'Yes, that's me.'

'When did you become the proprietor of Golden Travels?'

'That's a company I want to start sooner than later. I gave you the card because it has all the four phone numbers—the first number is mine, the rest are of my children. You can call any of the numbers if you want me to be at your service.'

'But why print cards when the company is not even in place?'

'How long does it take to open a company? I have enough space at home and I will turn one of the rooms into an office and hire a woman to run it. Women are always good at running offices. Anyone who is familiar with the computer will do. I know nothing about computers. I barely know how to operate the phone.'

'How much does your present employer pay you?'

'He gives me 3,000 rupees a month.'

'That's it?' I found the words erupting out of my mouth.

'I manage to make some extra money. For example I took you to Ferozepur yesterday. Now imagine you had booked a one-way trip, in which case my duty would have been to drop you at Ferozepur and return to Amritsar. Do you think I would have driven back in an empty car? I would have picked up passengers along the way and easily made at least a thousand rupees. I always do that when I drop guests off at the airport. I pick up passengers looking for a ride into the city. Is that a crime? It's not.

'So, even though my salary is 3,000 rupees,' he continued, 'I end up making 10,000 to 15,000 a month. My sons are earning too. My in-laws take good care of us. So that way I am fine, but how long can I go on working for someone else?'

Given a choice, no one would like to work for someone else. Nothing like being your own boss: you don't have to follow timings set by someone else, you don't have to chase targets set by someone else, you don't have to have your own worth assessed by someone else. And at the age of sixty, when it is all over, you don't have to regret that you spent your entire working life living up to—actually, trying to live up to—someone else's expectations.

But becoming your own boss requires one quality that

the majority of us do not have—or else the world would be full of masters who would have found it hard to get servants. That quality is courage. I certainly don't have that quality, or else I would have followed the footsteps of the writers I admire—Ernest Hemingway, Graham Greene, V.S. Naipaul, Anthony Burgess, Ruskin Bond—who refused to take up a regular job so that they could just write, even if that meant not knowing where the next meal was going to come from.

So how did Babu get the courage to print business cards that proclaimed him to be the proprietor of Golden Travels when the company was still an idea in his head? Was he born courageous, or did growing up in Punjab make him so? I decided to ask him, but even before I could frame my question, he pointed to an elderly Sikh riding a bicycle.

'Do you see that old sardarji?' he asked.

The cyclist, whose flowing white beard was in sync with his white salwar-kameez and turban, could have been anywhere between sixty and seventy. He could have been even eighty—with sturdy Sikhs you never know.

'What about him?' I asked.

'He is someone you can call a free man. He has no one to fear, no loans to repay, no debts to clear. Don't you see he has his head held high? Sikhs are like that, very proud people, they work hard to buy what they want to buy, rather than buy it first and then repay the loan.'

'How much of a Sikh are you by now?'

'Not much,' Babu laughed, 'but I am always learning from them. Sikhs are the most wonderful people on earth, but there is one thing that is eating into Punjab these days.'

'What's that?'

'Heroin.'

Drug addiction is indeed a problem in Punjab, amply evident from—and acknowledged in—the Independence Day messages of the administrators of the state, including the governor and the chief minister, carried in this morning's papers. They all talked about how determined the state government was in fighting the menace of drugs, and about measures being taken to rehabilitate addicts.

Some months before this trip, I had happened to meet a senior bureaucrat from Punjab who, over dinner, told me that policemen often paid huge bribes to get posted in police stations along the border because of the highly lucrative nature of the assignment. According to him, if they seized 50 kilograms of heroin, they showed a seizure of only, say, 20 kilograms, and the remaining 30 kilograms still filtered into the market, making every stakeholder happy.

He told me: 'Punjab always served as the transit point for drugs, but it was never the consumer. It was the use of opium—we call it *puki*—that was more common in Punjab. Mostly bus drivers would take *puki*, apparently it kept them steady. In fact, studies showed that drivers who were on *puki* were less prone to causing accidents. It would be easily available in Rajasthan, so any driver going to Rajasthan would get the supply not only for himself but also his colleagues. The addiction to heroin is fairly recent. I really don't understand how Punjab became the consumer, but it is clear that the drug business cannot thrive unless people who are supposed to crack the whip are involved in it.'

The bureaucrat had requested me not to mention his name in case I ever chose to write what he said. I promised him I wouldn't, mainly because, back then, I did not foresee myself writing this book and therefore being concerned about Punjab. Back then, I did not even know that until 1966, Indian Punjab comprised Haryana and Himachal Pradesh as well or that Simla was its capital city.

After reaching Punjab, the thought of following the drug trail did cross my mind. But I reminded myself that I was on the Radcliffe trail. Moreover, the drug problem was now so deeply—and dangerously—entrenched in its soil that it merited a separate book, best written by a seasoned crime reporter who would know how to charm cops into telling the story. Though after over two decades in journalism I have come to the conclusion that more often it is the cops who charm reporters into buying the stories they spin.

At the village of Nag Khurd, our destination, Dalbir Singh waved us down right outside his house. Unlike that day at Attari, when he was formally attired in a checked shirt and black trousers with black shoes, he was today clad in a shabby salwar-kameez and had his yellow turban tied casually around his head. I wouldn't have recognized him had he not waved at us.

I got out of the car and greeted him. He asked me, '*Roti-shoti khaani hai*?'—'Would you like to have lunch?'

I told him I was not hungry and was more eager to meet his Pakistani cousin. Upon which he asked me to get back into the car and he too got in. It turned out that the cousin and his wife were not staying with Dalbir Singh but with Dalbir's elder brother, Kashmir Singh, who lived further down the lane.

At Kashmir Singh's house, which stood like an island amidst green paddies, Babu and I were met with great warmth, as if we were relatives resurfacing after decades. I had asked Babu to follow me into the house so that he could serve as an interpreter in case I needed one.

Refreshments were served. In a quintessentially Punjabi home, they don't ask you whether you would like to have tea or coffee—or how much sugar you would prefer to have with the beverage. Trays, laden with cups of either tea or coffee and sweets and savouries, materialise as soon as you have taken your seat.

We now sat around hot samosas and gulab jamuns and a variety of savouries. Babu and I shared one couch. On the other couch sat Dalbir Singh and his Pakistani cousin Yakub Masih. The drawing room also had a cot, on which sat Kashmir Singh and his wife, along with Yakub's wife Shehnaz.

'I am told you were at Attari the day we arrived,' Yakub said as we shook hands.

'That's right. I would have waited for you, but I had no idea when you people were going to clear immigration.'

'Even we had no idea,' Yakub said.

'How many people were on the train that day? I didn't notice too many passengers.'

'There were 165 in all, including us.'

'And how was the journey?'

'The train left Lahore at eight in the morning and reached Wagah station at nine. After all the checks and formalities at Wagah, we could reach Attari station only at one in the afternoon. Once again we were frisked, our luggage was checked, and we had to go through the paperwork all over again. By the time we came out of Attari station it was five in the evening.'

From eight in the morning to five in the evening, that's nine hours—just to cover a distance of a little over twenty kilometres, whereas on the treadmill I can clock five kilometres in forty minutes.

Yakub Masih wore a grey salwar-kameez over his broad frame and even had a pen clipped to his breast pocket. He stood apart from his Indian cousins not just because of his build and the pen, but also because he was clean-shaven and did not wear a turban while his eyes were kohl-lined. He was fifty years old. From his surname I gathered he was a Christian and not a Muslim, but in order to be sure I asked him, as politely as possible, 'So you are not a follower Islam, are you?'

'No, we are Christians. But Muslims are like our brothers.'

Yakub's mother and Dalbir's mother were sisters who belonged to a Sikh family living in a hamlet called

Fatehgarh Churian near Amritsar. One of the sisters—it was not explained to me why—got married to a Punjabi Christian who lived near Lahore and worked as a driver for Bata, the shoe company.

Partition happened, years rolled on, the Bata driver died. After his death, all his five sons became drivers for Bata. Today, three of the older sons are dead, and the elder of the two surviving ones happens to be Yakub Masih, who no longer works for Bata but, like Babu, works for a car rental agency. His wife Shehnaz was also born as a Christian in Pakistan.

'So how is life in Pakistan?' I asked Yakub.

'Life is good, no problem at all.'

'Do people there see Indians as enemies?'

'Not at all. We love Indians. I have been wanting to come to India for a long time. Finally god has fulfilled my desire.'

'Is life easy for you there as a Christian?'

'Of course. There are 200 to 300 Christian families in the town we live, about 20 kilometres from Lahore. Even Muslims, when they face difficult situations in life, come to our churches and ask the pastor to pray for them,' he said.

This sort of a thing, it struck me, is quite common in the subcontinent: people going to the shrines of other religions in times of personal crisis—illness, unemployment, infertility. It need not necessarily mean that they have abandoned their own gods; it's just that they are temporarily expanding their faith to include other gods as well, in the desperate hope that at least one god will listen.

'But I often hear about churches being burnt in Pakistan,' I said.

'That's the handiwork of miscreants,' Shehnaz, the wife, answered. 'Such people don't spare even mosques, do they?'

I was impressed by her response, and since I was looking at her while listening to her, I also realised she was exceedingly attractive.

'How old are you?' I found myself asking her.

Yakub butted in, 'She is quite old by now. She is forty-six, correct?' He looked at his wife. She blushed.

'You know, I am a big fan of Rajesh Khanna,' Yakub said, 'I used to sing his songs for her. You know the song, *Yeh reshmi zulfein, yeh sharbati aankhen*? I sang that for her shortly before we got married.'

She blushed again. *Yeh reshmi zulfein, yeh sharbati aankhen*—These silken tresses, these syrupy eyes. Yakub had chosen just the right song.

Yakub himself must have been quite handsome back then. In fact, even now, he bore a faint resemblance to Rajesh Khanna, and I told him so. He looked pleased and said, 'I was a little hesitant to mention that myself, but during my younger days, people did think I looked a lot like him.'

The Rajesh Khanna-compliment put him at ease. His demeanour became friendly. Not that he had been unfriendly until now, but I could sense a mild unease in him which was understandable. After all, who was I, why should I show interest in his life, and why did I choose him, of all the people who travelled in the Samjhauta Express that morning, to interview?

'So when did you get married?'

'We got married in—when did we get married?' Yakub asked his wife.

'Trust you to not remember. We got married in 1991,' Shehnaz replied.

'And how many children do you have?' I asked her.

'We have four sons. The eldest is now twenty-one, he works as a welder. The one after him is a plumber. The other two are still studying. The youngest one, he is ten now, has come with us. He is sleeping at the moment,' she said.

'So tell me,' I asked Yakub, 'are Hindi films popular in Pakistan?'

'Very much,' he replied. 'But when I was growing up, the theatres would not show Hindi films. So I grew up on Pakistani films. I grew up watching the films of Sultan Rahi and Mustafa Qureshi, both very big actors at the time. Today Shaan Shahid is the most popular actor.

'My introduction to Indian films happened because of the video. We would rent the videos (VHS tapes). Then came cable TV. Today our theatres show films of Akshay Kumar, John Ibrahim (Abraham) and Salman Khan. And now because of the dish antenna, we also watch Indian channels, especially Star Plus and Colors.

'She'—he pointed to his wife—'is forever glued to the Colors channel. Every time I ask her what's going on in the house, she tells me, "Wait, wait, the serial is about to end." Her life revolves around the serials.'

'As if you don't watch *Comedy Nights with Kapil*,' she chided him. There was laughter in the room.

'For that matter,' I said, 'even I have watched quite a few

episodes of *Comedy Nights with Kapil*, and that's because my wife watches it regularly.'

'Precisely my point,' Yakub said, 'if the wife happens to be sitting in front of the TV, it is very natural for the husband to join her once in a while to watch what she is watching.' Laughter filled the room again.

I asked him, 'So how does it feel to be in India?'

'It's been only a couple of days,' he said, 'but I am touched by the warmth of the people. Given a choice I would settle here, but our visa expires in a month. Pakistan is actually an expensive place to live in. There, a kilogram of mutton costs Rs 600; here it is only Rs 250. There, a dozen bananas cost Rs 100; here it is only Rs 50.'

'But then, one hundred Pakistani rupees is equal to about sixty Indian rupees, have you considered that?'

'All I can say is that, *yahaan aakar dil ko tasalli mili hai* (I find great satisfaction coming to India).'

'Did you ever watch the parade at Wagah from the Pakistani side?'

'Of course I have. Twice.'

'And are you now going to watch it from the Indian side as well?'

'By all means, I have already told them'—he pointed to Kashmir Singh and Dalbir Singh—'that I want to watch the parade next Sunday.'

'Very few Indians and Pakistanis get to see the parade from both sides of the border,' I told him, 'I must say you are really fortunate.'

Yakub Masih said with the flourish of an actor: 'Fortunate are those who get to come to India.'

# 14

Ms Blue Eyelids asked me, 'Sir, have you been to Dera Baba Nanak?'

I had come down to the reception to ask her if there was anything else to see in Amritsar other than the Golden Temple and Jallianwala Bagh. Perhaps there was some place nearby where I could make a day trip.

Dera Baba Nanak rang a bell. I remembered spotting it on the map, a desolate dot, when I was looking at places in Punjab that sat close to the Radcliffe Line. Since it had appeared desolate—perhaps the map hadn't downloaded fully to show finer details, or maybe because I was looking at the map sitting in remote Chennai—I wasn't very sure whether an outsider could just walk in there, considering that it touched the border. So Dera Baba Nanak, in my head, had remained just that: a dot on the map.

'How far is it from here?' I asked her.

'Hardly 60 kilometres, sir,' she said. 'We go there often on Sundays. And today is Sunday, a good day to be there. Shall I book a cab for you?'

'Is there anything to see there?

'You can see the Kartarpur Sahib Gurdwara through binoculars.'

'Why through binoculars?'

'That's because Kartarpur Sahib is located in Pakistan.'

Ah, *that* Kartarpur Sahib, built on the spot where Guru Nanak died. The gurdwara, along with the one built at his birthplace, fell in Pakistan after Partition.

'Shall I book a cab for you?'

'Sure.'

Only after she had dialled the number I remembered that Babu had asked me to call him directly if I needed a cab. It was too late now to stop her.

After breakfast—Amritsari kulcha and chana, served in the dining hall—I returned to my room and spent the next three hours reading up about Guru Nanak and Dera Baba Nanak.

Guru Nanak was born in 1469 in a village called Rai Bhoi Ki Talvandi, 65 km southwest of Lahore. When he was in his late twenties, already married with two sons, he set out on a series of spiritual journeys through India, Arabia, and Tibet that lasted about thirty years. He preached that there was only one God, and that all human beings could have direct access to God with no need of rituals or priests, and that everyone was equal, regardless of caste or gender.

Upon completing his first journey, he joined his wife and the two children who were living in her maternal village, on the banks of the river Ravi. There, seated near a well in a farm belonging to a man called Ajit Randhawa, he would give discourses. Randhawa became one of his first followers, and as the number of followers grew, Guru

Nanak moved to a nearby piece of land, which he named Kartarpur, and set up a community there.

Kartarpur kept growing while Guru Nanak continued with his journeys, each lasting several years. In 1531, he finally settled there to lead the life of an ordinary householder, tilling the land, even as he continued with his teachings. He died there in 1539, at the age of seventy, but not before he had named one of his disciples, Bhai Lehna, as his successor, choosing him over his sons, Sri Chand and Lakhmi Das, who were also his disciples. After his cremation, a monument was built on the spot where his ashes were buried. Bhai Lehna, christened Guru Angad, moved out of Kartarpur to spread his master's teachings, while Guru Nanak's sons returned to their mother's village, which soon earned the name Dera Baba Nanak. Today Dera Baba Nanak is a town in Gurdaspur district of Punjab.

During British rule, Gurdaspur was a large district that was subdivided into four administrative zones: Shakargarh, Gurdaspur, Batala, and Pathankot. Since it was a Muslim-majority district, Radcliffe, without second thoughts, placed Gurdaspur in Pakistan. He was merely doing his job.

But Gurdaspur going to Pakistan meant that India would lose the only road that connected the subcontinent to Jammu and Kashmir. This was unacceptable to Nehru, a Kashmiri himself, who had been offered a look at Radcliffe's map. Once again it fell on Mountbatten to convince Radcliffe to tweak the line. So Radcliffe placed Shakargarh, which lay across the Ravi, in Pakistan and awarded the rest of Gurdaspur district to India. Along with Shakargarh, the settlement of Kartarpur also went to Pakistan.

Radcliffe's line, when he drew it, passed through a string of three districts in Indian Punjab—Gurdaspur in the north, Ferozepur in the south, and Amritsar in the middle. By going to Dera Baba Nanak, I would be earning the small satisfaction of setting foot in all three. Thanks to Ms Blue Eyelids.

The cab arrived. It was the same cab, the same driver, who wore the same pink shirt.

'So tell me, Babu,' I asked him as we hit the highway, 'do you ever go back to Bihar?'

'Of course,' he said, 'I try to attend every wedding I am invited to. If I don't go there, how will my relatives know that I live a good life?'

There was no doubt that Babu led a good life. He had everything that a man aspires for: a loving family, well-to-do in-laws, a house of his own, and soon perhaps, a company to run. He had earned all this in spite of being completely illiterate. Had he stayed on in Bihar, he would have probably led a wretched life, most likely carrying bricks on his head at a construction site. But some of the credit must go to his labourer-father for choosing to migrate to Punjab. When Babu's grandson grows up he will most likely live in luxury, and when the grandson has children and those children grow up, the humble and Bihari origins of the family would perhaps be forgotten.

'Have you ever driven around a lone woman passenger,' I asked him.

'Several times.'

'Do you chat with them? Do they tell you about themselves?'

'Two or three years ago, I drove this lady from Delhi to Shimla. She was from your part of the country.'

'My part would mean?'

'She was a Bengali. She was going to stay in Shimla for two days and I was supposed to drive her back as well. We got talking on the way. I told her everything about myself. She told me everything about herself. We sort of became friends. At Shimla, she checked into a hotel and I stayed in my car. In the evening she called me to her room and said, "You have driven me all the way, how can I not take care of you. You are going to have dinner with me." She ordered fish, chicken and what not. After dinner as I got up to leave, she said, "Why do you want to sleep in the car? Sleep here."'

'And then?'

'What then?' Babu kept a straight face, 'whatever was expected to happen, happened. I have had many experiences like this.'

'Tell me some more.'

'Many years ago—at the time I used to drive a bus—I happened to take a group of college girls from Old Delhi on a trip to Kashmir. There were forty or fifty girls in the group. One afternoon they were supposed to visit a garden, so I took them there. I remember it was winter, biting cold.

After the girls got off the bus and went into the garden, I bought myself tea and returned to my seat. One girl from the group came back into the bus. I thought she had come to collect something she had forgotten, perhaps a shawl or a sweater. But she came up to me and asked, "Why are you sitting here alone?" I told her, "It is very cold, I am having tea." She said, "So what if it is cold, I will heat you up." Those were her exact words.'

'And then?'

'What then? Whatever was expected to happen, happened.'

'Not bad, Babu.'

'I told you something the other day, right? Two things never get old.'

I had expected the journey to take much longer, but soon we were driving past shops whose signboards gave the address as Dera Baba Nanak. A number of shops and establishments were named after the founder of Sikhism: Guru Nanak Nursing Home, Nanak Dairy, Guru Nanak Stores. One also got to see a lot more turbans here than in Amritsar.

We came upon a large gurdwara with a gold-plated dome, called Darbar Sahib, built on the spot where Guru Nanak, sitting near a well—and drinking its water when required—gave his first discourses. I wouldn't be way off the mark if I said that Sikhism originated at this spot and established itself as a faith in nearby Kartarpur.

The well has been preserved in the basement of the shrine and is considered a shrine by itself. An elderly woman attending to the hand pump connected to the well pressed the rod twice as I cupped my palms under the nozzle. Cold water filled up—what a relief in the heat—and I drank it. The water tasted sweet and I drank once more. Babu followed suit.

We then climbed up the stairs back into the main hall where the Granth Sahib was placed in a golden palki or palanquin—which, along with the golden dome, had been gifted by the Sikh emperor Ranjit Singh. Also in the hall stood plaques in the memory of soldiers who died at Dera Baba Nanak during the 1965 and 1971 wars.

Watching me look around curiously, the granthi—the one who reads from the Granth Sahib in gurdwaras—walked up to me and introduced himself. He was a jovial man called Randhir Singh, a farmer by profession, who lived in a nearby village. Together we stepped out to the foyer for a chat. He spoke fluent Hindi and kept insisting that I have some tea but I asked for water, which arrived within moments in a steel tumbler.

'How old are you?' I asked Randhir Singh.

'I was born in 1960, so that makes me what, fifty-five years old?'

'So you have any memories of the two wars?'

'I was only a child, but some images remain in my mind. In 1965, I remember watching villagers carry on their heads boxes that contained lassi and other refreshments for our soldiers. In 1971, I remember people moving out of the village, with buffaloes carrying their belongings. What I also remember is—this is what I heard people talking at the time—that in 1965, the Indians were taken aback by the scale of the Pakistani attack. *Woh sambhal nahin sakey* (they floundered initially). But soon they were back on their feet and they beat the enemy. In 1971 there was no such problem here, our soldiers were well prepared. But in Hussainiwala the Pakistanis did manage to come forward.'

His facts were astoundingly accurate. At one point during the battle at Dera Baba Nanak in 1965, the Indian Army had indeed found itself on the back foot and had to seek the help of the air force. The battle, in fact, accorded the Indian Air Force a chance to prove that it could be a lethal force that was capable of tilting the balance during a war.

Randhir Singh was still recalling the wars when he paused to greet an elderly Sikh—in shirt and trousers—walking into the gurdwara.

'I am seeing you after a long time, all well?' Randhir Singh asked him.

He replied, 'All well, by the grace of Waheguru. I was visiting my daughter in England.'

Randhir Singh introduced him to me: 'Meet Sardar Kulwant Singh, he has served in the Indian Army.'

We shook hands. Kulwant Singh, seventy-four years old, told me that his house was barely two kilometres away but that he hardly lived there now because he and his wife spent most of their time with their daughter in England and son in Jalandhar.

'We come here once in a while, to see if the house is in order and to catch up with friends,' he said.

'Did you fight the 1965 and 1971 wars?'

'Of course I did.'

'You must have been a sepoy then?'

'I was a sapper, the engineering equivalent of a sepoy. My job was to build bridges, build roads, maintain water supply, and to lay and clear minefields. I never got to serve in Dera Baba Nanak though. During the 1965 war, I was sent to Baramulla in Kashmir, and during the 1971 war, I was posted in Sri Ganganagar in Rajasthan.

'What a horrible thing war is,' he continued, 'that too with your own people. Politicians don't want the people of the two countries to be together, because if the people come together, the politicians will lose their importance. That is why they keep working on creating a divide.

'India has already gone to the dogs. Look at Britain, where law is law, nobody can break it. But in India, the powerful people always manipulate laws, turning the truth into lies and lies into truth. Nice meeting you.'

We drove out of the bustle of the town into the fields and were soon flagged down at a BSF check-post where a sentry noted down my name, address and the car's registration number. The border between India and Pakistan, the sentry told me, was exactly a kilometre away.

The Indian side wore a festive look. Villagers flocked to the small gurdwara that sat by the barbed wires. Stalls sold pictures of Sikh gurus, scarves, steel bangles. One particular shop sold only toys, and most of the toys happened to be plastic guns. Meanwhile, on an observation post, easily thirty feet tall if not more, with the Indian flag flying over it, stood men with real guns.

Beyond the fence was farmland—interspersed with patches of wild grass—that seemed to stretch right up to the sky. Not a human in sight there, only buffaloes grazing at a distance on an untended piece of land, though I did notice an observation post with the Pakistani flag flying on it.

'Those are Pakistani buffaloes,' a young Sikh told me as I climbed up a mound where a platform has been built by the BSF for pilgrims to have a look at the Kartarpur Sahib Gurdwara. Said to be about four kilometres from where I stood, the gurdwara was visible to the naked eye—a white smudge between the blue of the sky and the green on the ground—and its features became clearer as I zoomed my camera to take pictures. I could make out the dome, the minarets and the arcade. The distance and the inaccessibility gave the gurdwara an extra halo: it could have been the Taj Mahal.

Pilgrims, as they ascended the platform, joined their palms and bowed in the direction of the smudge. Suddenly a pair of binoculars materialized out of nowhere. No one knew whom the binoculars belonged to, but people took turns, some more eagerly than the others, to have a look at the gurdwara.

I managed to get hold of the binoculars twice—for a few seconds at a time—and I felt as if I was watching a photograph of the gurdwara and not a live image. Even for a powerful pair of binoculars, four kilometres is too long a distance to convey real-time action: you can at best see magnified images but not the action on site.

I handed back the binoculars to the elderly woman I had taken it from: she now had tears in her eyes and wanted to have one more look at the spot where Guru Nanak had died. For her it was a case of being so near and yet so far—the obstacle being the Radcliffe Line that ran between the gurdwara and the platform where we stood now.

There was something else that ran between the two—the River Ravi, not visible from where we stood but certainly visible to the BSF men occupying the watchtower.

Presently one of the BSF men climbed down the ladder to use the phone installed at the base of the tower. From the badge stitched onto his chest, I could tell he was a Bengali.

'Is the river visible from up there?' I asked him, in Bengali.

'Yes it is, but who are you?' he asked me, sounding surprised and wary at the same time.

I introduced myself, emphasising on the fact that my ancestral village lay in Murshidabad. He said he was from Siliguri. We chatted for a while and I found out that he had to sit on the tower for twelve hours a day, six hours at a time, with a six-hour break in between. Sentries like him formed India's first line of defence.

Babu and I climbed down the mound and, covering our heads, walked into the modest gurdwara that sat right by the fence. Today being a Sunday, families from nearby villages had gathered there, lending the site a festive air.

This gurdwara is named after a saint-warrior called Baba Sidh Singh Randhawa, who died battling Muslim oppressors, fighting even when his head had been severed. The gurdwara came up on the spot where the urn containing his ashes was buried.

'Have you ever eaten at a langar before?' Babu asked me.

'No, but I have always wanted to.'

'Today you shall,' he said.

Langar is the community kitchen run by a gurdwara where a simple meal is provided, free of cost, to just about anybody who is hungry. The system, driven purely by sense of service to mankind, had originated in Kartarpur when Guru Nanak was setting up the township.

Babu led me to a verandah where people sat cross-legged in rows, on the floor, eating. We joined one of the rows and I eagerly observed Babu to make sure I did not break langar decorum: the volunteer never bends down to serve you food; instead you will have to stretch out your palm to receive the rotis and hold up the steel bowl to get the dal or kheer.

'Have some more kheer,' Babu insisted, 'It's the best kheer you will ever have.'

So I ate at a langar for the first time, even though I had spent the first thirty years of my life in north India, where gurdwaras dot the landscape, and the next fifteen years in Chennai where the sole gurdwara in the city is located barely two kilometres from my home. What made the meal even more special was the location: we were right on the border, with Pakistani buffaloes grazing just a couple of hundred yards away.

Villagers who had had their lunch sat on the floor in small circles inside the gurdwara compound. Some even napped. Babu and I approached one small circle that comprised three generations of a Sikh family: Baldev Singh, sixty-seven years old; one of his six sons, Harnam Singh, forty-two; and one of Harnam's two sons, a twelve-year-old boy called Satbir.

Baldev Singh was born a year after Partition, before which the family lived on the opposite bank of the Ravi, close to the Kartarpur Sahib Gurdwara. 'We had a lot of land there, much of which got eroded as the river changed course. Whatever little was left had to be abandoned during Partition when we were given land on this side of the border,' Baldev Singh said.

He has remained a farmer all his life, growing wheat, paddy, and maize and transporting the produce to the nearest market on a bullock cart. His sons have inherited his profession, only that they now transport the produce in a Bolero. The Bolero was strictly used for this purpose and not as personal transport.

'For personal transport we use motorcycles. We still can't afford a car,' Harnam Singh, the son, said.

I asked Harnam whether he or his brothers ever considered working in a city. 'Nahin ji, we always wanted to stay close to our land. Not just us, this is the thinking of the people in our village.'

One reason for this, perhaps, could be that the farmlands, because they are on the border, can never become real estate and so it makes sense for the villagers to focus on farming.

'How does it feel to be living on the border?' I asked them.

Baldev Singh said, 'Now the security is very tight. We must leave our fields by six in the evening, and by eight o'clock, this gurdwara must also empty out. If someone leaves behind a wallet or bag, they will find it the next morning in exactly the same place they had left it, so tight is the security.

'But before the fence came up in 1986, not many people knew where the border lay. Even Indian soldiers, when they came to fight the war in 1965, had no idea where the border was. We villagers had to guide them.'

I asked him whether descendants of Guru Nanak still lived in Dera Baba Nanak.

'Yes, they do,' Baldev Singh said, 'you will find them around the Chola Sahib Gurdwara.'

'Do you revere them?'

'Why should we revere them?' his son Harnam said, mildly agitated. 'Our guru is the Guru Granth Sahib. By the way, that tree you see'—he pointed to a banyan tree in the compound—'Guru Nanak would rest there when he would travel between Dera Baba Nanak and Kartarpur.'

On my way out, I sat under the tree and asked Babu to take pictures.

The story goes that when Guru Nanak was travelling through Arabia, he was gifted a chola—robe—by a local king. During his final years when he anointed Guru Angad his successor, he handed him the chola as well. Guru Angad too passed on the chola to his successor, and this went on until Guru Arjan Dev, the fifth guru, gifted it to a man called Tota Ram Arora for the services rendered by him during the construction of the holy tank at Amritsar. He gifted Tota Ram, a resident of Bukhara (in Uzbekistan), not only the robe but also a handkerchief stitched by Guru Nanak's sister Nanki for her brother on the occasion of his wedding.

Centuries later, Guru Nanak is said to have made an appearance before a ninth-generation descendant, Kabli Mal, and ordered him to bring back the chola and the handkerchief. Kabli Mal promptly complied, bringing them back from the family of Tota Ram in 1884. Ever since then the two relics have remained with the first guru's descendants and are today displayed in a glass case in the Chola Sahib Gurdwara.

Chola Sahib lay barely two kilometres from the Darbar Sahib Gurdwara, but away from the bustle of the town. It turned out to be a fairly recent and highly modest construction. There, even as a granthi softly read out from the Granth Sahib, a sevadar urged me to come over and take a look at the glass case. As I looked at the intricate embroidery, wondering how the two pieces of cloth survived all these centuries, the sevadar handed me a pamphlet and opened the page that contained Guru Nanak's family tree. The sevadar's finger stopped at

No. 17—seventeenth-generation descendant—against which were printed two names, Baba Lakkha Singh Bedi and Baba Gurpreet Singh Bedi.

'That's Baba Lakkha Singh Ji,' he mentioned the name with a hushed reverence and pointed to a pudgy man seated on a mattress on the floor.

I reckoned Lakkha Singh to be about my age, if not younger, given the streaks of grey in his beard. He wore a white turban and a white kurta and churidar—and not salwar-kameez—and I detected a collared blue T-shirt under the kurta. As I watched him from a distance, I saw that most people who came into the gurdwara touched his feet and some even gave him money: mostly twenty rupees, fifty rupees and occasionally hundred rupees. An assistant kept putting the money into a briefcase.

When the stream of visitors had thinned I sat cross-legged in front of him. I was face to face with a descendant of none other than Guru Nanak.

'Did you go to school?' I asked him.

'Haan ji.'

'Did your classmates know that you are a descendant of Guru Nanak?'

'Haan ji.'

'Did they respect you because of that?'

'Haan ji.'

'Did you have any other interests at school, such as sports?'

'Nahin ji. Home to school, school to gurdwara.'

'How was the atmosphere at home? Religious?'

'Haan ji, father used to tell us stories about Guru Nanak.'

'These days a lot of young Sikhs don't like to wear the turban.'

'Haan ji.'

'What do you have to say about that?'

'Now what can I say about it.'

'Do you have a message for the younger generation?'

'*Lagan se kaam kiya jaaye to nateeja achha hota hai*'—If you put your mind into your work, the results will be good.

'Can I take your picture?'

'Haan ji.'

Finally I pulled out my wallet and handed him a hundred-rupee note.

As I got back into the car, I wondered whether Lakkha Singh was actually dull or just pretended to be dull to discourage me from asking difficult questions. Leafing through the pamphlet now, I realized he was anything but dull—he was actually a shrewd businessman who had turned his lineage into a source of living.

The bilingual pamphlet, in Gurmukhi and Hindi, said: 'We give laung prasad (blessed clove) to women who don't have sons or whose newborn sons don't survive or those who have only daughters. They must have the clove after bath on an empty stomach. On the day she takes the clove, she must not take salty food but only sweet food. Repeat the procedure the next month if required. Once you are blessed with a male child, bring it to the gurdwara for the blessings of Guru Nanak's family and make donations for the upkeep of this building.'

Was the intake of clove alone sufficient for a woman to become pregnant with a boy, or was the ingestion of the clove supposed to be followed by sexual intercourse? The pamphlet was silent on that.

It was not hard to imagine naive young women from villages swallowing the clove in the belief that the clove alone was potent enough to make them pregnant—that too with a male child. Baba Lakkha Singh was exploiting their naivety. He also perhaps knew that if a woman gave birth to a girl child in spite of having ingested the blessed clove, she would not dare question a descendant of Guru Nanak.

Lakkha Singh was everything that Guru Nanak wasn't.

Guru Nanak had proved that devotion was thicker than blood by overlooking his sons when it came to choosing his successor, whereas Lakkha Singh lived off his lineage. Guru Nanak was against superstitions and rituals, whereas Lakkha Singh was promoting them with impunity. Guru Nanak was all for gender equality, where Lakkha Singh made his money by promising women a male child.

I regretted having added to his income by handing him that hundred-rupee note.

# 15

Monday morning. I wanted to stay in bed all day and kill my last twenty-four hours in the city doing nothing. But something was nagging me.

The pencil of Sir Cyril Radcliffe ran a distance of 553 kilometres as he sliced Punjab into two, but Partition is today symbolized by a small dot on that line: the Wagah border crossing. And yet I had spent not even thirty minutes there, watching the flag-lowering ceremony from a distance by standing on my toes and subsequently elbowing my way through the crowd for a closer look at Pakistan. If someone were to ask me whether I had witnessed the ceremony, the honest answer would have to be a no. What stopped me from going back there this evening?

I decided to call Babu, but instantly realized that merely going to Wagah wasn't going to serve my purpose. The idea was to watch the ceremony from close, which meant I needed a connection in the BSF. Why, I did have a connection! My classmate from school—we would even hang around together as kids—was now a senior officer in the BSF. We fall out of touch periodically, but remain good friends. Why had the thought of calling him not occurred to me before?

Fortunately he answered my call. You can never take the location or phone number of a man in uniform for granted, they keep changing every few years. My friend was still posted in Delhi, as he was when I had last spoken to him. I told him I *had* to watch the flag-lowering ceremony at Wagah this evening at any cost.

'Give me ten minutes,' he said, 'I will call you back.'

I spent those ten minutes or so standing by the large window and drinking the most perfect tea the hotel had served me so far. Until now, the tea had been milky, in spite of my telling the waiters to go easy on the milk. That's the thing with hotels: they suddenly become far more agreeable when it's time to leave. So far, I never thought of standing by the window, nor was I served with tea that was to my liking. But right now, with barely twenty-fours to go before I checked out, I felt like extending my stay by a few days.

My friend called back. The officer in charge of the Wagah border crossing happened to be his course mate, so everything had been arranged, only that I had to get in touch with the officer at once.

The officer, when I called him, told me, 'The parade begins at five-thirty, try to reach here by four. A vehicle will pick you up at three.'

'Thank you so much!'

'Most welcome.'

Greatly relieved, and feeling immensely grateful towards my friend and his course mate, I ordered alu and puri for breakfast and then asked for one more cup of tea.

I didn't realize when I dozed off, but I distinctly

remember the dream: Ms Blue Eyelids, in her starched white shirt and blue skirt, standing by my bed and gingerly tapping on my shoulder. 'Sir,' she said, 'please wake up, sir. You're about to miss your flight. I kept calling your phone but you never responded.'

Daytime dreams are always up to such mischief. With your brain going off to sleep but your senses wide awake in the daylight, such dreams often feel very real, right to the slightest of sensations. I could actually feel Ms Blue Eyelids' hand on my shoulder—and I woke up. In great panic I checked my phone. It was still Monday, and only half past noon.

At 2.45 the BSF driver called to say he had reached the hotel. I hurriedly got dressed and went down. Ms Blue Eyelids greeted me with a saccharine sweet hello. I smiled back and stepped out to the parking lot.

As I walked towards the olive-green jeep, the driver and an armed guard, both dressed in combat fatigues, instinctively stood at attention, their clenched fists pointing backwards. I sat next to the driver and the guard got into a seat behind. We drove in total silence. I was a guest of the big boss of the Wagah border, so there was no question of any of them attempting small talk. I felt important.

Soon I grew weary of the silence and asked the driver, whose name was embroidered as Rafiq on his chest, where he belonged to.

'Nadia district, sir, in West Bengal.'

'Oh Bengali! I am also a Bengali.'

'I figured that from your name, sir,' he grinned.

'Can I smoke in your jeep?'

'By all means, sir.'

After sitting straight for long, pretending to look important enough to be the guest of their big boss, I finally relaxed. The journey under the scorching sun—the jeep, being a jeep, only had a small fan fixed on the dashboard—became somewhat agreeable.

Shortly after we crossed we approached a barricade, but no one stopped us. Instead, one of the sentries saluted me tentatively. The driver finally stopped at a subsequent barricade where, only three days earlier, I had to show my ID and walk through the metal detector. Today I wasn't required to do any such thing: the sentry accompanying us led me straight to a conference hall, behind the galleries that were filling up.

One of the boundary walls enclosing the conference hall stood right on Radcliffe Line. If you stood against the wall and extended your hand, your fingers would come under the jurisdiction of Pakistan. I was shown into the hall and introduced to the big boss, my benefactor, the course mate of my classmate. He was a tall, gracious and affable Sikh.

'Partition is a very emotional issue in Punjab,' he said. 'Some years ago I was posted in Khem Karan, where a colonel from the Indian Army came often just to take a look at his ancestral house that sat right across the border. He would stand at the fence and stare at the house; sometimes he had tears in his eyes.'

'He had never even lived in that house,' the big boss said, 'because he was born long after Partition. He must be around our age. The house belonged to his grandfather. But he felt emotionally attached, you see. I was told his father, also an officer in the Indian Army, did the same—he would come to the border and stare at the home where he grew up.'

I have read all about the horrors of Partition, and seen movies and TV serials depicting it: those mindless murders and rapes; deaths due to hunger and exhaustion; the grievous injuries inflicted to one's body and mind due to the overnight displacement. I was horrified all right, but not really affected, simply because Partition was too remote for me, in terms of time as well as distance.

But the story of the colonel—a simple account of a man gazing at his ancestral house from a distance, which involves no violence at all—brought me close to tears.

Perhaps because it made me think of my own house, back in Kanpur. My parents lovingly built it, with a lot of sweat and sacrifice, way back in 1985 when I was fifteen, with the hope that it would serve as the family fortress. But I was the first one to leave home, followed by my brother: Kanpur was not the kind of place where you could build a career in English journalism. But we made it a point, no matter where we were, to spend Diwali in Kanpur.

In 2009, my mother passed away, quite untimely, and my brother returned to Kanpur to be with my father, whereas I continue to live in Chennai. Occasionally I advise my father to sell the house and buy a flat in Calcutta, where I myself hope to settle eventually. But each time I give him the advice, I simultaneously imagine our house already being sold. And then I imagine more: Would I ever visit Kanpur once the house is sold? If at all I do, would I visit my house, to look at it from a distance? How would I feel looking at it from a distance, knowing that we no longer own it? Would the new owners let me in?

Fortunately, the Kanpur home still remains my permanent address. But think of those millions who were forced to abandon their permanent addresses. Nothing like losing your home, worse if the home still exists but no longer belongs to you. That, in my opinion, was the saddest part of Partition.

Inside the conference hall I found the door flanked by two plates fixed on the wall, one bearing the flag of India and the other that of Pakistan. Mounted directly above each plate was a clock showing the time of that country: India is ahead of Pakistan by thirty minutes.

'We hold our flag meetings in this hall,' the big boss said when he saw me looking at the plates. 'We keep alternating, one month the Pakistanis come here and the next month we go there.'

A bearer served us tea. Soon we were joined by another tall officer who was in civvies. He represented the BSF's 'Q' branch, the intelligence wing. I asked him about the smuggling of heroin.

'Smuggling is not possible without the involvement of

villagers,' he said. 'I am not saying all villagers are bad, but there are bad elements in every village on both sides of the border. These people have a clique, often they are related, and they have been active for generations. Smuggling is their family business. Earlier they smuggled gold, now they smuggle heroin.'

I felt inclined to believe him. The village is one place where the arrival of an outsider is noticed immediately: word spreads within a matter of minutes that a stranger is in their midst. No nefarious activity, therefore, is possible without the involvement of the black sheep. What he did not say was that there are black sheep even among uniformed men—to err is human, after all.

It is the black sheep, in different garbs but working in tandem, who allow heroin-smuggling to thrive. Their primary obstacle is usually the barbed-wire fence, which is not insurmountable.

I tried imagining life in these villages without the fence but couldn't. Even though it was erected long after India had fought its three wars with Pakistan, the fence now looked so eternal as if it had existed from the time of Nehru and Jinnah.

Now as a sentry led me out of the conference hall to seat me in the front row of the VIP enclosure so that I could get a ringside view of the flag-lowering ceremony, I came face to face with Jinnah. His portrait, facing India, hung from the Pakistani arch. Similarly, Gandhi's portrait, facing Pakistan, hung from the Indian arch.

One could understand Jinnah's presence. He was the founder of Pakistan. But why was Gandhi's picture there?

He was against Partition, and even went on a fast shortly after Partition, demanding that India release the sum of Rs 55 crore that was due to Pakistan following the division of assets. But then, if not Gandhi's portrait, whose?

The two fathers of their respective nations, who hardly got along with each other while they were alive, are today united by their near-irrelevance in the countries represented by their portraits.

Patriotic songs split the air as I waited for the choreographed confrontation to begin.

It was truly a clash between the music of the two nations as Pakistani songs pounded my left ear and Indian songs my right, the irony of Partition betrayed by the fact that the playlists of both countries were dominated by Punjabi lyrics set to Bhangra beats.

I hoped, against hope, that the Pakistanis would play Nusrat Fateh Ali Khan's '*Pakistan, Pakistan*'. The tune was still playing in my head. But this was not Hussainiwala but Wagah, the international museum showcasing Partition, where each side needed to keep the tempo high.

Since I do not understand chaste Punjabi I was spared the nuances of the musical confrontation, but also since I do not understand chaste Punjabi, it was all noise to me. On top of it all was the sun, brutal even at this hour. It was lowering itself slowly, very slowly, on the Pakistani side, but was still so blinding that I had to squint each time I wanted to have a look across the Radcliffe Line.

What I saw across the border was no different from what I saw on the Indian side: galleries being filled up fast by people who must have planned their entire day around the thirty-minute treat of nationalism. Thirty minutes, that's how long the flag-lowering ceremony lasts, but it reminds both sides of the seventy years of love-hate relationship they have shared—more of hatred and less of love.

The border crossing—as I had learned from the poster at Sarhad—formally came into existence on 11 October 1947, when sentry boxes and flag masts were erected and a swing gate was propped up by drums. Population migration was still continuing and both countries felt the need to demarcate the imaginary Radcliffe Line that now dissected the GT Road so that people knew where each country's extent ended and the other's territory began.

Since protocol dictated that the national flag could fly only between sunrise and sunset, and that the flag should always be lowered slowly and ceremoniously, one can safely assume that the flag-lowering ceremony dates back right to the time of Partition.

By 1965, metal gates had long replaced the humble swing gate, and it was through these gates that the Indian tanks rolled into Pakistan on the morning of September 6 that year, in retaliation to Pakistani attacks in Kashmir. The war lasted about three weeks, following which both countries returned to pre-war positions after a compromise was reached at Tashkent.

But the gates were shut thereafter, and opened again only after India and Pakistan had fought another war, in

1971, which resulted in the creation of Bangladesh. Even then, they were thrown open not for the public, but only to facilitate the exchange of the prisoners of the 1971 war—an occasion thus described in a dispatch sent by the *New York Times* correspondent on 1 December 1972:

> WAGAH, India: The sound of bagpipe music filled the air. Women threw rose and marigold petals. There were tears of joy all around.
>
> For seven years, since the Kashmir battles of 1965, the heavy iron gates that mark the India-Pakistan border at this town 300 miles north of New Delhi have been closed but last Friday they were swung open briefly to permit the exchange of 1,156 prisoners of war held captive since last December when the two nations fought over East Pakistan (now Bangladesh).
>
> India released 540 Pakistanis, each bearing a package of tea inscribed: 'For your family, as a gesture of friendly feeling from the people of India.' Pakistan freed 616 Indians, each of whom was given a gift of a new suitcase.

In the dateline you see the reporter placing Wagah in India. Not his fault. Even seventy years after Partition, the border crossing continues to be known as 'Wagah border' and that's because the Radcliffe Line grazes past the village of Wagah.

No one I asked seemed to be sure when exactly the gates reopened for traffic—though it must have been around the time when Samjhauta Express was started; or when exactly did the sombre ritual of flag lowering transform into a choreographed confrontation and become a public spectacle. All I was told was that nearly 15,000 people occupied the Indian galleries on a weekday, and that the number went up to 25,000 during the weekend. Construction was on, I could see, to add more galleries.

It is here in Wagah—where you get to compare India with Pakistan first hand on the basis of the appearance of their people—that you realize the diversity of India. People occupying the Indian galleries belonged to different races and religions, spoke different languages, wore different attires and yet were cohesively bound together by an identity called Indian. The Pakistani side, on the other hand, represented sameness.

Vendors moved around selling ice-cream and potato wafers and water bottles. To kill time I bought an ice-cream and then wafers. Before I could finish the wafers the music stopped and the BSF emcee, clad in a white T-shirt and white trousers, took over. He shouted 'Bharat Mata Ki', and the crowd roared 'Jai!' He shouted 'Hindustan' and the crowded roared 'Zindabad!' He shouted 'Vande' and the crowd roared 'Mataram!' Chants could be heard from the Pakistani side too: 'Pakistan Zindabad!' and 'Jeevey jeevey Pakistan!'

The music resumed again as the emcee conducted an extempore performance that involved women from the audience. He asked the women, of varying shapes and ages and fitness levels, to run up and down the tarmac in pairs while holding aloft the tricolour. It would only be honest on my part to say that it was a funny spectacle, but one must hand it to the women: many of them had clearly never run in their lives but were now doing so, dropping all inhibitions in front of a crowd of some 20,000, just because they believed they were performing national duty. The rest of the audience, of course, did not find the sight funny: they wore the glasses of nationalism and cheered loudly.

Sharp at five-thirty the music stopped and now the words of command—a contest of lung power between the two countries—split the air as their sentries participating in the ceremony stood to attention, all set to go charging at the gates when ordered to.

The word of command, for the uninitiated, is the loud and prolonged shout—always indecipherable to the layman—directed at troops during a drill. Since this was Wagah, the drill master on either side of the border did not have the luxury of cutting corners: each of his commands had to rend the air for the same duration as his counterpart's.

The prolonged shouts continued for a while before the gates dramatically swung open and the mock showdown began: high kicks, stamping of the ground, flexing of biceps, menacing stares. To the ecstatic multitude, each of the BSF men raising his leg high enough for the boot to touch the pleated fan-shaped top of his turban was a national hero.

Finally the flags began to slide down, criss-crossing each other as they were lowered against the setting sun. Once the flags were carried away by slow-marching sentries of the respective countries, the platoon commanders of the BSF and Pakistan Rangers marched resolutely in each other's direction, as if headed for a collision. But they ended up saluting each other and shaking hands briefly before withdrawing, after which the gates were slammed shut. End of the drama.

'Let me show you around,' said Sunil Sharma, a young platoon commander who, since he did not participate in today's parade, was dressed in combat fatigues instead of the ceremonial BSF uniform.

The crowds had nearly dispersed and we strolled past the empty galleries that were littered with water bottles and empty Lay's packets. 'So much for their patriotism,' Sharma laughed when he saw me looking at the strewn rubbish.

We walked up to the gates, from where I could see a lone Pakistani sweeper clearing the mess in their galleries, and then turned right for a stroll along the Radcliffe Line, marked here by a white line and an iron railing. Across the railing lay a lawn, where a tea party was in progress. The women, elegantly dressed in salwar-kameez, sat together—separately from the men—on rows of chairs bearing white covers and black sashes. The men, most of them attired in shirts and trousers, stood in small groups across the lawn.

We walked up to the nearest boundary pillar—tapering and four-faced—where a Pakistan Rangers sentry standing across the railing saluted Sharma.

Sharma returned the salute and asked him, '*Kaise ho*?'—How are you?

'I am fine, sir,' he replied shyly.

I asked Sharma if I could take a picture of the man.

'Why not,' he replied.

The Pakistan Rangers sentry, his finger on the trigger, smiled as I clicked him against the sun that now sat on the horizon like a bright yellow ball. He seemed to be a nice sort, and going by his looks, I guessed that his ancestors must have come from either Uttar Pradesh or Bihar.

As Sharma and I walked back towards the galleries, I asked him whether such powerful stamping of feet affected the knees.

'It does,' he replied, 'even though we are given boots with triple soles embedded with horse-shoes. But stamping is something we are used to because that's also a part of our regular parade. The real challenge is to raise your legs and touch your toes to the turban. For that we need to do a lot of warm-ups and stretches. Our thigh muscles, especially the muscles on the back of the thighs, must be flexible. But when you are performing in front of a crowd of 20,000 people, you think of the pride and not the pain.'

Sharma, twenty-five years old, hails from a town in Madhya Pradesh, and his childhood dream was to join the army. But when he could not clear the tests required to join the army, a friend suggested that he apply for the paramilitary forces, and that's how he joined the BSF, three years ago, as a sub-inspector. His first posting happened to be in Kashmir.

'I still remember my first day in Kashmir,' he said, 'we were in Bandipora, travelling in an armoured vehicle. A crowd of local people was following us—I can never forget the hatred in their eyes. Then suddenly, the children started throwing stones at us.'

After facing hostile crowds in Kashmir for two years, Sharma found himself posted at the Wagah border where, every sunset, a much larger crowd treated him as a hero.

'Wagah is a prestigious posting because it represents the entire force. Not many people get to be a part of the flag-lowering ceremony. Every year a batch comes to train for the ceremony—they are chosen on the basis of their height, personality, and fitness. But nearly 50 per cent of them drop out. Even though I was selected, I was nervous initially. You cannot afford to get even one step wrong. I watched others and practised and practised. On my first day at the ceremony, I looked at the crowds and told myself, "I cannot let the BSF down." It went off well and I gained confidence.'

'Do you get extra perks for being part of the ceremony?'

'Nothing like that, only on some days we are given a special diet.'

'Do you also practise with the Pakistanis?'

'Of course, we have to practise with them too. We spend hours practising together. If one of our boys gets a step wrong, they point it out; likewise if someone among them gets a step wrong, we point it out. It is a coordinated exercise.'

Now that's something most spectators do not realize: that the Indians and Pakistanis actually spend hours practising together to look like enemies at sunset.

I was still talking to Sharma when his superior—an officer with a handlebar moustache, wearing the ceremonial uniform—happened to pass by. He was the one who stood on a pedestal holding a sword and took the salute during the flag-lowering ceremony. Sharma introduced me to him. The officer, it turned out, was the commander of the border outpost nearest to the Wagah border. He invited me to his office.

The outpost was barely a kilometre away, located in another village on the Radcliffe Line. Over tea we discussed the role of the BSF on the Pakistan border. 'If Pakistan attacks,' he said, 'we will be the first ones to retaliate. The army will come only later. The nearest army formation is 20 kilometres away, in Amritsar. Then, our job is also to check smuggling and infiltration. There is easy money in drug trade, so poor people don't mind even risking their lives. You saw the parade today, I don't know if you carefully noticed the people of Pakistan. From their very looks you can tell they are poor people. It is easy to brainwash poor people into becoming terrorists, it is easy to entice them into smuggling.

"These days our biggest fear is what if there is a rocket attack by terrorists from that side while the ceremony is on. Only last year a suicide-bomber blew himself up at Wagah, not very far from the gates, minutes after the ceremony had ended. More than sixty Pakistanis died, women and children included.

'Actually the ceremony was not a part of our duty, it just got added to our list,' the officer said.

It was dark now and I got up to take leave. 'Can I take a look at the border?' I asked him, 'I wanted to see how it looks when lit up.'

'Come, I will show you.'

He led me into a structure—a sort of a bunker—from where, through the loopholes, I could see the illuminated fence at a distance. The bright light gave the impression of busyness: as if the fence was a highway or one of those markets that comes alive only after sunset. In reality, there wasn't a soul around there, except for lonely BSF sentries manning the observations towers.

'And there,' the officer pointed to the left, 'that's the new stadium that is coming up.' By stadium, he meant the new galleries being constructed to accommodate even more visitors to watch the flag-lowering ceremony. The ceremony, quite unfortunately, has overshadowed every other role of the BSF. Spectators merely watch the choreographed showdown, applaud, and go home. Not many are aware that lowly sentries, earning slightly better than a pittance, stand guard at the fence round the clock, with no shelter to protect them from the summer and winter of Punjab—both known to be very cruel.

We stood in the sort-of-bunker in darkness, gazing at the floodlit fence, our faces illuminated by the same light that streamed in through the loopholes. I noticed a sudden unease descending on the officer's face. He said, 'Let's go, not a good idea to linger here. You never know if there is a snake around.'

My mind instantly went back to the day I had landed

in Amritsar, when Husanjeet, the cab driver, took me to his aunt's house in a border village called Udhar Dhaliwal, where he had encouraged me to get into a bunker. How wise I was to not have stepped into it.

# 16

Husanjeet and Sunny, nice chaps after all. Babu, I would never forget him for the rest of my life. Ms Blue Eyelids, I couldn't have been more grateful to her. Then there was Ramesh, who not only took me to Attari station so that I could witness the arrival of Samjhauta Express but also had me connect to folks who contributed to the narrative. I thought of these people as I reclined on the bed, nursing my drink, on my final night in the 'executive suite' of the hotel. These people were total strangers who weren't obliged to be nice to me, but they were. I guess that is how travel books get written: not so much because of the enterprise shown by the writer but more because of the kindness shown by strangers.

The driver woke me up at four in the morning. He sounded irritated.

The previous evening, upon returning to the hotel after watching the flag-lowering at Wagah, I had told the male receptionist—Ms Blue Eyelids' shift had ended—that I wanted to be at the Golden Temple at four in the morning and that he should book a cab for me. 'Sure,' he had assured me, 'the cab will be here at 3.45 sharp.'

It turned out that the driver had been calling me since 3.45: quite natural for him to be irritated because his calls had remained unanswered for fifteen minutes. I swiftly got ready and packed a hotel towel and a change of clothes in a plastic bag and hurried down.

By four-thirty I was at the Golden Temple. Hundreds of Sikhs were still fast asleep on the marble floor outside the precincts of their holiest shrine. I navigated through the sleeping masses into the gurdwara compound and found it as crowded as it would be at four-thirty in the evening. Only the air smelt different.

Wearing only a headscarf and my underwear, I stepped into the tank—the pool of nectar. The water was pleasantly warm and after bathing in it I felt my sensory system sufficiently refreshed to appreciate the magical hour of dawn. I suddenly saw better, heard better, felt better. I reflected upon life as I lingered in the water, listening to gurbani, the words of the gurus, being sung in the sanctum sanctorum. That's when I realized why I felt so good. I had bathed in the tank at this hour voluntarily, only because I wanted the experience and not because I saw it as a ritual that had to be followed. Sikhs don't believe in rituals or superstitions anyway, they bathe in the tank out of sheer devotion for their gurus—and the water was perfumed with devotion. The Ganga, on the other hand, reeks of superstition: people treat the river as a drain carrying all their sins. The Ganga stands for blind belief, the pool of nectar stands for blind devotion. There is a big difference between belief and devotion: belief can change, devotion doesn't.

I changed into fresh clothes and joined the long queue eager to pay respects to the eternal guru. Day had already broken by the time I could reach the sanctum sanctorum and bow before the Guru Granth Sahib. I came out of the Golden Temple feeling humbled as well as triumphant.

The taxi driver, a Sikh himself, showed no irritation for being kept on wait for so long. On the contrary, he held the door open as I got into the cab.

Back in the hotel, I ordered a cup of tea and pondered over my next destination: Bengal. The line that Radcliffe drew to partition Punjab was only 553 kilometres long, but the line he drew to separate East Pakistan from the rest of India ran up to 4,096 kilometres. As many as five Indian states today sit on that line, and I planned to visit all five.

I packed my bags and after breakfast and another cup of tea, went down to the reception to settle my bills.

'I hope you enjoyed your stay, sir,' Ms Blue Eyelids said.

'Absolutely,' I replied.

'Do stay with us if you come to Amritsar again.'

'Without doubt.'

Only after I got into the cab did it occur to me that I had not even asked her name.

At the airport there was a large crowd of people who had come to see off their loved ones. Most passengers queued up to enter the departure hall held passports. Apart from me, almost everybody seemed to be flying abroad, even to places I did not expect to be directly connected to India, leave alone Amritsar: 'Passengers travelling to Ashgabat by Turkmenistan Airlines flight no. 35528 are requested to proceed to gate no. 5.'

Soon my flight was announced. It turned out to be a Dreamliner again. As I glided up the escalator to the boarding gate, I noticed a woman chasing her tiny daughter who was sprinting across the departure hall. The woman was calling out, 'Simran! Simran!' Ah, the sweet sound of Punjab.

# East

This map is not to scale and its borders have not been verified or authenticated independently.

# 1

The fuse may have been lit in Calcutta, but Bengal itself saw little bloodshed when the bomb of Partition exploded. It was Punjab that bore the brunt. For most Bengalis, the Radcliffe Line was a destiny-altering line that had materialized on their palms overnight. No choice but to accept it.

If only they had displayed such stoicism on 16 August 1946—when the strike called by the Muslim League to demand creation of Pakistan triggered the Great Calcutta Killings—Partition itself might have been averted.

The province of Bengal, at the time, had a Muslim League government led by the charismatic Bengali nationalist H.S. Suhrawardy. He was all for a separate country for Muslims but at the same time was against the division of Bengal: he wanted Bengal to be an independent nation, an idea that never caught fire.

Suhrawardy was one of the key speakers at the rally held at the Maidan on the day of the strike, and even before it could end the riots had begun. No one knows for sure whether the speeches made at the meeting were inflammatory enough to instigate the rioting, but it is generally believed that his government did not do enough to stop Bengalis from butchering one another in the name of religion.

The death toll was so high—at least 5,000 said to have been killed—that the British began to see the point in Muslim League's argument in favour of Partition: that Hindus and Muslims cannot coexist peacefully in India. Exactly 363 days from the day of the strike, Pakistan came into existence.

Unlike in Punjab, where millions uprooted themselves and moved to the other side of the Radcliffe Line, the transfer of population in Bengal took place on a far lesser scale. But while the migration was a once-and-for-all affair in Punjab, it turned out to be a staggered process in Bengal, where a large number of Hindus initially chose to stay back in Pakistan-ruled East Bengal but began migrating once they found the political climate not too conducive for them.

After 1947 there were two more waves of migration. The first in 1964, when Hindus were targeted in the riots that broke out in East Bengal (by then renamed East Pakistan) after the Prophet's hair went missing from the Hazratbal shrine in Kashmir. The rioting was perpetrated by thuggish politicians who eyed and—with the blessings of the government—managed to grab the property of a number of Hindus.

The second—and a much, much larger—wave came in 1971, when East Pakistan fought its subjugation by West Pakistan. This time the refugees were mostly Muslims, escaping the murderous non-Bengali Pakistani soldiers who were shooting men and raping women on whim. At least one million Bengalis were killed in the genocide.

That year in December—when nine million refugees had already poured into West Bengal, Assam, and Tripura—the Indian Army formally joined the Liberation War that the Mukti Bahini, the guerrilla force made up of Bengalis, was waging against the troops of West Pakistan. Until then, the Indian Army had only been training the guerrillas.

[One of the most distinguished trainers of the Mukti Bahini happened to be a Sikh officer, Brigadier Shabeg Singh, who was to later meet with a very tragic end. A day before the highly-decorated officer was to retire, as a major general, he was dismissed from service on charges of irregularities. Deeply pained, he went on to join the Sikh separatist movement led by Jarnail Singh Bhindranwale, and died at the Golden Temple during Operation Blue Star, felled by the guns of the Indian Army].

Once the Indian forces marched in, the war was won in no time and East Pakistan became an independent nation called Bangladesh. Culture had prevailed over faith.

Illegal migration from Bangladesh is said to be continuing even to this day—though there is no solid proof, only suspicion—and has long been a political issue in Assam and more recently in West Bengal, where nationalist groups say the influx is altering the demography of these states.

But right from the time of Partition to until very recently, hardly anyone spared a thought for those thousands of families who remained stranded in no man's land for nearly seven decades, their existence forgotten by both India and Pakistan. These people were mere pawns in the game of chess—quite literally.

The story goes that sometime during the eighteenth century, the king of Cooch Behar would routinely sit down to play chess with the governor of neighbouring Rangpur state, which was a part of Mughal-ruled Bengal. On stake would be the most fertile pieces of farmland in their respective domains.

The king must have been a better player, because by the time the two stopped playing chess, the kingdom of Cooch Behar had 111 enclaves in Rangpur, whereas Rangpur had only 51 enclaves in Cooch Behar.

After Partition, while Cooch Behar acceded to India, Rangpur came under East Pakistan which subsequently became Bangladesh. As a result the ownership of the enclaves—called *chhit* locally—also changed hands.

*Chhit* means a sprinkle, a definition that goes well with the joke that the enclaves were created by a drunken British clerk who spilled ink while drawing the Radcliffe Line on the map. The truth is that the British had no hand whatsoever in their creation, but the line drawn by Radcliffe—and the animosity between the two new nations that were created by his line—reduced the enclaves, basically villages, into near-prisons.

For close to seven decades, their residents were left to fend for themselves, surrounded by the territory of another country and having no administrative access to what was supposed to be their own country. Stepping out of their village technically meant illegally stepping into another country, which could land them in prison. Life in a prison can be better: you may have to remain confined within its walls but you are taken care of.

Freedom for them came as recently as in 2015—also at the stroke of midnight, as July melted into August—when the 51 Bangladeshi enclaves in Cooch Behar merged with India and the 111 Indian enclaves in Bangladesh dissolved into that country following the ratification of the long-pending land swap by the two countries.

I was now headed for Cooch Behar.

Most places remain just names for us. We spend our entire lives and eventually die having only heard about them, not even knowing where they exist on the map. This trip allowed me to strike Cooch Behar off the long list of such places, and I found its location on the map most fascinating: a little below the Himalayas and right above the crown of Bangladesh. My first ever visit to the geographical entity known as north Bengal.

I flew from Calcutta to Bagdogra, a tiny town seated on the cusp of Bengal's tea gardens and forests. The airport at Bagdogra, even though small and shared by the military, is a busy one: it not only connects north Bengal to Calcutta and therefore the rest of India, but also serves as the gateway to Darjeeling, Sikkim, Nepal, and Bhutan.

It was at the parking lot of the airport that I noticed, for the first time, a foreign car on Indian soil: a Nepalese car with a red number plate bearing a registration number in the Devnagari script. Who knew there could be a Bhutanese car too hiding among the dozens of cars parked there? One of the cars, a humble Tata Indica, was now going to take me to Cooch Behar.

'It won't take us more than three hours,' the friendly driver, a native of Bihar, assured me.

I had half a mind to stay back in Bagdogra to take turns in visiting Nepal and Bhutan, and Sikkim and Darjeeling—and also spending a couple of nights in a dak bungalow amid the famed forests of north Bengal. But I was equally curious about Cooch Behar.

At first we drove past tea gardens and then lush green fields before running into the bustle of cities—Siliguri and then Jalpaiguri, two more cities that had been mere names for me until now. Then came the rivers—Teesta, Jaldhaka, Torsa—which looked at once beautiful and intimidating. They had just descended from the Himalayas, no longer pretty streams but full-fledged wide rivers whose waters still bore the momentum of a stream. They all flowed in the direction of Bangladesh.

It rained on and off as we drove, slowing down with every shower, and by the time we reached Cooch Behar the sun had long set. Arriving in a new place after dark is like receiving a gift that must remain wrapped until dawn. It is at daybreak that the place takes off its mask and reveals it true colours to a newcomer.

I checked into what had been recommended to me as one of the best hotels in town, and there I chose one of the best rooms in the hope that at least the bathroom would be large and clean. I don't mind staying in a cubbyhole as long as the bathroom is clean, but in India that's often a luxury even money can't buy.

As soon as the room boy—actually a man almost my age—showed me into the special room, I peeped into the bathroom.

'Can you have the bathroom cleaned?' I asked him.

'It is clean,' he insisted. But I could see the ghost of the previous occupant perched on the commode and standing under the shower.

'Is there a problem getting it cleaned again?' I insisted.

'Not at all,' he said.

A sweeper arrived with a broom and a bottle of disinfectant. Once he left, I began to unpack. The room boy showed up again: 'What would you like to have for dinner?'

'Get me tarka-ruti,' I told him, tarka-ruti being fried daal served with rotis, 'but first get me a bottle of whisky.'

After he had delivered the goods and left, I poured myself a drink and stepped out to the balcony—one of the perks of the room. I oversaw the evening bustle of Cooch Behar: people bargaining with hawkers under yellow lights, people making purchases, people hopping onto battery-operated trishaws to get home.

I felt tempted to join the bustle, but I had just spent four hours on the road and my back ached for comfort. I had a few more drinks and returned to the balcony a couple of hours later to find myself surveying the darkness that now represented Cooch Behar. There was a knock on the door.

'Can I clear the plates, sir?' the room boy asked me.

'But I haven't even eaten yet.'

He looked at me incredulously and then turned his gaze to the table where the food lay untouched, sealed in aluminium foils. He had obviously not come across a guest who was yet to have his dinner even though it was close to midnight.

He told me to leave the plates outside the door once I was done eating, and then asked me, 'What would you like for breakfast?'

'Get me an omelette and two slices of bread, and maybe two alu parathas?'

'*Ato khete paarben ki*?' he asked me out of genuine concern—Will you be able to eat so much?

'Why do you ask?' I asked back, in great surprise.

'Our parathas are quite big in size.'

'Fine, get me only parathas,' I said.

I instantly became fond of him. His concern for me was a very Bengali trait: there have been occasions in Calcutta when I have stopped by at a shop to ask for samosas only to be warned by the shopkeeper outright that they had gone cold. Customer satisfaction was more important to him than profit.

# 2

I woke up at seven and stepped out into the balcony to a steady drizzle. Not the kind of weather you would like to wake up to on your first morning in a new place. Rain, sunrise, sunset, darkness—all may become agreeable but only once you have experienced the place in broad daylight. Right now the cup of tea in my hand was my one comfort. That's the thing with Indian tea: it tastes nearly the same no matter where in India you are and often one sip is sufficient to make you feel familiar with a new location.

Right across the road from the balcony stood a mosque and a building that served as the local branch of the Allahabad Bank. Beyond these buildings was a large pond, visible because of the vacant plot between the mosque and the bank. Lungi-clad men, holding umbrellas over their heads, sat fishing on its banks—a picture of patience. Further down the road, at an intersection, stood a rectangular three-storied yellow building that identified itself as Cooch Behar Hotel.

So this was Cooch Behar, the erstwhile capital of the erstwhile kingdom of Cooch Behar that hadn't acceded to India until 1949. Today the capital is known as Cooch

Behar Town and the kingdom is known as Cooch Behar district—one of the many districts belonging to the province of West Bengal.

I have been familiar with the name ever since I was a child because while devouring the sports pages of the newspaper I would often come across cricket scores related to the Cooch Behar Trophy. Much later in life I learned that one of the most beautiful women in India, Maharani Gayatri Devi of Jaipur, hailed from the royal family of Cooch Behar. The familiarity ended there. Here I was, standing on the balcony of what was considered to be one of the best hotels in Cooch Behar, called Yubraj, or prince. Whether the name was a tribute to Cooch Behar's royalty or the famous cricketer Yuvraj Singh, I wasn't too curious to find out.

I called up Diptiman Sengupta, chief coordinator of the Bharat Bangladesh Enclave Exchange Coordination Movement, an NGO responsible for creating public awareness about the plight of the people living in the *chhit*s. He was the man of the moment, considering that his sustained campaign had finally borne fruits. Meeting him was absolutely essential before setting out for the *chhit*s.

Sengupta, however, didn't sound very eager to meet yet another journalist—he must have been besieged by reporters during the days preceding and following the midnight that saw the land swap—but he relented when I told him I had come all the way from Chennai just to meet him. He lived in Dinhata, a settlement almost touching Bangladesh, about twenty-five kilometres south from downtown Cooch Behar. 'Almost every driver in Cooch Behar knows where I live,' he said.

Relieved, I sat down for breakfast: two exceptionally large alu parathas served with curd and mixed-vegetable pickle. I had just begun eating when the room boy brought in an omelette as well.

'Why the omelette?' I asked him.

'I could sense you like omelette for breakfast.'

With my free hand, I reached for my wallet and pulled out a fifty-rupee note to tip him.

'Anything else you would like to have?' he asked.

'One more cup of tea.'

At nine, chauffeured by a pleasant young man called Gautam, I set out for the countryside that hugged the northern border of Bangladesh.

I crossed River Torsa again—I had crossed it way upstream the evening before—then it was mile after mile of paddy fields, punctuated by clusters of settlements. The intermittent drizzle made it a beautifully gloomy day, the grey of the sky deepening the green of the land.

After a drive of nearly an hour, shops started showing up, indicating that we had entered a settlement that was too urban to be a village but too pastoral to be a town—the kind of place where everybody knows everybody. A large chunk of India lives in and around such settlements: urban yet rustic, modern yet traditional, and far-flung yet well-connected today.

Gautam parked his car on a vacant stretch of land by the road and said, 'That's where Diptiman babu lives.' He pointed to a house across the road. I pushed opened a large gate and stepped in. The house was a very old construction, single-storied and built around a garden. There was no one to be seen as I wandered around the garden wondering where to knock or ring a bell, worried all along about stepping on a snake that might have slithered out of its water-logged dwelling.

After several minutes I spotted a woman—rather she spotted me—and she asked me to wait on a sofa in the verandah that was enclosed by grilles. As I sat there gathering my thoughts, jotting down questions I had in mind for him, Diptiman showed up: a bearded man, clad in a traditional vest and a dhoti casually tied around his waist, looking every bit an angry communist who wasn't capable of a smile. He was my age, forty-five, but could have passed off as one of those student leaders who hang around the campus even after graduating.

He lit up a cigarette and said, 'What happens in Las Vegas today has been happening in our society since time immemorial. Even Yudhishthir gambled. No man, no matter how great, is perfect. Everyone has their vices, but in a feudal society people accept the vices of their rulers. The boss is always right, after all. The rulers of Cooch Behar and Rangpur, whenever they sat down to play chess, would have at hand the documents of the most fertile lands. You will find that every enclave is not more than 100 metres away from a water body and tests have shown that their soil has 12 to 25 per cent more minerals than the soil in other places.'

The land swap, he said, should have ideally happened when the British were partitioning India, but then Partition was done in such a hurry—'what should have taken at least four years was completed in a matter of five weeks!'—that the future of the enclaves remained unsettled.

It drizzled steadily as we spoke. The woman I had encountered before—she seemed to be the domestic help—brought us tea. As I took a sip and put the cup down and looked up at Diptiman to resume the conversation, I was startled by a strange face, pressed against the grille, blankly staring at us. Moments later another face materialized, and then another. In a matter of minutes there were about a dozen people clutching the grille like prisoners and listening to us, their faces weary and eyes blank. With every passing minute there was a new arrival. I gathered that they were all people from the enclaves, who had come all the way, in spite of the drizzle, to find out from their hero what the future held for them.

For all of them Diptiman had the same answer, often delivered in the form of a rebuke: 'Your first priority should be to get the [Indian] citizenship, everything else comes later. How many times will I have to repeat that?'

The land swap required the residents of the enclaves to choose between Indian and Bangladeshi nationalities and relocate accordingly. While those living in Bangladeshi enclaves in India—a little over 14,000 people—are all staying back to become Indian citizens, nearly 1,000 of the 37,000 living in Indian enclaves in Bangladesh have chosen to come to India. For the 14,000 people awaiting Indian citizenship—they have never known governance and have always lived in fear—Diptiman is a father-figure they can turn to at this defining hour. Before Diptiman came into the picture, they had looked up to his father, Dipak Sengupta.

Dipak Sengupta belonged to the Forward Bloc, an ally of the Communist Party of India (Marxist) that ruled West Bengal for thirty-four years until 2011, and represented the nearby Sitai constituency in the State Assembly for four consecutive terms. He was sensitive to the plight of the residents of the enclave and frequently wrote to those in power presenting their problems—but with no success.

'In 2009, my father fell ill,' Diptiman said, 'and he asked me if I would carry forward his work. Since he was unwell, I said yes, just to console him. At the time I was working with a telecom company—an MNC—and earning nearly eight lakh rupees per annum, which was not a small amount back then. But my father persisted. He would say, "You have to carry forward my struggle. The government has to listen to you." I finally resigned, just to assure him.

'A few days later, on October 2 that year, he died. He was seventy-eight. I decided I would rejoin the company. On the day of his shraddho'—the ritual on the thirteenth day from one's death—'we were expecting about 10,000 people, but 18,000 turned up. The additional 8,000 were all from the enclaves, they seemed deeply affected by his death. That was when it struck me that he had been their sole hope.

'My wife has a government job, so there was no question of us starving in case I did not go back to my job. It was she who asked me to go ahead and take the plunge. So I started this movement and our organisation, made up of members from both sides of the border, began to grow.

'In mid-2011 we carried out a census in the enclaves. It was a great step towards creating a public awareness because until then people did not even know that the *chhit*s were inhabited,' Diptiman said.

On the face of it, the historic land swap was the culmination of an official process that was set rolling way back in 1974—twenty-seven years after Partition—when Indira Gandhi and Sheikh Mujib ur Rahman were the prime ministers of India and Bangladesh respectively. But nothing came of it for the next forty years until the movement led by Diptiman brought these long-forgotten pockets in the public eye.

His campaign and the subsequent ratification of the land swap, therefore, cannot be dismissed as a mere coincidence—certainly not when you see a crowd of 100-plus *chhit*-residents flocking at his door on a rainy morning.

'The time has come to dissolve the organisation,' Diptiman said. 'Its existence is no longer required. Now we will need to look at other things, such as making those people literate, making them aware of their rights. They have lived in darkness for far too long.'

'I would like to visit some of the *chhit*s. How do I get there?' I asked.

'Why, one of these boys will take you,' Diptiman said pointing to the crowd as he lit up another cigarette.

# 3

Half-a-dozen young men, eager to guide me to the enclaves, accompanied me as I walked out of Diptiman's home. I told them I could take along only three people at the most, and that they should decide among themselves which three it would be.

I was convinced that each of them wanted a free ride home, considering that Diptiman had nothing new to say to them this morning other than asking them to wait for Indian citizenship. If not a free ride, maybe just a joyride?

The men moved away from me and got into an argument which, to my surprise, ended rather quickly and amicably. Finally only two of them got into the car with me: one sat next to me and the other sat next to Gautam, the driver.

Gautam, far from wondering who they were, looked rather pleased that he now had two extra passengers. He had mostly been quiet throughout the journey, but now he started talking to the man sitting next to him. He was probably familiar with them.

I observed the man sitting next to me. He had hazel eyes, so prominently hazel that you didn't notice anything else about him. But there was something else as distracting as his eyes: his torn trouser that exposed a few inches of his thigh. Either he wasn't aware of the tear or didn't have a choice. The second was more likely because he, in spite of his handsome face and hazel eyes, was a picture of poverty. His name was Bashar Sheikh, thirty-one years old, who belonged to an enclave called Paschim Moshaldanga.

'Have you come from Calcutta?' he asked me.

'Yes, in the sense that I took the flight from Calcutta, but I live in Chennai. Heard of it?'

'Of course, but I have never travelled that far. I have been to Delhi, and I worked in Noida for a few months at a construction site. Then one day my landlord asked me for ID proof and I had none. He asked me to vacate. I approached other landlords, but they too asked me to produce ID proof. So I had to come back. Now I do odd jobs in the farms here,' Bashar said.

'Odd jobs such as?' I asked.

'Sometimes I work as a labourer, sometimes as a plumber, sometimes I drive the tractor. Only last month I was asked to take a tractor to Cooch Behar Town for repairs. The police stopped me and asked to see my licence. Now how was I to produce a licence? They let me off after I paid them a bribe of Rs 600. Fortunately my employer had given me sufficient money to get the repairs done.'

'That's very sad,' I remarked.

'Why do you think we are so happy now? We have always lived in fear.'

'Are you married?'

'Yes. My wife is from the Indian side.'

'And her parents agreed to marry her off to someone living in a *chhit*?'

'The thing is her family is even poorer than us. One day the elders in my village and her village got together and told her parents, "*Chhele ta bhalo, biye diye dao* (he is a decent chap, marry your daughter to him)." The parents had no choice but to agree.'

Presently we hit the bustle of a marketplace. 'This is Nazirhat,' Bashar said, 'the biggest market in this area. Everything we need to buy—from salt to clothes—we buy it from here. This is also where we sell our produce. You can say that this market is our lifeline.'

By 'our' he meant people living in the *chhit*s. It would take him a while to get used to the fact that the Bangladeshi enclaves in Cooch Behar were now part of India and that he himself was an Indian citizen-in-waiting.

We left behind the market only to once again cut across ripening paddies, freshly washed in rain. The sun was out now and there was a sparkle in the crop. Only when you find yourself in the midst of the countryside do you realize how small our cities are—and how small the minds of people living in it are. I had thought Bashar Sheikh was seeking a free ride back home, whereas he was actually doing me a great favour by coming along.

All through the journey he told me about the pathetic life in the Bangladeshi enclaves: Bangladesh had no direct access to them, India ignored them, and the residents—poor, hardworking peasants—remained stranded in no-man's land for several generations.

They survived the seven long decades as non-entities largely because of the human instinct for survival—and sometimes because of the kindness shown by friends or relatives living on the Indian side. The kindness was dispensed mostly in the form of false address proofs and forged identity cards that showed the *chhit*-residents as Indian citizens and allowed them to meet the most basic of human needs: earning a living, sending children to school, getting treatment in a government hospital… The kindness also came in the form of illegal electricity connections—chargeable, of course.

Life for those living in the Indian enclaves in Bangladesh, I presumed, must have been just as pathetic. Or maybe I am wrong. While all the 14,000 people living in Bangladeshi enclaves in India have decided to stay back and opt for an Indian citizenship, only 1,000 of the 37,000 living in Indian enclaves in Bangladesh have chosen to move to India. In other words, 36,000 Indians did not opt to move out of Bangladesh. Numbers always tell a story.

Right now I was overcome by the urge to give Bashar Sheikh some money so that he could buy a new pair of trousers. I even had enough cash. But what if he took offence? Worse, what if he was not even aware of the gaping hole? There can't be a graver crime than pointing out to a poor man that his trouser is torn. Moreover, notwithstanding his poverty, we were equals: I the journalist and he the activist who, as one of the many faceless faces, had campaigned for the freedom of the enclaves.

Gautam presently brought the car to a halt under a tree where half-a-dozen men, smoking *beedi*s, were seated in a circle. We had arrived in Paschim Moshaldanga, a hamlet of twenty-eight houses, in one of which Bashar lived. Close to where the men sat, lay a brick framework that had held up the mast when the Indian tricolour was unfurled here just days ago. Bashar introduced me to the men and slipped away.

I began by talking to Kadam Sheikh, thirty-six years old, who spends months away from home working as a construction labourer in cities such as Gurgaon, Noida, Amritsar, and Dehradun.

'I carry a fake voter ID because there is always the fear of getting arrested as an illegal migrant when I go to work in those places,' he said. 'But the card is of little use to my children because it gives my age as twenty-five. My daughter is already nineteen and my son seventeen—they can't have a father who is twenty-five, can they? Hopefully I should be getting a new voter ID soon—a genuine one this time.'

His neighbour Jamal Sheikh, fifty-five years old, chipped in: 'Our very existence depended on fake documents. Even hospitals would turn us away if they came to know we are from the *chhit*s. Why, even pregnant women have been turned away. You have no idea how difficult life has been for us. At least I never went to jail, but five people in our village did—for no fault of theirs. They were merely going to Dehradun to find work.'

'Can I meet them?'

'One of them was here until a few minutes ago,' Jamal Sheikh said, 'wait, I will send for him.'

A young man who was part of the semi-circle that had formed around us set off on his bike to get the man who had been to prison. Meanwhile, tea arrived from one of the houses.

The man who finally appeared was elderly, bespectacled, and wore a long beard. He looked too distinguished to have toiled under the harsh sun at a construction site. He could have been the imam of a local mosque. His name was Amir Hossain, sixty years old. One night in 2006, he and four fellow residents of Paschim Moshaldanga were picked up by the Border Security Force from Nazirhat. They were on their way to the New Cooch Behar railway station, where they were to board the train to Dehradun. They expected to easily find work in the capital of the newly-formed state of Uttarakhand, which was witnessing a boom in construction activity at the time.

Hossain recalled: 'The train was at two in the morning, and we were picked up around ten in the night. We were brought to the BSF camp at Digaltari, not very far from here, and beaten up all night. They even pulled our beards. Our crime: we had train tickets but no IDs. They told us we were illegal migrants from Bangladesh who were trying to sneak into India. The next morning they handed us over to the local police. We spent twenty-six days in jail before we got bail, thanks to our relatives living on the Indian side.'

'How were you treated in jail?' I asked.

'Wait, this is only the beginning of the story. After we

were out on bail, the case dragged on for two years, and finally in 2008, the magistrate sent us to jail for two years and fined us Rs 10,000 each. Failure to pay the fine meant an additional two months in prison. We spent three days in Dinhata jail, then four days in Cooch Behar jail, then seventeen months in Jalpaiguri central jail, and finally nineteen months in the new jail at Alipurduar. That adds up to three years. Three years in jail just because we did not have proof of identity!'

'Are you happy that you are now a part of India?'

'Happy? That's an understatement. There is no limit to our happiness!'

The poor in India have very little rights—and their dignity is like a dhoti that comes off at the slightest tug.

A rickshaw-puller can get slapped by just about anyone who stands higher than him in the social ladder. A patient suffering from poverty, apart from a life-threatening condition, can die just because the doctor on duty chooses to step out for tea when an emergency surgery is required. A pavement-dweller can be picked up by a cop looking for a thief or murderer.

I remember reading about a poor villager who spent nearly thirty years in various Bihar prisons just because he was caught travelling in a train without a ticket: once he landed in jail he was promptly forgotten by the world outside, pretty much how the enclaves were forgotten after Partition.

For people living in the enclaves, their poverty had been compounded by their statelessness. They merely happened to be born and grow up in the same land where their fathers and grandfathers were also born and had died. *Chhit*s, for that matter, don't even have burial grounds. People simply buried their dead in their backyards.

'There, that's my house,' Mohammad Naushad Ali, an elderly farmer, pointed to a tin structure at a distance. 'Do you see two graves just outside the house?'

I did spot two graves, a tarpaulin protecting them from rain.

'That's where my parents lie buried,' Naushad Ali said. 'We have no other place to go.'

Graves of loved ones in the backyard—did that double their emotional attachment to their lands?

As I got ready to leave, Bashar Sheikh, the hazel-eyed man who had accompanied me, showed up. He carried three paper boxes: he gave one to Gautam, the driver, and pressed two into my hands. 'Something for you to eat,' he said with a smile that made me at once happy and sad.

When I got into the car, he slipped something else into my hands: a packet of Sheikh brand of cigarettes, made in Bangladesh.

'You must eat them,' Gautam said when he noticed me looking into the boxes. Each contained a samosa and a rossogolla. 'They are village-made, very tasty.'

'Later,' I said, 'first let me smoke a Sheikh cigarette.'

'There's another *chhit* nearby, shall we go there?'

'By all means.'

The cigarette tasted smooth. I examined the packet. It was manufactured by Dhaka Tobacco Industries. I wasn't surprised at all that I was smoking a Bangladeshi cigarette without stepping into Bangladesh. The border lay close by, and since Bangladesh, unlike Pakistan, is a friendly country, and since the border is not entirely fenced, it is not unusual for villagers and petty smugglers to sneak in or out. Until the land swap, *chhit*s were legally out of bounds for the BSF or local police and are said to have been considered havens by smugglers and other criminals.

The enclave—former enclave—we drove into now was Madhya Moshaldanga, where the men were about to leave, on motorbikes, for Potarkuti, yet another (former) enclave about 25 kilometres away to attend an event celebrating their independence.

I asked one of them, Joynal Abedin, how he got his bike. 'This is my uncle's bike. He lives on the Indian side, and is right now posted in Delhi,' said Joynal, twenty-three, a third-year BA student at Dewanhat College in Cooch Behar.

'How did you get admission in the college?'

'I had to give a fake address. But for the past couple of years I have been publicising the fact that I live in a *chhit*. Is it a crime to live in a *chhit*?'

The village nearly emptied out as most of the men left for the function. The women went into their homes upon the arrival of a stranger. I sat on a cot—overseeing a vast expanse of paddy fields—along with Mohammad Asghar Ali, who gave his age as 106.

From two parallel ropes marking the pathway to Ali's house hung clothes as well as jute fibre, left to dry in the sun that was shining now. On the pathway a calf suckled its mother's udders.

'I was born in Mymensingh (now in Bangladesh),' Ali said, 'and my father moved to this place when I was nine or ten years old. All my life I have been a farmer.'

I calculated: his father must have settled in this village ninety-six years ago, sometime around 1919, when the massacre took place at Jallianwala Bagh.

'You must have seen a lot in your long life,' I told him. 'Do you have memories of Partition?'

'I am 106 years old,' he said. '*Aeto kotha ki mone thhakey*?'

*Aeto kotha ki mone thhakey*: Do you expect to remember so many things?

He was right. At 106, he had witnessed, as an adult, the process that saw the subcontinent becoming free from British rule to eventually being split into three nations; but since he was 106, it was unfair to expect him to remember everything.

'All I remember is that Jinnah saheb and Gandhi divided the country,' Ali finally said.

'How do you feel, now that Moshaldanga is part of India?'

'I will die any day now, how does it matter to me. But my children will hopefully see better times, that's the only consolation.'

# 4

If I were to see my real-time location on the map right now, I would find the blue dot moving along the jagged line that defines the northern extremity of Bangladesh.

What I wanted to do right now was go right up to the border, stare at Bangladesh, spend some time in a village on the Indian side, and get an elderly resident to reminisce about Partition. Basically what I had done in Punjab: to visit the line drawn by Radcliffe.

It is a different matter that in the places I visited in Punjab, I encountered not a soul who had witnessed Partition as an adult. Anyone who had witnessed Partition as an adult should be close to ninety today, and it is not easy to find a healthy and loquacious ninety-year-old in locations you choose or happen to visit.

'Take me to a village from where I can get a view of Bangladesh,' I told Gautam.

'And what's the purpose?' he asked.

I told him.

'I don't think the BSF people will allow us to get close to the border. You may need permission.'

'Just keep driving in the direction of the border, let's see what happens. You know in which direction Bangladesh lies, right?'

'I do.'

'Then drive on.'

Gautam complied. As we drove, I found it impossible to tell whether we were passing a (former) *chhit* or an Indian village: vibrant greenery all around. After about a kilometre's drive he brought the car to a halt and, pointing to cultivated pieces of land ahead of us, said, 'I think all that is Bangladesh.'

'How do you know?'

'Because I can see a BSF camp, just look to your left,' he said, 'I don't think we can drive further without permission.'

'Let's go to the BSF camp.'

Gautam drove up to its gates where I introduced myself to two young recruits clad in white collared T-shirts and shorts. This was a border outpost in the village of—as I could tell from the signboard—East Digaltari. The boys, since they must be spending their entire days staring at the green fields and dealing with villagers and smugglers, were evidently happy to be visited by a fellow countryman from the city. They were, however, puzzled by my request that I be allowed to visit a border village.

'But this is a border village,' one of them said.

'Yes, but I would like to visit a home,' I explained, 'I have heard there are homes that have the border running right through their courtyard.'

The two looked at each other and then led me into the

camp. I was offered a chair in the tent of the commanding officer, or CO, who seemed to be away, and—in keeping with the BSF hospitality—served with water and subsequently tea. Then the questioning began: What is your name again? Which paper did you say you work for? What is your designation? Why do you want to visit a border village? May I have your visiting card? May I see your ID card please?

I dropped names, but unfortunately they hadn't heard of my friend in the BSF or of the officers I had met in Punjab. But fortunately for me, both the men, who appeared to be in their twenties, thought very highly of the paper I worked for.

'Where should we send him?' one of them asked the other, 'Shall we send him to Paglabari?'

'But we need to get CO *saab*'s permission,' replied the other.

'Yes, you are right. Let me call up CO *saab* then,' the one who suggested Paglabari said and stepped away to make the call.

Pagla, in Bengali, means a crazy or eccentric man; bari means home. A crazy man's home, that too on the border: not to be missed. Who was Pagla? Why was he called Pagla? In which period did he live? Did he see Partition? My mind throbbed with these questions, but the most important question was: would the CO agree?

I heard my name and designation being repeatedly mentioned over the phone, and once he hung up he came up to me and said, 'Okay, one of our men will accompany you. And no photographs please.'

I headed to the car followed by a BSF man in plainclothes, and on my way out, I noticed the signboard again and it struck me that this was the same camp where Amir Hossain, the *chhit*-resident who had spent three years in jail, had been detained for a night. Soon we were driving on a path that was asphalted once upon a time but was now a bed of stone chips. Every now and then we passed a boundary pillar. Sometimes it would be to our right and sometimes to our left, sometimes half-submerged in a pond and sometimes half-hidden behind crops.

Since the imaginary line joining the pillars happens to be the Radcliffe Line, sometimes India lay on the left and Bangladesh on the right, sometimes India on the right and Bangladesh on the left, and sometimes India on both right and left. To me it all looked the same: it was like being in the midst of one vast farmland sprinkled with clusters of tin houses from whose roofs sprouted the ubiquitous dish antennae. When nature intends a region to be homogenous, manmade demarcations can look invisible—even insignificant—to an outsider.

'Now you get an idea how zigzagged the border is,' the BSF man, who was drawing my attention to the pillars, remarked. The zigzaggedness makes the India-Bangladesh border the fifth-longest land border in the world, even though Bangladesh is about half the size of Uttar Pradesh.

'How do you remember where the pillars are?' I asked him.

'It's our job to remember where they are,' he laughed.

BSF constables, posted in pairs along the path, saluted

us: 'Jai Hind!' They saluted because they recognised the man in plainclothes.

'Look at these boys,' the BSF man said, 'They have to be here round the clock, rain or shine. Do you see any Bangladeshi guard around?'

'No.'

'They take it easy because they know we are guarding the border. It's the same situation even on the Pakistan border: you will only find the BSF.'

We stopped outside a cluster of tin houses. One of them belonged to Pagla who, clad in a vest and lungi, rushed out to greet us. So there was no legend around Paglabari.

I shook Pagla's hand and asked him if he had a proper name.

'I do, Nadir Sheikh.'

'Then why are you called Pagla?'

'I have been called Pagla ever since I was a child. I have no idea why.'

We walked past Pagla's house into his courtyard that was shared by an identical house barely ten feet away. From the shrubs separating the two houses sprouted a weather-worn pillar that was inscribed: '977 | 7-S IND'. So Radcliffe had run his pencil between the two houses. Pagla's house was in the village of East Digaltari—in India. His neighbour's in South Bansjani village—in Bangladesh.

The children and the chicken running about in the courtyard did not recognize the border. Even the adults did not seem to, though right now everyone was in their respective countries because of the BSF man's presence.

Pagla said, 'There are about twelve or thirteen houses in this cluster, some in India, some in Bangladesh. We always visit one another's homes during weddings and funerals. This place is like my own village.'

Members of his neighbour's family—they had by now gathered outside their house out of curiosity—agreed vehemently. 'We are always together in times of need,' a male member from that side said.

Pagla, now sixty, was born in this house and his family consisted of his wife, son, daughter-in-law, and a grandson. He also had a daughter, who was twelve. There is no one in the family old enough to have witnessed the drawing of Radcliffe Line.

As a child, Pagla had studied in a nearby madrasa and went on to become a farmer, growing paddy, jute, and sometimes wheat. His son, who studied in a nearby high school, worked in a brick kiln near Delhi. About 30 per cent of the men in this cluster worked in big cities in north India, mostly as labourers. They came home once a year to lend a helping hand during the harvest season.

'Life is good, I have no complaints,' Pagla said.

'What do you do for entertainment?' I asked him.

'Why, I have a dish antenna. I watch movies.'

'Do you watch Bangladeshi programmes too?'

'I watch everything.'

Suddenly, a bare-chested boy from across the border cried out: 'We also have dish antenna, Airtel.' His name was Sujan, fifteen years old, studying in the tenth standard.

'Do you watch Indian films?' I asked the boy.

'As many as I can, especially films of Ankush and Dev (both present-day Bengali actors).'

'What about Hindi films?'

'Yes, Hindi films too.'

'And your favourite hero?'

'Salman Khan!' he spat out the name ecstatically.

As I tested his knowledge of Salman Khan—he was indeed a fan—it struck me how, even during moments of excitement induced by hero-worship, not once did he come closer to me. He remained in his part of the courtyard, standing about five feet away, respecting the divide established by the Radcliffe Line. Same people, same culture, same religion, same customs, same sources of joy and suffering—yet an imaginary line dividing them into two nations. How cruel and meaningless.

'If I go stand where the boy is standing now, will I be entering Bangladesh?' I asked aloud, to no one in particular.

'Yes!' came the answer in unison.

I looked at the BSF man, who didn't look very pleased.

Pagla's neighbours urged me, '*Aasen na*! *Aasen na*! *Kichhu hobe na*'—Please come over, please come over, nothing to worry.

Pagla too egged me on, '*Jaan na*! *Kichhu hobe na*!'—Go ahead, nothing to worry.

I took two strides and I was in Bangladesh.

One of Pagla's neighbours suggested I have tea with them. 'What's the hurry?' he said. I turned to the BSF man for approval but he looked nervous and motioned me to come back. I complied.

Relieved that I had listened to him, he smiled: 'So you just travelled to a foreign country. Congratulations!'

As we walked out of Pagla's house, with boys of varying ages escorting us to the car, the BSF man pointed to the paddy field right across the road—a Bangladeshi paddy field—where a number of women and children, all farmhands, stood as if they had suddenly frozen into statues. They looked nervous.

'Do you see them?' the BSF man said. 'They were about to cross over but stopped when they saw us. They will cross over the moment we leave.'

'But why do they want to cross over?' I asked.

'To get to their homes. I told you the border is zigzagged, right? There is a narrow strip of Indian territory between their fields and their homes. We are standing on that strip. If they cross this strip, they will reach home in no time, whereas if they keep to Bangladeshi territory, they will have to take a long detour, seven or eight kilometres, to get home.'

'20 kilometres,' one of the boys who had escorted us out corrected the BSF man.

'The boy is right, 20 kilometres.'

I felt sad and angry. It is always the poor who are the worst sufferers of calamities—natural or manmade. At the same time, I found it heartening that the BSF usually turned a blind eye to such harmless violation of the Radcliffe Line: it was the victory of humanity over hostility.

# 5

So the Radcliffe Line, even though imaginary, has a colour: green. Pretty much like water, colourless but which acquires the hues of the sky. Green is the opposite of red, the colour it represented while being drawn. Seventy years is a long time. The generation that witnessed Partition has passed on, and the succeeding generations have moved on.

But I noticed a vital difference between the green of Punjab and Bengal. I don't know if the difference is real or in my mind: I found Punjab's green radiating happiness, whereas Bengal's conveyed melancholy. Punjab's was a loud song, Bengal's a gentle poem.

The clouds had completely cleared as we drove back. It felt as if it had never rained. I opened the boxes that had been given to me in Moshaldanga. The samosas had gone cold, but I ate them anyway. Then I ate the rossogollas. What I had in my mouth was the flavour of north Bengal, in its most humble and raw form. And in my mind was a strange elation: of having stepped across the line that partitioned Bengal.

Culturally, there are two kinds of Bengalis—West Bengalis and East Bengalis—and the distinction existed even before Partition. They speak different dialects, their food habits aren't the same, and many of their customs vary. It is pretty much like the cultural differences between western Uttar Pradesh and eastern Uttar Pradesh, or between north Kerala and south Kerala.

Post-Partition, when the geographical entity of East Bengal went to Pakistan and many of the Hindus from there migrated to West Bengal, Bengalis in India came to be split into two cultural groups: Ghoti, the natives of West Bengal, and Bangal, who had migrated from East Bengal.

The lay Ghoti and Bangal maintained their distinct identities for the longest time. Each group thought itself to be superior, did not marry the other, and privately poked fun at each other's food habits. The Ghoti took pride in eating prawns, the Bangal swore by the hilsa. The Ghoti supported Mohun Bagan, the Bangal was a fan of, naturally, East Bengal.

Today, after seventy years, the distinction has almost ceased to exist. Why, I happen to be a Ghoti who married a Bangal. I don't remember asking her whether she was a Ghoti or a Bangal: to me she was a Bengali from Calcutta.

It was only after I got married that I became acutely aware of her Bangal identity: my mother-in-law, who was born in Assam but had spent the best part of her youth in what was to become Bangladesh, would tell me stories about her younger days—she still does—and thus was born my fascination for the land she grew up in. Bangladesh continues to hold a mysterious charm for me, and now I had at least stepped into it, if not visited it.

These thoughts crossed my mind during the drive back to Bagdogra airport the next morning. As I crossed the rivers again—Torsa, Jaldhaka, Teesta, I asked myself: won't it be worthwhile to watch the conclusion of their journeys? Why just theirs, even of the Ganga and the Brahmaputra, which merge in a town called Shivalaya, some seventy kilometres east of Dhaka. Bangladesh also has a town by the name of Bishwanath. A long visit, therefore, was a must for me.

Right now though, I was to stick to the Indian towns and villages bordering Bangladesh. My next destination was Agartala.

# 6

When I boarded the flight for Agartala, I knew as much about the city as most educated Indians do: that it is the capital of Tripura, one of the seven states that constitute northeast India.

I knew one more thing, because I had taken a close look at the map: Agartala sat right on the border with Bangladesh, perhaps the only Indian state capital to be located on an international border. By flying from Calcutta to Agartala, I would be crossing the breadth of Bangladesh in just about an hour.

The farmland that came into view as the plane descended to touch down was waterlogged. I wondered if I had come to Tripura at the wrong time. Assam was reeling under floods and it was quite possible that parts of Tripura were inundated too. I decided to ask the man in the next seat.

'Hello, are you from Agartala?'

'I am from Dhaka,' he gave me a friendly smile.

'So you are now headed for Dhaka?'

'Yes, Dhaka is barely two hours by road from Agartala.'

'And what brought you to India?'

'It was a business trip. I work for a cement company,

we make Seven Rings cement. I had a meeting in Chennai last afternoon.'

'Chennai? That's where I live!'

'Oh really? I had a meeting at the L&T office there. So what brings you to Agartala?'

I told him.

'In all probability I will spend the night in Agartala. If you are free this evening, we could perhaps catch up.'

'My evening depends entirely on my hosts, but let me have your number, just in case I happen to be free.'

'Certainly,' he said. 'My name is Mujibur Rahman and my number is—'

As my fountain pen scribbled his name, I couldn't help thinking about his illustrious namesake—the founding father of Bangladesh—who too, incidentally, had an Agartala connection and a very important one at that. It was in the capital of Tripura that his representatives met Indian officials in the late 1960s to seek help in freeing East Pakistan from the domination of West Pakistan. The plot was discovered and thirty-five Bengali politicians, military officers and civil servants—including Sheikh Mujibur Rahman—were arrested. But they had to be released following a mass uprising and it was upon his release, in February 1969, that Sheikh Mujibur Rahman was accorded the title of Bangabandhu, or Friend of Bengal.

Thereafter public resentment against West Pakistan only began to pile up, and once its soldiers sought to suppress the Bengali anger with mass murder and rape, the Bangladesh Liberation War began, in March 1971, with India joining it in December that year. The end of the war saw East Pakistan becoming an independent Bangladesh—the country whose breadth I had just crossed.

I asked my neighbour about the flooded farmland.

'What you see below is all Bangladesh. No floods in Agartala,' he assured me.

Later that evening, I was told by my host that many Bangladeshi citizens, when they travelled within India, preferred to cross the border at Agartala and take a domestic flight because it cost a lot less than an international flight from Dhaka.

A BSF man in plainclothes waited for me outside the arrival hall. I did not want a repeat of the questioning I was subjected to at Digaltari camp in Cooch Behar, so I had asked my BSF officer-friend, my classmate from school, to put me in touch with his colleagues in Agartala. One of those colleagues—I shall call him Suraj—had sent the plainclothesman to receive me.

Two things instantly struck me about Agartala: its abundant greenery and laidback charm. It seemed to me a city without ambition, content with the way it was, having long made peace with the fact that it hardly mattered to the world outside of the northeast, showing no great desire to find prominence on the map of twenty-first-century India. A place with such an attitude can only be endearing, especially when much of urban India changes beyond recognition every new morning.

Driving out of the airport I passed colourful hoardings: Mayfair jeans and trousers, Frooto—not Frooti—mango drink ('Any Time, Frooto Time'), Swarnakamal Jewellers, Shyam Sundar Jewellers, Airtel. In less than twenty minutes we were at the BSF officers' mess, in a neighbourhood called Salbagan, where the butler brought me tea after I had a shower.

I sipped the tea gazing at the manicured lawn that my window overlooked. The skyline was marked by sal trees. I could have been in the midst of a jungle. Only that I wasn't. Until this morning, the northeast had been remote. Now it was real and—because of the tea, served in a cup and saucer emblazoned with the BSF insignia—all too familiar.

I had barely finished the tea when the butler, a middle-aged and potbellied man from Punjab, brought in a tray bearing lunch: rice, rotis, dal, and green beans. He looked grumpy; it was past three in the afternoon and perhaps he was eager to be relieved of his duty.

After lunch I stepped out to meet my benefactor, Suraj, whose office was located in a building that was a minute's walk from the mess. We had only spoken on the phone before, and now we shook hands. He was in civvies and belonged to the 'Q' branch, the intelligence wing of the force.

The border with Bangladesh, he said, posed a different set of challenges. Unlike in Punjab, where the BSF guards against infiltration and narcotics being smuggled *in* from Pakistan, here it watches out for cattle and cough syrup being smuggled *out* of India. I had been told this by even the two young recruits at the Digaltari camp; one of them had said, '*Yahaan goru ka chori bahut hota hai*'—Cow theft is rampant here.

Cattle smuggled from India feeds the beef industry of Bangladesh which, being a Muslim-majority country, also happens to be dry and therefore the demand for cough syrup. I wanted to talk more about the trans-border crimes but Suraj reminded me that I must leave for the flag-lowering ceremony that began at five. The plainclothesman who had received me at the airport was already waiting to take me there.

'Don't expect what you saw at Wagah,' Suraj cautioned me. 'I will see you tomorrow morning.'

The flag-lowering ceremony takes place barely a couple of kilometres from the city centre, at the Akhaura border-crossing, Akhaura being the town on the Bangladesh side of the border.

I arrived well before time at the check-post and was instantly served with tea. This was the first time I did not have to travel thirty or forty kilometres from a city to meet the Radcliffe Line; here the line grazed past the city, in the form of a white strip painted across the narrow road leading from Agartala to Akhaura. Mobile barricades guarded the white line so that the layman knew where the border lay. A blue signboard erected on the Indian side of the line read: 'Please visit again. Indian territory ends. Bangladesh 0 km.'

*Please visit again*: Indian courtesy for departing guests.

A red-and-green signage stood across the border, a bilingual one: Welcome to Bangladesh. The welcome was extended by 'Bangladesh Police, Brahmanbaria District.'

The BSF inspector giving me company told me that each day, anywhere between 100 and 200 people from each side crossed the border on foot. Also that a pair of buses now ran daily between Agartala and Calcutta via Dhaka.

I saw Bangladeshis, easily distinguishable by their lungis, showing their passports to the BSF sentry on duty and strolling past the barricades into their land. Many of those crossing the border on foot usually had relatives living nearby, on the other side. If one had a visa, it was possible to live in Akhaura and shop in Agartala: many seemed to be doing that, evident from the bulging plastic bags they carried. At the same time, shoppers in Agartala can also buy produce from Bangladesh—including potato wafers, fresh fish and RFL brand of plastic furniture—which arrives through the border-crossing.

Presently about a dozen plastic chairs were arranged on the pavement for people to watch the lowering of the flags. I got to sit in the front row. On the other side too, men, women, and children had gathered. I heard drumbeats, one beat every thirty or forty seconds, melancholic and not jingoistic, as if part of a sombre tribal ritual taking place at dusk, in a forest village. The word of command that followed reminded me that this was actually a martial ritual. But no stamping of feet or high kicks, no patriotic cries, no cheering: only a solemn and relaxed ceremony that ended with people from both sides pressing close to the barricades.

One elderly man from Bangladesh, raising his voice, asked the people on the Indian side, to no one in particular though, '*Bhalo achhen toh*? *Bhalo achhen toh*?'—How are you? All well?

His query, however, was drowned by the women who had begun talking to familiar faces across the border.

'How your daughter has grown up! She was just a child till the other day.'

'How is aunt doing? Please convey my regards to her.'

'How is your mother's health now? Better than before I hope?'

'Come home someday, it's been long since you visited us.'

It was the kind of chatter that takes place when you bump into an old acquaintance on the road. But here the women stood about ten feet apart and couldn't get any closer because the white line stood between them.

'You want to have a picture taken with the BGB officer?' the BSF inspector asked me. BGB stands for Border Guard Bangladesh, formerly known as BDR, or Bangladesh Rifles.

'Sure!' I handed him my camera and walked up to the BGB officer and told him, in Bengali, that I would like to pose with him. We smiled at the camera and then I shook his hand, which I felt was a little too soft for a uniformed man. But his face more than made up for the softness of his hand: he clearly looked the man in command, stern and dignified.

'How is your relationship with the BGB?' I asked the BSF inspector as I claimed my camera.

'Very friendly at the moment,' he said, 'it all depends

on which party is in power there. Usually, our relationship is cordial when Sheikh Hasina is in power. Things are a little different whenever Khaleda Zia comes to power, but on the whole we remain friendly.'

Soon we were sitting in a small circle that included some of the sentries who had just participated in the ceremony. They hailed from different places—Rajasthan, Haryana, Uttar Pradesh, Bihar, West Bengal—but were united at the moment by duty and by the dusk of Agartala. Tea was served again.

Stray dogs, meanwhile, had taken over the border-crossing, which was now deserted: they pranced about the white strip that denoted the Radcliffe Line, as if the stretch belonged to them.

# 7

The butler appeared to be in good spirits when he brought me tea the next morning. The tip I had paid him after he had brought me drinks and dinner the evening before seemed to have worked. Over tea, I read about a murder in the local paper:

> SONAMURA: Thirty years old Rina Begum was murdered allegedly by her Bangladeshi husband Billal Miah last night. Rina Begum was residing at her father's house at Kulubari along with nine years old son.
>
> Her husband Billal Miah of Bangladesh came in the father-in-law's house in the evening yesterday. In the night Billal Miah strangulated her and left the house at night itself. Her brother Bijnur Rahman filed an FIR against the husband Billal Miah. Sonamura Police Station registered the case under Section 302.
>
> Sonamura Police Station said after committing the crime Rina Begum's husband Billal Miah left for his homeland in Bangladesh.

I tried to picture Billal Miah. He had been mentioned five times and his nationality three times in a report that wasn't even hundred words long. The report, if anything, raised more questions in my mind than the information it provided: Is marriage between Indians and Bangladeshis common in border areas? Why did Rina Begum choose to marry a Bangladeshi and not someone from the Indian side? Likewise, why did Billal Miah choose to marry an Indian and not someone from his country? Or, were they neighbours, living in a cluster of houses that had the Radcliffe Line running through it? Was theirs a love marriage? Why did she leave her husband's home to stay with her father? What provoked the husband to kill her? And now that he had escaped to his homeland, what could Indian police do about it? What would be the nationality of the child?

The answers would remain unknown. The newspaper had done its bit by recording the murder and the matter ended there. No one—not the press, not the police, not the public—would be interested in the life, or death, of a poor villager. Their deaths, unlike the death of someone rich and famous, are an occurrence and not an event.

Incidentally, I was going to Sonamura this morning. Suraj, whose home, like his office, was in the campus, was going to pick me up at nine. In an ideal situation, I would have stopped at the Sonamura police station and found the address of Rina Begum and visited her village. But Suraj had taken a day off from work so that he could take me to some villages on the border, and it would be criminal on my part to impose a detour on him. A visit to a border village is next to impossible unless you live in the village, or know someone living in the village—or know someone in the BSF.

Tripura means the land of the Tripuri, a tribe that traces its origins to western China and today is distinguishable by the surnames Deb and Deb Barma, conferred to them by their king. The ruling family used the surname Deb Barman, also written as Dev Burman.

They ruled Tripura from the fifteenth century until 1949, when the kingdom acceded to India. Even though their mother tongue was Kokborok, they had immense respect for the Bengali language and got Bengalis from neighbouring Bengal to perform administrative work and conduct rituals. The liberal patronage extended to the Bengali language over the centuries resulted in its absorption into the cultural identity of the ruling elite. I, for one, had always believed that Sachin Dev Burman and his son Rahul Dev Burman—two of India's most celebrated music composers—were Bengalis. They weren't. But they will be remembered as the creators of some of the finest Bengali and Hindi songs that exist on this planet.

Until 1947, Tripura was 70 per cent tribal and 30 per cent Bengali. Today, seventy years and two waves of migrations later, it is 70 per cent Bengali and 30 per cent tribal, with Tripuris forming the majority of the tribal population.

Needless to say, Tripura has had its share of insurgency, which peaked in the late 1990s but got defused quickly thereafter due to thoughtful action on the part of the state government. Unlike other insurgency-hit states, it did not bring in the Army to fight the insurgents and therefore prevented further alienation of the tribal population, and at the same time took concrete measures to integrate the tribal population into the mainstream. Manik Sarkar, a Marxist and Tripura's chief minister since 1998, is considered the most honest—and therefore the poorest—politician in the whole of India.

'One of my course mates was martyred somewhere near here,' Suraj pointed to a spot on the pavement as we passed an intersection where a policeman stood on a canopied pedestal, diligently regulating traffic even though there was hardly any traffic to be regulated. 'But now Tripura is peaceful.'

Peace, if considered synonymous with quietness, was amply evident on the roads of Agartala. But quietness is also synonymous with fear, and I had no idea what Agartala must have looked like during the peak of insurgency. This morning, however, it appeared to be inspired by peace, considering that there was a traffic constable doing his job with utmost seriousness. In times of fear, men in battle fatigues take over.

The peace became more pronounced as we left Agartala behind and hit the countryside. I had witnessed the happy green of Punjab and the melancholic green of Bengal, but Tripura was something else. Its paddy fields, even though their expanse was intimidating, represented an innocent smile that could have well belonged to the 1960s.

We were travelling on NH44, the sole highway that holds Tripura together, apart from connecting it to the rest of India via Assam. Tripura's location on the map is unique. It is surrounded on three sides by Bangladesh (the border is 856-km long). On the fourth side it is enclosed mostly by Mizoram (109 km) and partially by Assam (53 km).

It is through its border with Assam that NH44 enters Tripura and leads rights up to its southern extremity. We were headed south now, with one more BSF officer in civilian clothes—a young and hyperactive man whom I shall call Vikram—giving us company.

We had picked Vikram up from a BSF camp in the town of Bishalgarh, about 20 kilometres south of Agartala. Suraj had told me that Vikram knew the border villages like the back of his hand and was keen that he travelled with us.

Vikram, who sat next to the driver, was on the phone most of the time. Sometimes an informant would call to say that an unusually large number of Phensedyl bottles had been spotted at a pharmacy on the Indian side. Another informant would call to say that yet another pharmacist had been noticed stocking Corex bottles.

Both Phensedyl and Corex are popular cough syrup brands that sell in dry Bangladesh for four times the retail price. Each time he received a tip-off, Vikram would turn to Suraj for advice, 'Sir, what should we do?' Suraj, who had obviously spent more years in the BSF, would remain unruffled and offer his thoughts, in BSF jargon.

In a town called Bishramganj we diverted from NH44 and moved southwest, on a smaller road. After what seemed to be an interminable drive, the monotony of the green was broken with the arrival of yet another town, called Melaghar.

These towns too could have belonged to the 1960s, but shops selling mobile phones and mobile connections were a giveaway. Mahamaya Hardware, with its worn-out signboard, was placed next to Maa Mobile Centre, which boasted of two snazzy signboards, one sponsored by Sony Xperia and the other by Lava brand of phones. Sometimes amidst clusters of such shops and sometimes by the road, wiry artisans worked on Durga idols that were still in the skeleton stage.

From Melaghar we snaked alongside the River Gomti until we reached the town of Sonamura, where we crossed the river and after two or three kilometres ran into it once again at a riverside border outpost. The river looked still and green, but it was moving, making its entry into Bangladesh: the boundary line was a stone's throw, literally, from where we stood.

It is actually silly to say that the river was entering Bangladesh. Rivers precede mankind by thousands of years; it was man who started drawing imaginary lines across them. And Radcliffe's Line is probably the youngest of such lines: only seventy years old.

An orderly brought us water and then tea—an inescapable ritual if you are visiting a BSF installation, be it a base or an outpost. This outpost was located in a village called Srimantapur which, according to Suraj, also served as a border-crossing.

As I sipped my tea, I noticed a brown calf tethered to a tree. I was told that it had been rescued by the BSF two days ago when smugglers were trying to push it across the border. It was now waiting to be handed over, as per law, to the customs department, which would auction it. The calf did not look particularly unhappy: it had plenty of grass to munch on even while being tied to the tree.

Smuggling of cattle into Bangladesh has been thriving for decades. It is humanly impossible to prevent it along a border that is 4,096-km long, much of which remains—and most likely will remain—unfenced. The night I spent in Calcutta before I took the plane to Agartala, I browsed through news related to the cattle-smuggling and came across a report which said that as many as two million heads of cattle are smuggled into Bangladesh annually—the smuggling being a 600-million dollar industry.

I also came across reports which said the smuggling was on the decline ever since the Bharatiya Janata Party or the BJP, which considers the cow to be a sacred animal, came to power in 2014. The BJP government's crackdown on cattle smuggling, apparently, had crippled the beef business in Bangladesh, which was now looking at other countries to source cattle.

There were also voices advocating legalisation of the cattle trade, a move that would be immensely profitable for both countries. But that is unlikely to happen because most Hindus consider the cow to be a mother. Oddly enough though, India happens to be the world's largest exporter of beef.

Suraj said: 'Cows that are smuggled are usually not local cows but the ones that come all the way from Rajasthan, Haryana, and Uttar Pradesh. They are transported in trucks that travel, without being stopped, for hundreds of kilometres before reaching the villages bordering Bangladesh.

'Once they reach the border, it becomes the BSF's responsibility to stop them from being smuggled. My question is, if they are serious about putting an end to cattle smuggling, why allow them to reach the border in the first place?

'All the BSF can do is to seize the cows and hand them over to customs. The customs holds auctions and the smugglers buy the cows back and manage to push them across the border. So ours is actually a futile exercise. If you really want to stop the smuggling, you either don't allow the cattle to reach the border in the first place, or you legalise the trade. There is no other way.'

So the brown calf might still end up in an abattoir in Bangladesh. The smugglers have a code name for calves, which fetch more money because of their tender meat: Pepsi.

After tea we strolled down to the border-crossing where I saw two large yellow trucks set to return to Bangladesh after having offloaded their cargoes. One of the drivers had already climbed up to his seat after finishing the paperwork. His cargo had comprised 500 bags of Three Rings cement.

'Three Rings or Seven Rings?' I asked him, 'I met someone yesterday who works for Seven Rings.'

'Three Rings. Seven Rings is different.'

He turned on the ignition and crossed the border, marked by nothing except the presence of a lone boundary pillar, and sped away on an empty road that snaked through a vast expanse of greenery into Bangladesh. The road led to Comilla, where Sachin Dev Burman was born and spent his early life.

The driver of the other truck showed up. His name was Zakir Ahmed, and he had just finished offloading 400 bags of Tiger cement at the customs yard and was now headed home to Khulna.

'I make ten to fifteen trips in a month,' he told me. Barely had I started talking to him when a drunk shopkeeper—his shop was right on the boundary line—accosted Zakir and begged him to buy some chocolates from him and sell them in Bangladesh, where they are supposed to be expensive.

Zakir chided him, 'I have driven trucks in twenty places around the world, including four countries in Europe, but never have I come across a despicable character like you!'

As his truck, too, faded away into Bangladesh, I gazed at the road that was now empty. So empty that it looked inviting. There was even a green-and-red signboard at some distance, which said 'Swagatam' in Bengali: Welcome. But I was restricted by the pillar at my feet.

# 8

Standing in an enclosure made of sandbags, and built on an elevation, I surveyed the farmland, marvelling at the orderliness of cultivation.

On the face of it, what I saw was a green carpet of paddies. But within that green were several shades of green, marked by neat squares and rectangles. Each farmer knew exactly which square or rectangle belonged to him. From some of those neat squares sprouted neat cubes—in the form of sugarcane and banana plantations. Diversity in unity.

The sandbag enclosure within which I was standing belonged to yet another border outpost that lay seven or eight kilometres north of the border outpost we had just visited. The farmland I was gazing at belonged to the village of Kulubari, where two nights ago, a woman called Rina Begum had allegedly been murdered by her Bangladeshi husband Billal Miah.

I knew I was coming to Sonamura, but what a coincidence that I should be in the exact village where the crime I had read about in this morning's paper had taken place. I had no idea that Suraj had planned lunch at this border outpost. Should I climb down the mound and walk through the fields and ask those two men bending over their crop whether they knew Rina Begum or Billal Miah? In a village, everybody knows everybody. But the outpost was secured by a fence. Moreover, lunch was ready.

In a canopied area an orderly laid out hot food: rotis, rice, dal, cabbage, bitter gourd. Over lunch, my hosts talked about retired armed forces personnel protesting in faraway New Delhi to demand one rank-one pension.

Suraj said: 'An entire generation of army men has retired without going to war, and they talk about one rank-one pension. Whereas we in the BSF serve in hostile conditions round the clock, but we are not even entitled to pension.'

'What? BSF people don't get pension?' I asked.

'Only those who joined service before 2004 are entitled to pension. Rules changed in 2004. I am fortunate because I joined in 2001.'

The more I listened to them, the more I was convinced that their resentment against being treated inferior to the army ran deep—and not without reason. It is often said that people sleep peacefully at nights only because the army keeps awake guarding the frontiers. That is not entirely true. The army too sleeps at nights, at least on the borders with Bangladesh—and even Pakistan, which has been at war with India on four occasions.

Except for the Line of Control in Kashmir, which is guarded jointly by the army and the BSF, the remaining boundary line with Pakistan—in Punjab, Rajasthan and Gujarat—is defended by the BSF alone. And unlike army men, who get posted to comfortable locations after serving on the frontier for a couple of years, a BSF man, throughout his career, serves in locations where the weather can be harsh and the terrain hostile, where there are no cinemas or malls or restaurants but only villages and sometimes nothing. No one understands remoteness better than a BSF man.

And yet, in spite of having been trained to be the first line of defence, the BSF, raised in 1965, remains a police force, governed by the home ministry. That's not all. Unlike an officer in the army—or the air force or navy—who can always dream of becoming the chief someday, a BSF officer cannot harbour such an ambition. As per rule, the top boss of the BSF must be a senior officer from the Indian Police Service, and such an officer, until he is assigned the role—invariably towards the fag end of his career—usually has no idea about life on the border, leave alone the experience of policing the border.

It was therefore natural, for the BSF men to be sore, and in my opinion, they sought to mask the bitterness by taking extra pride in their work—which I thought, worked out well for the nation.

Once upon a time, in a village called Boxanagar that sat on the border between British Bengal and the princely state of Tripura, four brothers built a house each. The houses formed a perfect square, facing one another, with a common courtyard at the centre.

Then one day, shortly after Partition, government servants came and planted a pillar in the courtyard, as a result of which one of the four houses went to East Pakistan and the remaining stayed in Tripura. Today the border between India and Bangladesh runs through the courtyard.

After lunch at the Kulubari outpost we had travelled several kilometres north, along the border, to reach Boxanagar, where there were so many moss-coated, weather-worn boundary pillars amid houses that if you took a stroll through the village, you would be walking in and out of Bangladesh without realizing it.

The four brothers are long dead, but their descendants continue to live in those houses. The house that fell across the Radcliffe Line, made of brick and mud, looked frozen in time, while the three on the Indian side appeared to have undergone renovations in the seventy years that have lapsed since Partition.

A woman stood at the door of the brick-and-mud house when we arrived—Suraj, Vikram and I, along with two armed sentries posted in the village. She was chatting with a man seated on a chair outside one of the houses on the Indian side. He sprang up to greet Vikram: 'Welcome! You are coming after a long time.'

The man went in and brought out more chairs. He then brought out a table too. Tea and biscuits arrived. The woman, meanwhile, had vanished. Two tiny calves, barely days old, nibbled on leaves heaped in the centre of the courtyard. They stood a few feet away from the four-faced tapering boundary pillar.

Our host was Arfat Ahmed, who lived in the house with his parents, wife, and three brothers. He taught mathematics at a nearby government school.

'Are you constantly reminded that you live on the boundary line?' I asked him.

'Since the BSF people keep coming, yes, we are,' he laughed.

'And not because of the pillar?'

'I have been seeing the pillar from the time I was born. It is the presence of the BSF people that reminds us what the pillar is for.'

Arfat's father Haji Naseeruddin, who joined us presently, also grew up with the pillar: he was born nine years after Partition. But the father, a farmer all his life, has memories of the war that led to the birth of Bangladesh. He was fifteen then.

'Until 1971 I remember men from the East Pakistan Rifles coming here often. Then the war happened. The Mukti Bahini would go through this courtyard to fight the Pakistan Army. They would come mostly at nights and lay in ambush. Back then the villages were backward, no electricity, only lamps,' recalled Naseeruddin. 'We could hear the battles being fought.'

Naseeruddin's grandfather was among the four brothers who had built the four houses. When the officials had come to install the pillar, Naseeruddin's father had even objected.

'My father pleaded with them to move the pillar slightly westward, so that the entire family remained together,' he said, 'but one of the officials apparently told him, "I am following the map. If you interfere with our work, we are going to put this pillar right inside your house." My father kept quiet after that.'

Naseeruddin excused himself. It was time for his prayer. He was evidently a devout Muslim. He had the skull cap on and wore a flowing grey beard, unlike his son, who sported only a moustache. I noticed another contrast. The son, even though educated and a teacher himself, came across as unrefined, whereas the father, a farmer all his life, exuded grace. When it was time for his prayer, he excused himself firmly but very politely: it had not mattered to him that two BSF officers—and the BSF is the undisputed master of the people living along the boundary line—were sitting in his courtyard and had still not finished their tea. He personified what is known as old-world charm.

Haji Naseeruddin reminded me of three elderly Muslim men I knew when I was growing up in Kanpur. Two of them ran shops—four-legged wooden stalls known as gumti—while the third was a half-blind man who went around pushing a cart to buy scrap and old newspapers. They were all poor men, but there was—now when I think of it—something very elegant about the manner in which they spoke and conducted themselves.

Once the father withdrew, I asked Arfat, the son, if I could briefly step into the house on the Bangladesh side—just to take a look. He led me in. The air smelt stale. The woman I had spotted at the door was nowhere to be seen. I heard no sounds either. In the room we stood, there were wooden benches, one piled up over the other.

'There is no space in my home, so I used to give tuitions in this house. But now the high court has ruled that government teachers cannot give tuitions, that's why I have put the benches away,' Arfat said.

So while he taught at an Indian school, he conducted his tuition classes in Bangladesh. That's how it happens in villages like these: you could be standing in India but your shadow could be cast in Bangladesh—and vice-versa.

On the drive back to Agartala, I searched the internet for news related to Tripura. I was curious to know what kind of news of national interest emanated from a place as quiet as this. The top news thrown up by the search engine was: 'Tripura HC bans private tuition by govt. teachers.'

So I had inadvertently met an affected teacher—that too in one of its remotest villages.

# 9

Back in downtown Agartala, in a shop called Sherowali Sweets, I had the best samosa I had ever eaten. We had stopped there because Suraj had to buy sweets: he was expecting guests the next day. We stepped out of the shop and were about to get back into the jeep when a large procession came on, taking up every inch of the road. The processionists carried red Marxist flags and responded in unison ('Lal salaam! Lal salaam!') to the slogans shouted by their leader. I was witnessing a political procession after a long time, and as we waited for the road to clear, my eyes wandered to two signboards—Chakraborty Astrological Centre and Giri Homeo Hall—that firmly established the Bengali character of Agartala. There are countless Bengalis who, in times of trouble, seek succour in either astrology or homeopathy.

Back in the BSF campus, as we got off the jeep to say goodbye to each other, I asked Suraj if he could arrange for a car that would take me to Karimganj, my next destination. Karimganj, in Assam, also sat on the Radcliffe Line, but about 250 kilometres northwest of Agartala: the two were connected by NH44. Even if the driver maintained a speed of sixty, I would be there in about four hours.

Suraj did know a driver and called him up right away. The driver, when I spoke to him, said it would take me more than ten hours to reach Karimganj—'so bad the road is'—and accordingly quoted an exorbitant sum. I told him I would get back.

Suraj said there was a passenger train too, that also took about ten hours, but apparently a seat had to be reserved in advance with the help of a handkerchief. Those taking the train, he said, went to the railway station early in the morning and claimed their seats by placing handkerchiefs or other inexpensive belongings on them. They then went about their business and returned to the station only when it was time for the train to leave.

'If you want to take the train,' Suraj said, 'I could send one of my boys in the morning to hold a seat for you.'

'I need a drink to decide,' I told him and we shook hands.

As I reclined on the bed with a glass of whisky, the two scenarios kept alternating in my mind: ten hours on a bad road, and ten hours in a train where I, even if I got a seat, could not take a bathroom break without worrying about the safety of my belongings or losing my seat. The 250 kilometres seemed insurmountable.

I finally decided I would fly.

The air tickets—from Agartala to Guwahati, and from Guwahati to Silchar and back—cost me less than what the driver was demanding. From Silchar airport, Karimganj was just 55 kilometres away: a drive of perhaps forty-five minutes, at the most an hour?

What was more, I would get to spend a night at Guwahati, yet another place I had thought I would never visit in my lifetime. Since the flight to Guwahati for which I bought tickets was scheduled to leave only the day after tomorrow, I now had one more day in Agartala. Pleased with myself, I shut my laptop and ordered one more drink.

The next afternoon, after lunch, I set out for the Ujjayanta Palace. It was built in 1901 as the new home of the Manikya dynasty, which ruled Tripura for over 500 years until its accession to India in 1949. Tripura remained a Union Territory until 1972, when it attained statehood and the government purchased the palace to turn it into the legislative assembly.

Palaces are often lasting reminders of perishability. Whoever built such everlasting structures did so in the belief that they and their descendants would live in them, as rulers, until the time the sun had stopped rising. But time intervenes, and times change. In 2013, the Tripura royal palace became a public museum.

The museum, clearly, was the principal attraction of Agartala. People had come in large numbers and they were evidently not tourists but locals, posing for pictures against the stately building. Its charm lay in the fact that it was the former palace and had been out of bounds for general public until two years ago.

But what I found most charming about the place was the congregation of cultures in its premises: the visitors spoke dialects I was not at all familiar with, though I could tell the dialects belonged to northeast India and even though they sounded similar, they weren't the same. From time to time, I also overheard Bengali and Hindi being spoken.

The poet Rabindranath Tagore, deeply revered by the royal family, made the first of his seven visits to Tripura in 1899, the year the construction of the palace began, and it was he who christened it Ujjayanta. Needless to say, an entire gallery has been dedicated to Tagore in a museum that is otherwise a treasure trove of information about the northeast.

I learned that forests covered nearly 60 per cent of Tripura, whose population, as of the 2011 census, stood at 37 lakh, of which only six lakh were Tripuris. In other words, Bengalis largely constituted the remaining 31 lakh. I also learned that Kalyan Manikya was the first king of Tripura to hand out copper-plate inscriptions to Bengalis, granting them ownerships of land in the kingdom, way back in 1641. I learned something about Bengalis too:

> The exact origin of the word Bangla and Bongo or Bengal is unknown, though the word is believed to be derived from the Dravidian-speaking tribe called Bang that settled in the area around the year 1000 BC. It could also be derived from the word Vanga, which was a kingdom in the Bengal during the times of Mahabharata as mentioned in Sanskrit literature.

Today Bengalis have many identities: Bengalis of India, both living in Bengal and outside it; Bengalis of

Bangladesh; Bengalis of Tripura; Bengalis of Britain; Bengalis of America. And, of course, the Bengalis of Assam: I would soon be shaking hands with some of them in Karimganj.

# 10

In Guwahati, a city I had never set eyes on, I fortunately had a friend. Even though we had never met before, we remained in touch ever since he wrote to me some years ago after he happened to read one of my books. He was a Bengali who, incidentally, grew up in Karimganj.

'Tell the driver to bring you to Pan Bazaar, I am waiting for you here,' Anurag, the friend, told me when I called him as soon as I landed.

'Will he know where Pan Bazaar is?' I asked him.

'Everybody knows. It's the heart of the city.'

If Pan Bazaar, or betel-leaf mart, was the centre of the city, then what was the city going to be like? I had no previous visual knowledge about Guwahati—northeastern states are generally off the radar for television cameras of mainland India—and this piece of information, that Pan Bazaar lies at its heart, brought rather unflattering images to my mind. What I didn't know at the time was that Guwahati itself took its name from an ingredient that is inseparable from the betel leaf: guwa or areca nut, more widely known across India as supari.

Pan Bazaar, to my great surprise, turned out to be

what Colaba is to Mumbai. Situated on the banks of the Brahmaputra, it had its share of pan shops all right, but walking around it—which I did after checking into the hotel Anurag had booked for me—felt like taking a stroll through the colonial era.

Lakshmi Cabin, where we had samosas and tea, dated back to 1942. The Guwahati Baptist Church was built in 1845. Sheikh Brothers Bakery opened in 1885. The signboard of the Pan Bazaar police station proudly declared that it had been established in 1894. Mahamaya—'A-Class Restaurant'—opened in 1918. Indo Foreign Surgico, which sold medical products, in 1949.

Then there was Cotton College—in Assam, according to Anurag, who studied there, it is considered even more prestigious than the Indian Institutes of Technology—which had started in 1901. But many years before that, in 1883, had come up the Pan Bazaar Girls' Higher Secondary School.

These are just some of the many still-in-business institutions and establishments in Pan Bazaar that date back to an era whose remnants are hardly found any longer in other cities. A small number of them now function out of newly-constructed buildings, but their unchanged addresses preserve the old character of Pan Bazaar. In some cases, new buildings were necessitated by circumstances beyond the control of the owners.

'You see this building?' Anurag pointed to a shop next to the Baptist Church. 'This was flattened in October 2008, when a series of blasts rocked Guwahati. I was in college at the time, and I myself escaped death by a whisker.'

'And where did this blast happen—the one that almost killed you?'

'Come, I will show you.'

Soon we were walking along the river. 'This is where it happened,' he pointed to a spot by the river, close to the High Court. 'I was going to watch a movie, when I suddenly realized I had left my ID card behind in the college. So I turned around to return to the college and moments later I heard a deafening sound and felt hot air on my back.'

We sat on the riverbank, sipping tea, watching the Brahmaputra flow with a powerful and purposeful silence, as its waters turned golden in the fading light. The extraordinary calm I sensed now belied the impression I had formed of Assam over the decades: a state that was always jumping from one crisis to another, each crisis involving violence and each of the crises being about ethnicity. The only feel-good connection with Assam was Assam tea.

When the British left India, the province of Assam comprised almost the entire northeast region with the exception of Tripura and Manipur, which were princely states that chose to join India in 1949. In 1960, the Assam government declared Assamese to be the sole official language of the state, a move that did not go down well with its non-Assamese population.

Bengalis, who formed a majority in southern Assam, were the first to protest, but over the years various ethnic regions also began to feel neglected by the government of Assam, as a result of which smaller states began to be carved out of it: first Nagaland, then Meghalaya, and finally Arunachal Pradesh and Mizoram.

Then came a time when many in Assam began to feel neglected by New Delhi and this sentiment gave birth to secessionist movements that, over the decades, have been brought under control—at the cost of many thousands of lives—but are still far from being extinguished.

Another issue has been on the boil in Assam for a long time. Indigenous Assamese groups firmly believe that Bengali Muslims continue to sneak in from Bangladesh in large numbers, fast altering the state's demography. Of all the Indian states that border Bangladesh, Assam's share of the boundary is one of the shortest—262 kilometres—but it claims to be the worst hit by the 'illegal immigration', a term you come across frequently when reading about Assam.

In 1979, to demand the exclusion of non-natives of Assam from the electoral rolls, the All Assam Students' Union began an agitation that stretched on for six years before it signed the Assam Accord with the Indian government in 1985. As per the accord, those who had settled in Assam before 1966 would be considered as Assamese and the rest detected and weeded out.

But how to find out who settled before 1966 and after? As good as finding needles in a haystack. Needless to say, the Assam Accord remains unimplemented. The jury is still out on who exactly is an Assamese. But the fear, that the 'illegal immigration' was fast altering the demography of

Assam, did contribute immensely to the Hindu nationalist BJP establishing its hold in the region.

In short, the time is yet to come when Assam can breathe easy and say: 'The worst is behind us.'

We went for a short drive around Guwahati in an autorickshaw. Newly-constructed high-rises now sprouted in this earthquake-prone city, where many old houses, single-storied with slanted corrugated-iron roofs, stood as well. From a handicrafts emporium I bought a black silk tie and the Assamese gamosa, a thin white towel with a red woven border, which can also be used as a scarf, a bandana, or a waistcloth.

Back in the hotel I ordered drinks for myself and tea for Anurag. My introduction to Guwahati had been short and sweet.

At the Guwahati airport, when I was buying a burger after having cleared the security check, I heard my name being announced on the PA system. At first the name had merely sounded familiar, then I realized it was my name they were calling out. I was being asked to report to the security. Why me?

As I anxiously retraced my steps, I found my laptop on the security officer's desk. He had switched it on and the screen was showing my name. 'Yes, that's me,' I told him.

'Key in the password then,' he said.

We were both equally relieved—I, obviously, more than him—that the laptop had been restored to its owner. How absent-minded of me to have collected the laptop bag, but not the laptop.

We got talking. He told me his wife worked for the Central Reserve Police Force and that she was now on maternity leave and if I could suggest some books for her to read.

'No, she doesn't read the kind of fiction that is coming out these days. Suggest some non-fiction, preferably travel books.'

'Great,' I said and wrote down the names of ten books, including the three which I had authored.

We exchanged numbers and promised to meet again.

An hour later I was in Silchar. Outside the airport stood a row of shops where drivers had congregated, calling out names of various destinations to solicit customers. To my surprise, I heard no one offering a ride to Karimganj.

'Karimganj?' I asked one of them.

'2,000 rupees.'

'Why 2,000? It's barely 55 kilometres.'

'Have you seen the road?'

'No.'

'Once you see the road you will know. Okay, 1,800. Follow me to the car.'

We hit the countryside almost as soon as we drove out of the airport. Tea plantations showed up first, and then the trademark greenery of the ripening paddies. Beyond the green fields ran the mountains, seemingly blue from the distance, a strip of white clouds hanging over their peaks. No matter how hard you try to avoid them, clichés are the first thing that come to your mind when your senses are hit by something powerful, and the terrain we were driving through, if described in one word, was picturesque. The road was wide and smooth.

'You told me the road was bad,' I said to the driver.

'We are barely five kilometres out of the airport,' he laughed. 'We still have a long way to go.'

He was right, as I was to find out only minutes later, when the smooth road was behind us and what lay ahead was a collection of potholes masquerading as a road. The scenery remained just as pretty but the highway clearly belonged to hell.

The car bumped ahead at the speed of ten kilometres an hour, my butt thrown off the seat at every jolt, the time lapse between two jolts being about thirty seconds. When you are forever bracing yourself for the next bump, no other activity is possible—you can't read, you certainly can't jot down thoughts, you can't have a conversation with the driver, and there is no question of catching up on sleep. I clenched my teeth and looked out.

So this was Barak Valley—made up of Cachar, Hailakandi and Karimganj districts—whose biggest town happened to be Silchar. The region has a strong Bengali population which is fiercely protective of its culture and language. Protests had erupted here when the Assam government, in October 1960, made Assamese the sole official language of the state and on 19 May 1961, eleven people, including a young woman, were killed when police fired at protestors at the Silchar railway station. Following the incident, Bengali was allowed to be the official language in the Barak Valley. I found all signboards to be in Bengali or English: I could have been somewhere in West Bengal or Tripura.

It took me four hours to cover the distance of 55 kilometres to Karimganj. The hotel where Anurag was supposed to have booked a room for me was located right on the highway: it called itself a 'landmark of luxury' on its website. Luxury was precisely what I needed at the moment, but pictures are usually deceptive when it comes to hotels in smaller towns.

The receptionist wore a 'you-need-me-more-than-I-need-you' expression as he ordered me to fill in my particulars in a register. In the corridor hung a solitary picture—that of the Golden Temple in Amritsar. When I was shown into my room, I found the sheets stained, the dustbin and the ashtray overflowing, and the towel in the bathroom looking more like a used doormat. This landmark of luxury turned out to be the antipode of luxury. But I knew I would be fine. I placed the towel by the bed, to be used as a mat, and, pulling out the brand new Assamese gamosa, went to shower.

# 11

Most towns have a centre, usually marked by a square or a clock tower that is surrounded by its most important buildings. A newcomer usually makes his way to the centre first and forms his own mental map of the town, and with the help of that map in his head, he navigates its streets. But Karimganj had no centre. Its nucleus lay across the border, in the city of Sylhet in Bangladesh.

The province of Sylhet, of which the city of Sylhet is the administrative centre, is one of the most fertile regions of Bangladesh, where tea-plantation was started by the British as early as in 1857. They had separated the region from Bengal and attached it to Assam even earlier, in 1814. In 1905, when Bengal was first partitioned, Sylhet became a part of a new province called Eastern Bengal and Assam. In 1912, Bengal was reunited and Sylhet went back to being a part of Assam.

During Partition, a referendum was held in Sylhet, since it was Muslim-majority and Bengali-dominated, to determine whether its people wanted the region to remain with Assam (therefore India) or join the Pakistan-ruled East Bengal. Sylhet voted to go with Pakistan.

There are Bengali Hindus who firmly believe that the referendum did not reflect the real sentiments of Sylhet. They contend that during Partition, Assamese leaders of the Congress, which was in power in Assam at the time, were themselves keen that Sylhet go to Pakistan. The reason being Assam, had Sylhet remained with it, would have become Bengali- and Muslim-dominated—something that indigenous Assamese fear even today. Such people seem convinced that the Congress government in Assam had looked the other way when Muslim League thugs sought to prevent Hindus from voting in the referendum.

Whether there is merit in their belief can be a subject for research, one that would not only be painstaking but also pointless considering that Sylhet's separation from India has been a closed chapter for seventy years.

Radcliffe, when he ran his scalpel across this fertile land, chose to leave behind a tiny portion of Sylhet—that already sat separated from the rest of Sylhet province by the River Kushiyara—with Assam. The tiny portion included Karimganj.

Several explanations are given for the choice Radcliffe made. One of them is that he did not want to cut off Assam's road link with Tripura. Another is that he was persuaded to do so by the Congress and the Jamiat Ulema-e-Hind, the Islamic organisation that was opposed to Partition.

Whatever the reason, Karimganj, in spite of its separation, remains emotionally connected to Sylhet through language. People on either side of the Kushiyara speak Sylheti, a dialect of Bengali not easily comprehended by people from other parts of Bengal. It's a thriving dialect, commonly spoken even in parts of Europe that have a sizeable migrant Sylheti population. Britian, at present, has a Sylheti-origin Member of Parliament, Rushanara Ali, who was born in 1975—in the Sylheti town of Bishwanath.

I now stood by the Kushiyara, on the Dashami Ghat, watching, for the first time, the Radcliffe Line assume a definite—and watery—form. Across the river, lay Bangladesh which, from the opposite bank, appeared to be nothing but a mass of tropical trees.

The air was laden with a citrusy fragrance. Labourers carrying transparent sacks on their head hurried down the steps of the ghat with practised gaits: they were transporting some kind of lime from a parked truck to a country boat that flew the Bangladeshi flag. Once the boat reached its capacity, the wiry boatman got his oars working and headed for the opposite bank, making way for another boat, on which the labourers now dumped their sacks. Boats left and boats came.

The export of the fruit, carried out solely on the muscular strength of the labourers and the boatmen, went on with clockwork precision under the watchful eyes of a harried-looking customs official in uniform. He hadn't noticed my presence for a while but when he eventually did, he asked me not to take pictures.

'Why, sir?'

'You are standing on the zero line, so no pictures. Normally we don't allow people to even stand here.'

Since he was sweating and looking irritable, I put my camera away, even though I saw nothing wrong in standing by the river and taking pictures of the boats crossing its breadth. Even Wagah and Hussainiwala sit on the zero line, but visitors are encouraged to take pictures there.

Perhaps India and Bangladesh could agree on a joint 'river ceremony' taking place every sunset. Such an exercise would not only produce a spectacular sight but also turn Karimganj into a tourist destination, thereby improving its roads. As of now, the Kushiyara meant nothing—absolutely nothing—to Karimganj: just the watery equivalent of a barbed-wire fence.

I stayed put, having put my camera away. I waited to see if the customs man had a problem with my very presence at the riverbank. But he went about his work, forgetting all about me. So I stood and watched. I assumed that whatever manmade construction I saw around the ghat—including the small Shiva temple at the ghat—was at least seventy years old. Ideally they had to be. Ground rules signed between India and Pakistan in the late 1950s, when Bangladesh too belonged to Pakistan, stated that no construction could come up within 150 yards on either side of the Radcliffe Line. Bangladesh inherited those ground rules once it became an independent nation and today, even though the India-Bangladesh border runs through homes and villages, new constructions are still not permitted along the border.

I watched many more lime-laden boats glide across the Kushiyara. I also watched an elderly Bangladeshi couple cross the river on a boat flying the Indian flag: they had taken the boat, I gathered, from an immigration booth located about a hundred metres downstream. The couple looked completely at ease, as if returning home on a cycle-rickshaw.

Had I been carrying the necessary documents, I too could have been on one of the boats, paying only thirty rupees to cross over to Bangladesh. It would have been so much fun—and rewarding too—to cross the border on foot or on a boat than fly to Dhaka. I would have understood Partition, and its ridiculousness, better that way: how, until 1947, we were all one people who now stood divided by an imaginary line. To fly to Dhaka would mean arriving in a foreign country as a foreigner, with no connection whatsoever to the soil that emotionally bound Indians and Bangladeshis.

'These orange-like fruits you are carrying,' I asked a passing labourer who had balanced two sacks on his head, 'what are they called?'

'Hatkora,' he said.

Unsure of what I had heard, I put the same question to another labourer passing by.

'Shatkora,' he replied.

'Shatkora or hatkora?' I asked.

'Shatkora! Shatkora!' he replied, wiping the sweat off his eyebrows.

'Where do they come from?'

'They come from Mizoram.'

Standing there I searched the internet and found that

both names were equally acceptable: hatkora as well as shatkora, the sour-bitter citrus fruit that made Sylheti fish and meat dishes famous, even in the West.

I had barely put the phone back in my pocket when I heard the calls of the muezzins, over several loudspeakers, on my side of the Kushiyara. Simultaneously, I heard their calls from across the river. It was a magical moment, to listen to the calls for prayers rising high into the sky—way above the humans, above the vegetation, above the geographical boundary—making you wonder which call came from which side of the river.

I had come to Dashami ghat, named so because it saw the immersion of Durga idols every autumn, on a cycle-rickshaw. The ride from the hotel had cost me ten rupees. But I decided to return to the hotel walking, so that I could stop at an eatery on the way for lunch. It was well past the time for an afternoon meal, but in small eateries in eastern parts of the country, lunchtime often stretched to dinnertime.

I had barely begun my walk when something forced me to jump off the road onto the sidewalk. An unkempt elderly man, who looked more like a beggar than a rickshaw puller, was ploughing a rickshaw through the crowded road and shouting, '*Ei shuorer bachcha ra*!'—you sons of a swine—'move aside, I am drunk as you can see. Ha ha ha! No one can stop me today, ha ha ha! *Ei shuorer bachcha ra*, move aside!'

It was impossible to tell whether the man, clad in a soiled shirt and Bermuda shorts, was a rickshaw puller who was drunk, or a drunken tramp out for a spin on a hijacked rickshaw. The latter seemed more likely because a rickshaw puller would never risk his livelihood by indulging in such antics, that too in the heart of the town.

The man, after creating a mild commotion, was soon out of sight while I found an eatery that looked decent enough from the outside. Inside, however, the air smelt stale but I decided to eat a vegetarian meal there anyway. I was the sole customer for a long time before a Muslim family occupied an adjoining table.

After eating I chatted with the owner at the cash counter. His name was Suman Dey, sixty years old, and it was his father who had migrated to Karimganj from Dhaka way back in 1941. The father had purchased a piece of land from a Muslim man for five hundred rupees to build this hotel.

'Is it true,' I asked him softly, 'that Hindus in Assam fear that they will soon be outnumbered by Muslims?'

'Well, the population of Muslims has gone up like anything,' he said. 'Whether that is because they produce more children, or because people are constantly coming in from Bangladesh, I am not sure. Earlier, not one customer of mine was a Muslim. Now they are the ones who mostly come. You can see them shopping till late in the night.'

'Does that worry you—their increasing numbers?'

'In the town we are in a majority, so nothing to worry. In the villages their strength is more. Earlier riots would happen, but now they don't.'

I scooped up a spoonful of fennel seeds kept at the cash counter and put them in my mouth and stepped out of the restaurant. As I chewed on them, walking in the direction of the hotel, I thought: Had I been a Bangladeshi, no matter how poverty-stricken, I would never sneak across the river to settle in Karimganj, one of the most depressing towns I had ever come across in India.

While I had no idea how Karimganj looked when viewed from across the river, Bangladesh had certainly looked pretty from the Indian side of the riverbank: I could only see a dense population of trees, and what lay behind those trees was left to my imagination. I imagined a place prettier than Karimganj.

Back in the hotel I switched on the air-conditioner—the only thing in the room that was brand new—and lay on the bed with a book, wondering at the same time what to do next.

Anurag, the friend I had met in Guwahati, had given me the number of one of his friends who lived with his parents in Karimganj, and had asked me to visit the family. But I hesitated to make the call because I knew they would invite me, and I was disinclined to venture out again. All I wanted to do was leave Karimganj this very moment. But to do that I would once again have to endure a four-hour-long drive, on India's most terrible highway, to Silchar airport. No other way out. I felt imprisoned.

A terrible road can be forgotten if the hotel is comfortable, a terrible hotel can be forgotten if the town is charming, a terrible town can be forgotten if the people are pleasant. But I was yet to connect with the local people mainly because I was still too put off by the painful journey to think kindly about Karimganj. Moreover, I did not understand Sylheti and also did not know a soul in town.

Could sex have rescued me from the gloom, I wondered. The thought of sex struck because the book open in my hands, *Out of Sheer Rage*, happened to mention it. Author Geoff Dyer, who is following in the footprints of his literary idol, D.H. Lawrence, all over the world, finds himself on the Greek island of Alonnisos where he and his 'almost-wife', travelling on a moped, meet with an accident. After the accident, there are two things they can't stop doing: replaying the crash in their heads—and having sex.

My tailbone hurt. The cumulative impact of a thousand bumps was as good as that of a collision. But I was without a companion. So I called the number Anurag had given me.

# 12

The sun had long set, but the sky was still orange, when I came down from my room and stood outside the hotel. Anurag's friend, whom I had called, was coming to take me to his home. His name was Soham and he was going to arrive any moment.

Ten minutes passed. No sign of him. I didn't mind the wait though. Dusk can make even the ugliest of towns look agreeable. The light is bright enough to let you see what must be seen, yet feeble enough not to let you see the details. Undesirable aspects of a town usually hide in the details.

Within my hearing distance were two men—one of them was sitting on his stationary scooter and the other stood next to him—who conversed animatedly in Sylheti. Had I known the language, I might have gained some undistorted information about life in Karimganj even while watching people go about their business under the orange sky.

There was still no sign of Soham. I impatiently looked at my watch and that's when the man seated on the stationary scooter asked me: 'By any chance are you Mr. Ghosh?'

'I am.'

'I am sorry I didn't realize it was you standing here all this while. I am Soham.'

We shook hands.

'Please get on the scooter,' he said.

He drove me through the entrails of Karimganj and stopped at a roadside stall selling chow mein when he spotted a friend standing there. After they had exchanged pleasantries, the friend, who had already ordered chow mein for himself, insisted that we join him. He ordered more chow mein and led us into a room—located amidst a row of shops behind the stall—that served as the dining area for the vendor's customers.

Over the noodles, Soham told me that he was essentially a musician at heart who, because of the lack of opportunities and more importantly encouragement, in a town like Karimganj, was saddled with a regular job. He had been a bright student at school—a gold medallist, he said—but once he moved to Calcutta to join college he was so taken with the culture of music bands prevailing in the big city that he lost interest in studies.

He started a band called Axis, of which he was the songwriter, composer, and guitarist, and subsequently became the founding member of another band, Eruption. But he remained without a degree, which he finally earned many years later from the Kanpur University before returning to Karimganj.

His father, wanting the son to stay at home and to find a regular source of income, opened a travel agency for him—at home. But the son hated it. 'How could someone craving to play the guitar sit behind the desk like a receptionist and book tickets?' said Soham. There was another problem: even if he created music, who would listen? Karimganj was no longer the place he knew as a child.

'Most of the good, cultured families had moved out, people from villages were moving in to settle here. It was impossible to find even a friend, leave alone someone who could appreciate your music,' he said. 'Then I thought: if I had to remain deskbound, why not get myself a regular job.'

He wrote a test and joined the Allahabad Bank as a teller at its branch in Dibrugarh. Eight months later he was moved to a branch in Dimapur in Nagaland. In Nagaland, he said, he had the time of his life because he would get to attend and play at underground parties.

But before long, he got transferred to Silchar, where he found his job 'horrible, absolutely horrible.' I didn't need to ask him why. Silchar—unlike Dimapur or Dibrugarh—was a big city, which meant more work, and someone who liked to juggle with musical notes was left counting bank notes all day.

One day, a tiff with an impatient customer made him quit his job. He was relieved to be back home, where he wrote the Teacher Eligibility Test: 'I scored 121 out of 150; the highest score in Assam was 129.' Today, at thirty, Soham, the musician, is a teacher, teaching students at a primary school every subject other than music.

'Had Partition not happened,' Soham said, 'I would have remained the son of the soil. Here I feel like an outsider. Have you read Albert Camus's *The Outsider*?'

'I have, but why should you feel like an outsider? You were born here, weren't you?'

'Somehow I am not able to relate to this place. I find people here conservative and narrow-minded. Here you are destined to lead an ordinary life. As I told you just now, the good families, the friends I grew up with, they have all moved out to other places. People from the villages are settling here now, so are illegal immigrants from Bangladesh. Sometime ago there was a football match between Bangladesh and Manipur, and I saw most of the crowd cheering for Bangladesh.'

His friend, who had ordered the chow mein for us, went a step ahead: 'Muslims in Karimganj these days support Pakistan.'

'I am not sure about that,' Soham said, 'but sometimes they do behave as if they belong to Bangladesh.'

I thought to myself: who would I support if I were a Sylheti from Karimganj watching a football match between Bangladesh and Manipur? The answer seemed at once easy and difficult.

Geographically, Karimganj lies in India, and therefore as an Indian, I would be expected to support Manipur. But considering that historically and emotionally Karimganj remains a part of Sylhet, which now belongs to Bangladesh, whom would the Sylheti in me support: the team with whose members I share everything except nationality, or the team with whose members I share nothing other than nationality?

No easy answer to that. But very easy to bring in religion

if a Sylheti Muslim from Karimganj is found supporting the Bangladeshi team. Had religion been such a strong adhesive, Bangladesh would have never separated from Pakistan. Culture is one's truest identity, nationality a mere technicality—something that the people who were partitioned understand far better than those who weren't.

Soham's father Somesh Das was not even a year old when Partition happened. He was born in 1946 in Sylhet district, in a town called Golapganj, where his father owned farmland and also ran a shop. Since Bengal had remained largely peaceful during Partition, his family, like countless other Hindu families, stayed on in Pakistan-ruled East Bengal.

'But rowdy elements from the Muslim League would threaten the Hindus from time to time,' Somesh Das, now nearing seventy, said when I met him at his home. 'They would say things like, "We will take away your daughter" or "We will grab your property."'

'I had a brother, who was about five years older than me, and a sister, who was ten years older. My parents were very worried about her safety. They began thinking of moving to India but it is never easy abandoning the home where several generations of the family has lived, knowing fully well it would be instantly grabbed by the hoodlums.

'In April 1950 the Liaquat-Nehru Pact was signed. Under the agreement, those forced to flee their homes during Partition or those who still wanted to migrate were allowed to dispose of their properties. My father saw this as a now-or-never opportunity. He sold our property for a measly eighteen or nineteen thousand rupees and we moved to Karimganj, where my mother's maternal uncle lived.

'My father wanted to recreate the life we had in Sylhet. All his life he had been a villager, so he wanted to settle in a village and even bought a piece of land. But my mother was dead against the idea of us going back to the rural setting. She wanted him to establish himself in the town. He sold the land and tried his hand at many things, but failed. In his hands, even gold would turn to dust, such was his misfortune. For me he was the ultimate tragic hero.

'He died in 1976, at the age of seventy-one. By then, fortunately, we two brothers and my sister had fairly decent jobs and a roof over our heads. But we siblings also had had our share of struggles.

'In 1955, when my sister completed her schooling, she got a job with the railways. But to complete the formalities she needed to travel to Guwahati, and a one-way train ticket cost twelve rupees. My parents did not have even that much of money to spare—so poor were we back then. So the railways job was ruled out.

'Soon afterwards she landed a job in the postal department, but a family friend whom my father looked up to advised her against it. The family friend felt that since the postal department dealt with money—those were the days of money order—it was best she did not take up a job that involved financial transactions.

'My father listened to his advice. Fortunately, she also

had a job waiting for her in the Public Works Department, and she took it up. Once she found employment, we were assured of two square meals a day.

'We two brothers, even before we could complete our schooling, enrolled with the employment exchange by pretending to be a few years older because we badly needed jobs.

'Eventually my elder brother was recruited by the Assam Rifles and got posted at NEFA, or the North East Frontier Agency, which later became Arunachal Pradesh. But he soon realized he wasn't cut out to be a soldier and quit once he found a job in the census department.

'Meanwhile, I got a call from the police department and for the selection process travelled to Shillong'—then the capital of Assam—'where the viva voce was conducted by none other than K.P.S. Gill, who later became famous for fighting terrorism. But I wasn't destined to become a policeman. Finally I got a job as an instructor in what was then called the National Discipline Scheme.

'The scheme was started in 1954 mainly to inculcate discipline among the children of refugees, and by the early 1970s it became institutionalised as the Department of Physical Education. I retired from the department as a district sports officer about ten years ago.'

The cotton vest Somesh Das wore—I now noticed—highlighted a once-muscular physique, and it was quite likely that his former profession had decided the drink I was offered at his home: the healthy lassi and not Assam tea.

The irony was too loud to be missed. In Punjab, where I

had expected a glass of rich lassi, I was served with coffee; whereas in tea-growing Assam, I was served with a tall glass of lassi.

Their son Soham, was not to be seen—he seemed to have gone out again after having brought me here—but Soham's elder sister Debashree sat with us, listening to her father reminisce about his days of struggle. She now lived in Agartala along with her husband, a civil servant, and child, and was visiting her parents in Karimganj.

I said to Debashree, 'Your brother seems to believe that many Muslims in Karimganj behave as if they were Bangladeshis. What do you have to say about that, considering that you too grew up here?'

She said, 'I don't know what exactly he told you, but I never sensed any difference between Hindus and Muslims as long as I lived here, which was until the mid-1990s. *Tokhon obdi aamra ek sutoye baandha*: until then we were stringed together. I had many Muslims friends.

'When I was in school, we would have a dance drama every year before the school closed down for Durga Puja holidays. The dance drama depicted Goddess Durga's victory over the demon king, and it was a Muslim girl called Zohra who would invariably play Goddess Durga because she happened to be the prettiest among us.'

Somesh Das said, 'Mr Ghosh, I will make one request to you. Please visit Bangladesh at least once. *Manush manush ke ato bhalo baaste paarey*'—how humans are capable of loving one another—'you will see for yourself. I go there often, and get so much love from the people.'

Debashree said, 'He is right. I had gone there with my husband a couple of years ago. I found them most hospitable. Bengalis in India, when they invite you for a meal, serve you only two or three varieties of fish. But in Bangladesh, they serve you six or seven varieties.'

Somesh said, 'And I find Muslims there more hospitable than the Hindus. They take offence if I don't visit them.'

'What takes you to Bangladesh?' I asked him.

He said: 'I have a maternal uncle living in Dhaka. He is a senior bureaucrat. But visiting him is only an excuse. The real reason is to trace my roots, to visit places where my ancestors lived, to search for people who are old enough to have memories of Partition and of my father.

'Some years ago, I went there looking for the grocery-cum-sweetshop that my father owned. I walked into a police station and gave them the address I knew. One constable hailed an autorickshaw for me and explained to the driver where exactly to take me. I not only found the shop but also a fish-seller who was ninety-two years old and had distinct memories of my father. He said, "I remember him, he was so fair-skinned that he looked like a sahib."

'The shop had changed hands several times but it remained a grocery-cum-sweetshop. It was, unfortunately, closed the day I went there. Then the fisherman told me something I can never forget. He said, "What was the purpose of Partition, babu? Before Partition, I would often get to eat maachher teler bora (fish oil fritters, a delicacy), but after Partition, I can count the number of times I have eaten it."'

'How do you travel to Bangladesh?'

'I take the bus. A one-way ticket costs eighty rupees.'

'Do you think illegal migration from Bangladesh is happening?'

'In my opinion that is a myth. Who would want to leave their homeland and settle in another place? There are people of East Bengal origin in Assam, that's true, but those are people who were once upon a time hired by the Assamese to work on their lands. They toiled on inhospitable terrains, braved cobras, braved malaria, and now that those lands have turned into gold, you want them to go back? No sir, they are not going to go back!

'Let me tell you an interesting story. Some months ago, while returning from Sylhet to Karimganj, I decided to have breakfast at a roadside shop there. I ordered parathas. The cook, when he saw me, came up to me and said, "Babu, don't you recognize me?" I could not recall having met him. He then said, "I have dropped you home a few times in my rickshaw in Karimganj."

'I asked him what he was doing there. He said he made more money working in the roadside eatery in Sylhet than pedalling a rickshaw in Karimganj. So every six months he would apply for a multiple-entry visa so that he would work in Bangladesh. He was so happy to see me that he put an extra spoon of ghee in my paratha.'

Soham arrived just when it was time for me to leave. As I got onto his scooter, it struck me: the son disapproved of those supporting Bangladesh, whereas the father loved Bangladesh; the son was born some forty years after Partition, whereas his father had been a direct victim of it.

# 13

I woke up around noon to realize that I still had an entire day left to spend in Karimganj. I was booked to fly back to Guwahati from Silchar only around noon the following day. How was I going to kill time in a place that seemed like a prison to me?

I had the numbers of two more people whom I could call and, provided they were available, go over to meet them. One number was that of a retired history professor called Kamaluddin Ahmed. The other was that of a local BSF officer with whom I had spoken some days ago. He had sounded very official and—unlike the BSF men I had interacted with so far—not warm. He had merely asked me to get in touch with him once I reached Karimganj. Perhaps I had got used to BSF drivers waiting for me at the airport and the comfort of the officers' mess, which actually were mere favours extended to me and not entitlements.

I called up the officer, realizing that he was not at all obliged to be nice to me and that it was I who needed him.

'Ah, so you have come,' he sounded mildly friendlier this time, 'where are you staying?'

I told him the name of the hotel.

'I will send one of my boys. He should reach you around three o'clock. He will show you around a bit. But remember, this is an international boundary, so there are certain restrictions in place.'

'Restrictions like?'

'You cannot take photographs. You cannot venture near the boundary line on your own. You will only go to places where my boy takes you.'

'I shall keep that in mind.'

About fifteen minutes past three a white Bolero pulled up outside my hotel. A young officer in civvies stepped out to greet me. He was shadowed by an armed sentry—a fellow Ghosh—who eyed me suspiciously until I told him that we shared the same surname.

'So sir, what exactly would you like to see?' the officer, apparently a new recruit, asked me.

'Nothing in particular,' I said, 'I just want to get a feel of the international border.'

'Very well,' he said and asked the driver to take us along the river.

After about a kilometre or so of a bumpy ride on the highway we branched off towards the Kushiyara and were soon driving parallel to it. The river was to our left, calm and colourless, defining the border; farmlands and the dwellings of villagers to our right.

There was a time when, if you gave a child a blank sheet of paper and a box of colours—I am talking about the time when I was a child, I am not so sure about today's children—he or she would invariably depict a river. Sometimes the river would flow from between two mountains, with the sun in the background; sometimes the riverbank would be dotted by trees or a hut or two. In their innocent imaginations, the river was essential to natural beauty. In Karimganj, however, the beauty of Kushiyara remained locked up: a barbed fence ran between the river and the path we were driving on.

After a point the river curved away and it was now farmland—Indian farmland—that appeared across the fence. I soon got bored of the situation—having to watch everything from the vehicle, and not being able to walk around or take pictures—and told the officer that I was done.

'In that case,' he said, 'we shall now go to the Dashami Ghat, very close to your hotel.'

I wanted to tell him I had been there the day before, but kept mum because visiting it in the company of a BSF officer might generate a different experience.

Once again we were back on the potholed highway and drove past the hotel to get to the ghat. There was no export of shatkora happening today, but an elderly Muslim couple, seated on a country boat flying the tricolour, glided past us. The boat clung to the Indian side as it went upstream.

'I find it very fascinating that you can cross over to another country in the humble country boat,' I told the young officer, pointing at the couple.

'They are not crossing over to Bangladesh.'

'I am confident that they are.'

'No, they are headed to a destination on the Indian side.'

'But they look like a Bangladeshi couple,' I said, 'I am sure they are headed home.'

We both kept our eyes fixed on the boat as the boatman, wearing a Vietnamese hat, pushed it upstream. Soon the boat disappeared behind a bend and the officer looked at me with a victorious smile.

Seeing him looking pleased, I asked: 'Can I take a picture of myself standing against the river—purely for personal use?'

'I will have to ask my boss,' he said and took out his phone.

'Please don't bother,' I pleaded, 'I have dropped the idea.'

The boat reappeared. It was now gliding across the river towards Bangladesh. The officer looked worried and he pulled out his phone again and stepped away to make a call.

Common sense dictated that the elderly couple was indeed headed for Bangladesh because the Kushiyara, serving as the international boundary, is not used as a domestic waterway—something he should have known better than me. Moreover, boatmen, when their destination happens to be on the opposite side of the river *but* upstream, row as close as possible to their side of the riverbank to beat the current. Once they reach a point when the destination becomes downstream, they take advantage of the current to cross over with ease. This was what was happening now.

The officer, looking relieved, returned to me and said, 'Actually they are bona fide passengers.'

I wanted to tell him: 'I told you so'. I merely said, 'I see.'

Suddenly the air smelt citrusy. I turned around to see

that a shatkora-laden truck had just arrived. As if out of nowhere, the customs man materialized too, the one who had prevented me from taking pictures the day before. He looked in our direction quizzically, perhaps wondering who I could be. What if he now walked up to the young officer and said, 'This man was here yesterday as well. He was taking pictures and I told him not to.' To prevent such a possibility I told the officer that we should get going.

'Now I would like to take you to the Steamer Ghat,' the officer said.

Just when we were about to get into the vehicle the call for prayers rose from mosques on both sides of the river. I paused—just to feel the moment.

The Steamer Ghat turned out to be home to a defunct warehouse belonging to the Central Inland Water Transport Corporation Limited, and also a camp of the Central Reserve Police Force, or CRPF. Once a part of the river-trade circuit that connected West Bengal and Assam via Bangladesh, it is today a ghost port.

'This place is haunted,' a CRPF constable told us, pointing at a river-facing building that once held the offices of the water transport company. In one portion of the building lived its manager who had drowned in the Kushiyara. 'His ghost is often sighted in the building,' the guard said.

'When did he drown?' I asked.

'Many years ago.'

'Have you ever seen the ghost?'

'No, I have not. But the caretaker sees it every now and then.'

'Are you scared that there is a ghost near you?'

He laughed nervously and said, '*Belt-dhaari ke paas bhoot nahin aata*'—Ghosts don't come anywhere near those who wear the belt. By belt he meant his paramilitary uniform.

'Can I see the caretaker?'

He led us into the building and we climbed to the first floor where the manager had lived. The caretaker, a Bengali man called Rupa Das, sat on a string cot that stuck out like a sore thumb in the otherwise-elegant drawing room. He stood up when he saw us. He said he had worked as a driver for the company for twenty-three years, until it wound up its Karimganj operations in 1997. He was left behind to look after the property.

'Yes, I keep sighting manager sahib's ghost,' Rupa Das said.

'When did he die?'

'I am unable to recall, but many years ago. He had slipped from the pier into the river.'

'What happens when you see the ghost?' I asked.

'Nothing happens. It does nothing to me, but I feel scared, even though now I am used to seeing it.'

'Where does the ghost appear?'

'Exactly at that spot,' he pointed to the space right outside the bedroom door. 'I see him emerging out of the bedroom and lingering there for a few moments before he disappears.'

'What time of the day?'

'Always at nights.'

We trooped out of the building and got into the Bolero. I asked the BSF officer to drop me at the main market so that I could have lunch at Ahar, which had been recommended to me by Anurag, my Guwahati friend, who had called this morning to find out how I was doing.

Ahar turned out to be an unpretentious, clean place. A standee outside its door urged patrons and passers-by to shun junk food. I had a vegetarian Bengali meal as I listened to Bengali songs playing softly on the restaurant's speakers. It was here I discovered that the popular Hindi song, *Na jaane kyon, hota hai yeh zindagi ke saath*, from the film *Chhoti Si Baat*, also had a Bengali version: *Paagol hawa, ki aamar moton tumio hariye geley.* I felt pleased at the discovery.

For three days the newborn nations of India and Pakistan did not know where their borders lay, because Lord Mountbatten had chosen to keep Radcliffe's maps a secret until power had been transferred. He released them only on 17 August 1947, to be published in the newspapers the following morning.

During those three days, Pakistani flags flew in several Muslim-majority towns that assumed they would join Pakistan but, ultimately, ended up with India. Karimganj was one such place. But on August 18 its citizens realized—much to the relief of the Hindus and also Muslims who were opposed to Jinnah's Muslim League—that they were staying with India.

One of the families rejoicing on that day was that of Kamaluddin Ahmed, the history professor whose number I had. He retired as the principal of Karimganj College in 2001 and lived in a neighbourhood called Kanishail: 'barely a kilometre away from your hotel,' he told me when I called him after returning from lunch. 'Once you reach Kanishail, you will find a tyre shop, they will tell you where my house is.'

That evening I got onto a cycle-rickshaw and asked to be taken to Kanishail—and instantly felt sorry for the elderly and emaciated rickshaw-puller. The roads inside Karimganj are just as bad as the road leading to it.

Twenty minutes later I asked him, 'Have we reached Kanishail?'

'Not yet, but we are almost there.'

We were riding through near-darkness. There was a power-cut—a frequent occurrence in Karimganj—and the road was deserted.

'Have we reached Kanishail?' I asked him again, after a bit.

'Yes,' he replied. 'Where do you want to be dropped?'

'I am looking for a tyre shop, but I don't see any.'

'You want to go to a tyre shop?'

'No, to someone's house that happens to be near a tyre shop.'

'Whose house do you want to go to?'

'Professor Kamaluddin Ahmed.'

'Ah, you should have told me earlier!' the rickshaw-puller said.

We were at the professor's home in less than a minute. Quite miraculously, electricity came back the moment I entered the gate. I asked the rickshaw-puller to wait for me so that he could drop me back to the hotel.

The professor, clean-shaven and clad in a shirt and lungi, seemed to be glad to have me over. A man—perhaps a caretaker—brought us tea and biscuits and just when he was placing the tray on the table, his mobile rang. The ringtone turned out to be the famous Tagore song, *Ami chini go chini*, in the voice of Kishore Kumar, my favourite singer. After serving the tea he withdrew to a corner of the room to listen to our conversation.

Professor Kamaluddin Ahmed said, 'I was born in 1941, so I was still a child when Partition happened. I didn't understand much of what was going on, except that we were going to be independent.

'All I remember is that Eid was round the corner—we were living in the village at the time—and our family was hoping that Sylhet would stay with India so that we could celebrate Eid with extra enthusiasm. My father was a member of the Jamait Ulema-e-Hind, which was strongly against Partition, whereas the Muslim League wanted Sylhet to go to Pakistan.

'Our family feared that if we came under Pakistan, we would be excommunicated by the Muslim League. By sheer coincidence, the boundaries happened to be announced on the day of Eid, and we learnt that Karimganj was staying in India. My father became a hero in the village.'

[When I checked later, I found that Eid in 1947 had indeed fallen on August 18, which also meant that in the just-divided Punjab, where Hindus and Muslims were still butchering each other, it could not have been a happy occasion.]

'But after Partition, did your family ever consider moving to East Bengal?' I asked.

'That was out of the question,' Professor Ahmed said, 'for two reasons. One, my father was an Indian nationalist. Two, this was our land. Our ancestors are buried here. We would have rather died here instead of migrating to another land. But many of our friends did migrate to East Bengal, so did some of my uncles. The uncles however, came back. Home is home, after all.'

He stood and walked into his study and emerged with a booklet. 'You have come all the way, I thought I must give you one of my books,' he said.

'Please sign it for me,' I said and gave him my pen.

The booklet was titled *Assam's "Doubtful Citizens": Fact or Fiction?* I read through the blurb:

> A misconception prevails among many people outside Assam that "lakhs" of "Bangladeshis" are residing in Assam and exercising franchise ... Dr Ahmed, with the help of mostly public documents, shows that all this is an emotional exaggeration, has no empirical or statistical foundation, and as such is nothing more than a self-composed chorus of some pseudo-intellectuals.

'So you don't believe people from Bangladesh sneak into Assam and settle here?' I asked him.

'Not at all,' he said. 'It is said that every year a few lakh Bangladeshis come to settle in Assam. At that rate, a large chunk of the Bangladeshi population would have been living in Assam by now.

'What we must keep in mind is that Assam is also the original home of countless Bengalis, both Hindus and Muslims. But every Bengali-speaking person is doubted to be an illegal migrant, which is very sad.'

'Do you have memories of the time when Bengalis rose in protest against the imposition of Assamese as the sole official language in Assam?'

'Very much,' he said, 'I was in college then. I remember going to the Kushiyara where they were immersing the ashes of the eleven people killed during the protests. It was an unforgettable sight: nearly 1,000 people were standing on the other side of the river to express their solidarity with the language movement.

'*Partition na holey bhaloi hoto*'—it would've been better had there been no Partition—'but it happened. Now it is history.'

# 14

The distance between Karimganj to Dawki, my next destination, is barely 50 kilometres as the crow flies. All I had to do was cross the River Kushiyara and drive across Sylhet to the border village of Tamabil, and then stroll across the Radcliffe Line into Dawki, a village in the Indian state of Meghalaya.

But this was 2015 and not 1945—and I wasn't carrying my passport. I must, therefore, drive all the way back to Silchar, fly back to Guwahati, drive down to Shillong, and then drive farther down to Dawki.

I left Karimganj at six in the morning even though my flight from Silchar was scheduled for departure at 12.45 p.m. Reaching the airport earlier than required wasn't going to harm me—airports are a rather nice place to kill time—but bearing the pain of a dreadfully slow and bumpy ride and at the same time panicking about missing the flight was certainly going to kill me.

The driver was a young Sylheti who couldn't have been more than twenty. I took a liking for him the moment I got into his weather-beaten car. He came across as a sincere and obedient boy—not flamboyant and cocky, as some young drivers can be—who wore faded and ill-fitting clothes which I was sure he had inherited from his father or some uncle.

I would have liked to know more about him—we had four hours ahead of us—but conversation was not possible because he spoke only Sylheti and also because I was constantly preparing my buttocks for the jolts that were being delivered by India's most-potholed highway.

We crossed a village called Bhanga not long after we left Karimganj behind. Bhanga, in Bengali, means broken or shattered, and even before I could wonder how a Bengali-speaking village acquired such a name, I came across a signboard: Bhanga Glass House. Call it the mother of all ironies.

Only when the chain of mountains showed up on the horizon did I breathe easy. I knew I was not very far from the airport. Then the farmlands gave way to tea gardens and the road got smoother. It was too late now to have an insightful chat with the driver but I decided to ask him a question anyway.

I asked him, in Bengali: 'Why is the road so bad?'

He replied, in a mix of Sylheti and Bengali: 'What can we do? The state government is asking [Prime Minister] Modi for money to build the road, but Modi is telling them, "First account for the money you already got from the Central government for the purpose."'

I wasn't sure whether to believe what he said—he could be absolutely right or horribly wrong. In my experience, however, taxi drivers often understand the politics of a land better than its long-time residents, leave alone lay visitors.

At 10.15 we were at the airport. I tipped the boy hundred rupees and then, on second thought, doubled the amount to two hundred. He looked happy and that made me happy.

From Guwahati airport, I took a taxi to Pan Bazaar to meet Anurag. We met at the Circuit House where, sitting on a bench by the Brahmaputra, we had tea. We sat facing a tree-covered hillock—a small island in the river—and on that island, Anurag said, was a seventeenth-century temple dedicated to Umananda, or Shiva. I was tempted to pay a visit—there was a ferry connection—but right now it was time for me to head for Shillong. Anurag had already called for a taxi.

'I have friends in Shillong as well,' he said as I got into the car. 'Do call me if you need any help.'

'I will. And see you soon.'

It took me a long time to wade through the peak-hour traffic of Guwahati—as bad as Bangalore's—and just when it looked like I had finally come out of the city, the driver got a call. The conversation that he had took place in Assamese but I got the drift. Even though I could not hear the caller, I was able to construct their conversation. It went a bit like this:

Caller: 'Where are you headed?'

Driver: 'Shillong.'

Caller: 'Shillong? But the road was shut due to landslides.'

Driver: 'What are you saying?'

Caller: 'It was supposed to reopen today, that's what I read in the papers. But I am not sure.'

Driver: 'Let me find out for myself. I am almost there.'

It turned out that the two lanes meant for the outbound traffic were still shut, but the remaining two lanes meant for the inbound traffic served as a two-way connection with Shillong, which lay about 100 km away. The sun had long set, it was nearly seven o'clock, and my only concern was to reach the BSF officers' mess at Shillong at a decent hour.

Every once in a while, the driver would draw my attention to the heaps of collapsed earth and boulders across the road divider: 'See, landslide.'

So far I had only read about people dying in landslides. Now the heaps of soil gave me a clear idea of how such deaths happened. The very thought was scary: you are driving on the highway one fine evening and suddenly a mass of soil and boulders descends on you and subjects you to an almost-instant burial while you are still alive. You can't even attempt to escape.

After we had driven for about 20 kilometres on the highway it widened back to four lanes and we now cruised in the direction of Shillong. Ahead of us was a lorry whose number-plate bore the letters 'ML.' 'Are we in Meghalaya yet?' I asked the driver.

'We have been in Meghalaya for quite some time.'

'Switch off the AC,' I told him, 'I want to smell the mountain air.'

The child in me felt elated, and the adult in me ashamed. Even though I was forty-five I had seen so little of my country that I was getting excited at the sight of 'ML' inscribed on the back of a lorry. During the drive from Karimganj to Silchar, I had come across a row of trucks parked by a lake: their number-plate bore the letters 'MN'—Manipur. On the highway from Cooch Behar to Bagdogra, I had spotted a truck marked 'NL'—Nagaland. Not to mention the two painful rides I just had in 'AS' cars. For a pair of eyes long used to 'UP', 'DL', 'HR', and 'TN', the sight of new combinations of letters was not only refreshing but also a sign that I was, finally, travelling.

'Are you planning to visit Cherrapunji?' the driver asked me.

'No, a place called Dawki. Heard of it?'

'I have. It's a slightly risky route. Make sure you get a good driver.'

When a professional driver considers a particular route to be risky, there's reason to worry. But after having just seen the piles of earth on the highway, the thought of tumbling down a mountain didn't scare me so much.

The air was fragrant and chilly. Every now and then, we drove through villages, their presence marked by brightly-lit shops flanking the highway. The shops were all run by women. The villages bore an air that was at once lazy and lively. No filth, no squalor, only content, cheerful faces—just the kind of place to settle down, or at least pause and have a leisurely smoke. But time was running out.

Finally I saw a puff of cloud drifting across a signage

that announced the arrival of Shillong, rather our arrival in Shillong—the capital of Meghalaya, the abode of clouds.

The orderly at the BSF mess said I had made it just in time: in another half an hour the cook would have left and the bar would have closed. 'What would you like to have for dinner?' he asked.

'What can you give me?'

'Anything you want, except chicken or mutton, because for that we need to be told in advance.'

'How about egg curry?'

'That's possible. And drinks?'

'Whisky. Three large whiskies.'

That night I slept under a blanket, warm in the knowledge that I was in the Scotland of the East.

# 15

The village of Dawki is 90 kilometres from Shillong, and even though it serves as an important border crossing, I had not been aware of its existence until about two weeks ago. The only consolation was that I shared my ignorance with the majority of Indians. I can at least name all the seven north-eastern states and their capital cities.

The driver taking me to Dawki turned out to be a twenty-something Bengali man who was born in Shillong and had roots in upper Assam but who looked more like a mountain-hardened Khasi born to drive in the hilly terrain. I had, in fact, taken him for a Khasi until I happened to ask him his name.

'Manoj Dey,' he had replied.

'Ah, a Bengali,' I had exclaimed. 'We should then be talking in Bengali and not Hindi.'

'Talk to me in any language you wish, sir. I can speak Hindi, English, Bengali, Sylheti, Assamese, Nepalese, Nagamese, Khasi, Meitei, and Mizo.'

Despite his fluency in several languages, Manoj turned out to be a man of few words, which suited me fine because Meghalaya is a place where the drive can be as scenic as the destination.

Khasi Hills is easily one of the prettiest places on earth. Once you leave the bustle of Shillong behind, the road is deserted and you have the whole place to yourself, hardly a soul in sight except the occasional fruit-picker or villager. And then you come across villages—quaint, charming, and clean.

The drive gets even more scenic once you cross the bifurcation where a section of the road curves away in the direction of Cherrapunji. I regretted, for a moment, having given up daytime drinking. Liquor stores are dime a dozen in Shillong, many bearing funny names (for example, Drowsy Wine Store), and I could have bought a couple of cans of beer to make the drive more pleasurable. But no, it would have been a terrible idea to absorb such pristine sights with alcohol-altered senses.

We drove past a roadside house where a number of well-dressed young men had congregated. Some sort of celebration seemed to be on. But Manoj announced solemnly: '*Manush maara gechhe*'—there's been a death in this house.

'Are you sure?' I asked.

'In Meghalaya things work the other way round. Here, when someone dies, people actually party before they bury their dead. And when people get married, it is the boy who goes to live in the girl's house.'

He slipped back into silence. About an hour into the drive, even though I had not consumed any beer, I felt the need to empty my bladder. I asked Manoj to stop at a place that might have a toilet, and he did so, after a few kilometres, at a wayside restaurant. I walked into the restaurant to seek permission to use its toilet, but found not a soul around even though the tables seemed to have been freshly laid out.

'Hello! Anyone there?' I said aloud, twice.

Finding no response, I used the toilet and walked back to the car.

Shortly afterwards he stopped at a typical forest village called Riwai, which seemed to be of interest to tourists because there were stalls at its entrance, selling fruits, snacks, and water.

'Go in, you will see a bridge made of living roots,' he said.

I walked in, bought a ticket for ten rupees from a booth and climbed down steep steps. Butterflies fluttered, insects called, birds chirped. On a wooden stall sat a child selling pomelos: he was most likely minding the stall in the temporary absence of his mother. When I aimed my phone camera at him, he said, 'One picture ten rupees,' and instantly blushed and turned his face away. It was evident that he had been tutored to respond in such a fashion only recently.

Eventually I came across a stream, the sky barely visible here because of the trees, and across the fast-flowing stream hung a bridge made of living roots. A bunch of noisy tourists was already on the other side, and I soon joined them by crossing the bridge. One tourist washed his face and rinsed his mouth with the water, so clean it was, and further downstream villagers washed clothes.

As I sat on a rock to observe and absorb, I felt grateful to Manoj for having brought me here. He need not have, because his brief was to drive me to Dawki. In India, you don't need a guide book if you have a good driver at your disposal. I have never bought a copy and probably never will: it merely directs you to the happening places, preventing you from letting things happen to you.

We stopped next at Mawlynnong, 'God's Own Garden', as the village, said to be India's cleanest, was described in the receipt handed to me by a local youngster after I paid him fifty rupees—my contribution to the upkeep of the village, which could have well belonged to the English countryside.

There I noticed a signboard, 'Bangladesh View Home Stay' and walked in the direction of the painted arrow. I entered a large compound and wandered around for a while. People clearly lived there, because clothes hung on the clothesline, but I heard or saw no one. I came across a bamboo tower—rising up to thirty, or perhaps forty, feet—which promised a view of Bangladesh.

As I began to climb—it involved walking up a set of bamboo ramps—I heard a man's voice: 'You will have to pay me twenty rupees for the view, is that okay? But you don't worry, pay me after you finish.' He was the owner of the place.

From the top of the tower I was treated to a view that I can never forget. Actually I saw nothing. All I could see, beyond the green canopy of Meghalaya, was a vast swathe of land that almost merged with the sky. I could tell the land from the sky only because of the hazy brown of the soil and the equally hazy grey of the rivers, with the brown and the grey seeming to occupy almost equal space.

The fact that I could see nothing made the view special, because the nothingness represented a foreign land, Bangladesh, which I couldn't enter without a passport. Had it represented another Indian state, I wouldn't have even bothered looking—and the Khasi man wouldn't have bothered building the bamboo tower in the first place.

I was still trying to make sense of the nothingness when I felt my phone vibrate in my trouser pocket. I took it out to find a text message from Airtel welcoming me to Bangladesh.

The Khasi man told me that he built the tower every year after the monsoon—ten labourers worked for twelve days to construct it using 'countless bamboos'—and he had been doing it for the past seven years to add to his income from the homestay.

'Khasi people are very hospitable people, you know,' he said as I handed him two ten-rupee notes. 'Stay with us sometime.'

'What's your name?' I asked him.

'Rishot. It's a Khasi word. It means a pillar. Whether a weak pillar or a strong pillar, that I don't know,' he laughed, his breath reeking of alcohol.

'Let's now go straight to Dawki,' I told Manoj. 'I want to get there before sunset.'

'Don't worry,' he assured me, 'we are not very far from Dawki.'

Thus began one of the most memorable road trips of my life. One moment we were curving around the hills of Meghalaya, the next we were overlooking the plains of Bangladesh. Half way through this drive I realized that the nothingness I had observed from the top of the bamboo tower at Mawlynnong was a mirage caused by height and distance—exactly what happens when you watch the details of your own city getting blurred shortly after a flight takes off. As we got closer to Dawki every passing minute, the details of the Bangladeshi terrain became clearer.

From time to time we stopped at waterfalls to take pictures: the waterfall would be located in Meghalaya but the water would be flowing into Bangladesh in the form of a river. Sir Cyril Radcliffe must have had no problem separating Meghalaya, then a part of Assam, from East Bengal: the line where the hills ended and the plains began became the natural border.

We climbed down the hills and were now almost on the plains, driving along a grey river across which lay the buildings of Bangladesh. Soon the river bifurcated and the section we continued to drive along, magically turned from grey to green—a very clean green—sprinkled with numerous small boats that carried anglers. It turned out that the grey part fell in Bangladesh and the green—River Umngot—in Meghalaya.

Then we crossed the green part on an old suspension bridge, and once again drove along the grey part and reached Dawki, which resembled a seaside English village without the sea. At the border crossing, I found a BSF officer, cutting a rather dashing figure in his green Ray Ban, waiting for me.

Until about a month ago, the officer said, about 500 trucks would go into Bangladesh each day, carrying boulders, stone, limestone and coal. But now there was a ban on the mining of the stones, and as for coal, Bangladesh imported it from elsewhere because they found Indian coal more expensive.

Right now, he said, only fruits and vegetables went from India—oranges, pineapple, tomato—apart from betel nut, betel leaf, and also bay leaf. From Bangladesh came potato wafers and biscuits (both from a brand called Potato), plastic crockery and cotton goods. There was also a weekly bus service, connecting Dhaka and Guwahati via Dawki and Shillong. About fifty people, from each side, crossed the border on foot daily.

We walked up to the barricade on the zero line to take a look. A green signboard across the line announced Tamabil to be 0 km away, Dhaka 300 km away and the city of Sylhet only 54 km away. Which meant Karimganj was only a stone's throw from here—well, almost.

On seeing us, a Border Guard Bangladesh sentry walked closer to the zero line and asked the BSF officer, in Bengali, 'How much does two kilograms of *barfi* cost on your side?'

'Two kilograms would cost about 1,100 takas—our taka, not your taka,' the BSF officer, a native of Bihar, replied in

Hindi. Taka is the currency of Bangladesh because Bengalis measure money in taka. Even Indian Bengalis refer to the rupee as taka.

The officer told me softly, 'He must have asked one of his countrymen to bring him sweets from India and now wants to check whether he has been overcharged.'

'Can I have a picture taken with him?' I asked.

'Sure, go stand with him. I take good pictures.'

I handed him my phone and, walking up to the boundary pillar, posed with the Bangladeshi sentry.

The BSF officer then got into his jeep and asked me to follow him. We were going to his office, the border outpost, barely a kilometre away.

At the outpost we sat on a raised wooden platform that overlooked the grey river and the Sylheti village of Borlapunji. An orderly brought us water and then tea. 'Get some biscuits as well,' the officer told the orderly.

I could sense that he was only too glad to have company. Life, particularly for an officer, can be lonely in a border outpost, which is usually in the midst of a remote village. Lower-rung sentries have one another for company, whereas the officer, who cannot get too friendly with his subordinates or with the villagers (the only other people he comes across), leads a near-solitary existence. For this officer, the location—the confluence of the Himalayas and Sylhet—might have been of some consolation, but then, one can safely assume that even in a place as pristine as Kashmir, tourists and soldiers view the terrain differently.

'You must miss city life,' I said to him.

'What can we do, our job is such,' he said. 'A layman should spend just one night in the kind of places we stay. Sometimes there is nothing but forests for miles around. Sometimes there is nothing but the desert for miles around. Sometimes our men stand in waist-deep water to keep watch.

'We fight militants in Kashmir, mosquitoes in Bengal, leeches in Tripura. There are times when food supplies have to be air-dropped for us. We cannot even take phone connectivity for granted. There are places in Rajasthan where we have to travel 100 km just to find a shop with a phone so that we can call home. There is never any respite from hardship, no matter where we are posted. Anyway, it is a part of our job. You tell me, which border area are you headed to next?'

'I am going to Mizoram after this. And then a few places in West Bengal.'

'Which places?'

'Malda, Murshidabad, and a place called Petrapole, which is about eighty kilometres from Calcutta.'

'I know Petrapole. A parade takes place there every evening, something similar to what you see in Wagah.'

Call it a coincidence: at the precise moment he mentioned Wagah, I noticed a lone sentry bringing down the tricolour that had been flying at the outpost. The sentry carried out his duty more as a chore, which was understandable, because he wasn't being cheered on by a crowd of 25,000. At the Wagah border, a sentry's life centres around the flag-lowering ceremony; here, lowering of the flag is just one of the many duties he is expected to perform.

The officer asked me, 'How about one more cup of tea?'

'No, I am fine.'

'No, you must have something, how about some jaljeera?'

'I wouldn't mind that.'

He summoned the orderly and asked him to bring jaljeera. I wondered why he had not offered me alcohol, considering we were in Meghalaya. Either the officer was a teetotaller or drinking was not permitted in border outposts. The latter was more likely to be the reason. Not that I was craving a drink, but I wouldn't have minded being served with whisky at this time, the magical hour of dusk, when the world around you looks beautiful—and this place *was* beautiful.

Over jaljeera, I asked him if smuggling was a problem in Dawki.

He replied, 'Smuggling happens in places where people on both sides of the border are of the same ethnicity. Here, Khasis live on one side and Sylhetis on the other. They have nothing in common.'

I now heard something from across the river, similar to the sound of a generator.

'What's that?' I asked the officer.

'That's the sound of a thresher,' he said.

I tried imagining myself in the land across the river, where the thresher was now at work: would life there be as rosy as it looked from here?

Suddenly, the call of the muezzin rose from that land, drowning the noise made by the thresher. Had I been drinking whisky instead of *jaljeera*, and had I been sitting in a place not as sanctimonious as a BSF outpost, I would have composed a poem or two in celebration of the moment.

# 16

It was dark when we began our return journey to Shillong. We were in the middle of nowhere, driving through silence, when my phone rang. A Bangalore number was flashing on the screen.

The caller was from a travel portal. He wanted to know whether I had enjoyed my stay at the hotel in Amritsar. Ms Blue Eyelids briefly flashed in my mind, but right now, driving through the jungles of Meghalaya, I was least inclined to get mentally transplanted to Amritsar.

'The stay was very good, that's all I can say,' I told the caller.

'No sir, that won't do. I have a questionnaire for you,' he persisted.

'Bugger off!' is what I wanted to tell him. Instead all I told him was, 'Sorry, you will have to call me later.' I hung up and marvelled at the progress of human ability: that my phone should be functional in the middle of nowhere, so that I could get a call from Bangalore from a total stranger, who knew where exactly I had stayed in Amritsar.

A few kilometres ahead we found the road invaded by clouds.

'Just what I feared,' Manoj, the driver, said.

He began to move very slowly, almost inch by inch, and I wondered if I would make it to Shillong in time to order drinks and dinner. As if by miracle, a red car materialized in front of us and Manoj blindly followed its taillights for some distance until we reached a village, where the car as well as the clouds vanished. We made it to the officers' mess shortly before nine.

I woke up in the morning to a disappointing piece of news. The BSF commandant in Mizoram with whom I had coordinated before booking my tickets to Aizawl called to say that it may not be a good idea for me to come to Mizoram at the moment.

'It's raining heavily here, there are landslides. We are even airdropping supplies to our men stationed on the border,' he said. 'I think you should postpone your trip for your own safety. And the particular place you want to go to is difficult to access even in normal times, right now it is impossible.'

I had planned to travel to a place called Parva, where India borders Bangladesh as well as Myanmar. For days I had been trying to picture the place in my head, but without success. Now I must put the idea on hold, if not abandon it all together.

I opened my laptop and cancelled my Calcutta-Aizawl-Calcutta tickets. Then I called up my BSF officer friend, my classmate, and begged him to find me a contact in

Petrapole, the border crossing closest to Calcutta and also the busiest on the entire border with Bangladesh. He assured me, as usual, that he would do the needful.

Relieved, I poured myself some tea and turned the pages of *Shillong Times*. An entry in the Lost and Found column caught my eye:

> LOST: Ladies bag containing mobile, ATM card, cash, mini purse. Somewhere between Nongrim Hills and Rynjah. Finder may contact—

The lady in question, who had lost practically everything, obviously nursed the hope that a Good Samaritan might just call up to say that her bag had been found. In other words, it wasn't uncommon in Shillong for lost items to be found and restored.

I set out to see the city after breakfast. I had hired Manoj for today as well. What a relief to play the tourist in a charming hill station after trudging remote villages and towns for days. Manoj even had a rough itinerary in mind.

He first took me to the Cathedral of Mary Help of Christians, built on an elevation, on the site of Shillong's oldest Catholic Church that was gutted in 1936. It stood surrounded by a vast open space that must have been the size of a football field, most of it concreted and the rest of it serving as lawns, now sprinkled with school children in their uniforms. But once I stepped into the church I found not a soul in there other than me.

Actually there was someone else too—a little Khasi girl, not more than six, in her school uniform. She was accompanied by a woman who waited at the door. The girl walked straight up to the altar, prayed fervently to Mother Mary with her palms joined and eyes shut, and wrote a short prayer on a register placed there. She looked over her shoulder once to see whether I was standing close enough to read her prayer. Once she was out of my sight, I had a look at what she had written:

> Dear God: I hope it is good for me to be friendly and please help me to love one another.

What had made the little girl write what she had written? I would never know.

Manoj then took me to Elephant Falls, a set of three waterfalls now enclosed within a garden that has its share of stalls catering to tourists. One of the stalls lent you traditional Khasi attire so that you could get photographed clad in it. I watched two tubby Gujarati men, wearing Khasi costumes, each holding a sword and a shield, trying to look fierce as a (real) Khasi woman clicked their pictures.

From the Elephant Falls we drove up to the Shillong Peak, from where, on a clear day, you can see the city spread out below you. Call it bad luck, but the moment we made it to the top of the peak it began to rain. Within minutes, however, the rain subsided into a drizzle and I was able to put my hand out of the window to buy tickets to the enclosed area that serves as the viewing point.

I couldn't resist buying roasted corn as soon as we got in there. Rains and roasted corn go together, and this was no ordinary rain, but rain in the land of the clouds. Munching on it, I took a look at the shops selling handicrafts and was about to buy a hat when I decided against it, for two reasons. One, the hat was made in China; two, the shopkeeper, a young Khasi woman, was in a trance. The transistor on her lap was playing a romantic Kumar Sanu song—*Mera chaand mujhe aaya hai nazar* (I have sighted my moon)—and she, with her eyes shut, was loudly singing along. I did not have the heart to break her reverie.

It was pointless to hang around here because the clouds were blocking the view of Shillong. And so what if I got to view Shillong? It wasn't out of bounds, but a city where I was staying. I would rather experience it than view it.

Driving out of the viewing point we ran into a row of vegetable stalls. The vegetables looked so fresh that I regretted not living in Shillong. At one stall I asked for a radish, something that I could eat right away. The owner of the stall scraped the pink radish clean before handing it to me.

'How much do I pay you?' I asked her.

'You don't have to pay me anything,' she replied.

Back in the heart of Shillong, Manoj slowed down the car and said, 'There is a Shiva temple right across the road, but you will have to climb down a bit. Would you like to go?'

'Why not,' I said.

I am an almost-atheist who rarely lets go of an opportunity to visit a Shiva temple—the lesser known the better. I climbed down the steps to find a saffron-robed sadhu squatting in the temple compound. He was smoking a chillum. He told me he had come all the way from Haryana and was on his way to the Kamakhya temple in Guwahati. Since he looked like an honest seeker, I gave him two hundred rupees, upon which he pulled out a rudraksha bead from his pocket and placed it on my palm.

'Keep this with you,' he said, 'it will bring you good luck.'

Later when I began the upward climb, I wondered about this thing called luck. There are people who probably consider me luckier than them, just as there are people whom I consider to be luckier than me. Does the holder of good luck ever realize how lucky he is?

With the bead in my pocket, I spent the rest of the day roaming Police Bazaar and Bara Bazaar, rubbing shoulders with tourists and marvelling at the fact that *all* shops were run by women. These women had a few things in common: they were good-natured, they were reasonably fluent in Hindi, they (at least the majority of them) habitually chewed betel leaf, and they wore a checked apron-like garment—called jainkyrshah—across their torsos.

I recalled what the BSF officer at Dawki had told me: 'Khasi society is matrilineal. It is the woman who inherits the property, who runs the household and who takes care of the family business. The man has no say in these matters. And if the woman is unhappy with the man, she can always dump him and take another. All she needs to do is pack his belongings and leave them outside the door.'

'Does that still happen?'

'I believe so,' he had said.

The following morning I set out for Guwahati.

Manoj was driving me for one last time, which kind of made me sad because he was the best driver—not just one of the best drivers—I had ever hired: cheerful yet non-intrusive, reticent yet knowledgeable, young but seasoned when behind the wheel. He was someone who would feel suffocated if you hired him to drive you from home to office and back: he was a free spirit who would rather take you from one end of the world to another.

On our way, we stopped briefly by the Umiam Lake, barely fifteen kilometres north of Shillong. I had missed it while driving into the city because it was already dark by then. The lake, beautiful but barely fifty years old, is a popular tourist destination. Presently, though, I did not spot any activity on it: I only noticed signboards, tied to trees, spelling out dos and don'ts for tourists.

We drove on at great speed, through one village after another, driving past young Khasi girls selling homemade pickles, slowing down once we neared Guwahati. Manoj dropped me at the Brahmaputra-facing Circuit House, where Anurag had booked me a room. It, however, was of little use to me because I would have to leave for the airport soon—but not before I had paid a visit to the Umananda Temple on the island visible from the Circuit House balcony.

Finally, as the taxi glided out of the Circuit House in the direction of the airport, I looked at the river. The setting sun, as usual, had left a golden streak across its width. I envied those who were relishing the sunset: what it must be like to have the mighty Brahmaputra feature in your daily life? A part of me, however, was glad that I was returning to the familiar arms of Calcutta.

# 17

My real introduction to Calcutta took place only ten years ago, when I got married. Until then I only had childhood memories of the city. My father-in-law and mother-in-law had both migrated to the city from what was to become Bangladesh—he in the late 1950s and she after the 1964 riots. They got married in 1969—it was an arranged marriage—and after living in north Calcutta for about fifteen years, built a house in Salt Lake City, a planned township that was coming up, at the time, in the northeastern fringe of Calcutta, not far from the airport.

My initiation, therefore, had taken place at Salt Lake City, which bore no resemblance to the Calcutta I had in my memories. A few years later, I set out in search of that Calcutta too and found it pretty much intact—a search that resulted in a book about the city.

It was on the highways skirting Salt Lake City that I would often come across the name 'Jessore Road' painted on blue signboards erected by the highways department. The name—at once familiar and foreign—would intrigue me, but I never pursued my curiosity. I had other interests to pursue at the time. Later, when I came to know that

Jessore was in Bangladesh, those signboards acquired a special charm: they indicated how close Salt Lake City was to Bangladesh. All I had to do was follow the arrows. How fascinating.

By then, something else had begun to fascinate me as well. My mother-in-law had a resident cook—as many Bengali families do—who hailed from a place called Bongaon, which literally means a village in a forest. Each time I heard the cook mention the name, I would picture a village untouched by time. It lay about 80 kilometres from Calcutta and—what I found even more fascinating—was connected by rail with Sealdah station. The best part: Bongaon bordered Bangladesh.

This morning, finally, I began to lift the curtain on the two unseen sources of my fascination as I set out on the road to Bongaon, the road being none other than Jessore Road. My destination was actually Petrapole—the busiest border crossing between India and Bangladesh—which lay barely five kilometres beyond the village of Bongaon.

As far as I knew, from what I had gathered of late, Jessore Road was a part of the ancient Grand Trunk Road, whose different segments now bear different nomenclatures assigned to them by the highways department. I had already touched its western extremity at the Wagah border, and now I was going to touch its eastern arm. Only that the same road in the west was about six times wider and smoother. This stretch still belonged to the time of bullock carts.

The driver, a forty-something native of Bihar, wasn't

used to long-distance travel. He drove for Uber in Calcutta and he had happened to be driving me home the evening before when I had asked him if he could find a driver to take me to Petrapole. He volunteered to take me there, provided I agreed to the fare quoted by him. Since it wasn't too unreasonable and his car was comfortable, I had agreed.

Jessore Road has often turned into a river of refugees, right from the time of Partition until the liberation of Bangladesh in 1971, when the river was in spate. That year, the celebrated Beat poet Allen Ginsberg, after visiting the refugee camps lining the road, wrote a lengthy, heart-rending poem titled *September on Jessore Road*, which began like this:

> Millions of babies watching the skies
> Bellies swollen, with big round eyes
> On Jessore Road-long bamboo huts
> No place to shit but sand channel ruts
>
> Millions of fathers in rain
> Millions of mothers in pain
> Millions of brothers in woe
> Millions of sisters nowhere to go
>
> Millions of Souls nineteen seventy-one
> homeless on Jessore under grey sun
> A million are dead, the millions who can
> Walk toward Calcutta from East Pakistan…

This was September too. But the year was 2015. No refugee camps but only crops bathed in the autumn sun. I heard not the howl of Ginsberg but a happy song of Kishore

Kumar playing on 94.3 FM. The radio station, which takes pride in calling itself a '100 per cent retro station', has this uncanny ability of reading the playlist on my mind, and its songs now made every mile melt away in a moment. By the time the signal weakened, we were already halfway to our destination.

At Bongaon, I found neither a village nor a forest. It was a bustling town that had mushroomed along the Jessore Road. It must have been a forest village once upon a time, but now from a roadside tree, hung a signboard advertising Ffreak Jeans: 'Way of Life. Exclusively available in Sivam Fashion Bazaar, Talatala Club Road, Bongaon.' The signboard also urged passers-by to follow Ffreak Jeans on Facebook and Twitter.

I saw shops selling lottery tickets, bicyles, toys, and musical instruments. When you spot a shop selling musical instruments you know you aren't exactly in a village. At another shop hung several shapely pairs of legs—basically torso-less mannequins—sporting colourful leggings. And as if to assert that this was a Bengali town, there stood a homeopathic clinic as well.

Once we left the bustle of Bongaon behind, the road widened and we drove under a large green overhead signboard that bore two skull-and-crossbones signs and in between them the warning:

YOU ARE ENTERING INTO
INDO-BANGLADESH BORDER AREA.
ALWAYS BE CAUTIOUS.

One could understand the warning, but why the skull-and-crossbones signs? It was as if the road led to death. Well, it did, in 1971, when hundreds of thousands of Bengalis fled in the opposite direction to escape death at the hands of Pakistani soldiers. It was through this road that the Indian Army marched in to liberate East Pakistan from West Pakistan, with Jessore becoming the first district to be freed.

No sooner had we driven under the signboard that we arrived in the village of Haridaspur, the last major village on the Indian side. Here we came across a row of parked trucks, each awaiting its turn to enter Bangladesh through the border crossing, which lay just a kilometre or two ahead, at the confluence of two hamlets: Petrapole in India and Benapole in Bangladesh. They are the Attari and Wagah of the east.

Right now we didn't have to go that far. The BSF camp, where the officer in charge of the border crossing waited for me, was located in Haridaspur. The officer, clad in a tracksuit, was admiring roses in the lawn when we drove in. Once we had exchanged pleasantries, he showed me into the guest house and excused himself.

He returned about ten minutes later, in uniform. By then, I had been served, in turns, with water, tea, potato wafers, onion pakodas, rossogolla and another Bengali sweet called pantua. I was having the pantua when he returned. 'That has come from Bangladesh, please have one more,' he said. I accepted one more piece.

We then got into his jeep and drove to the border crossing, which I found marked by two sets of stately pillars. One set was white-tiled: its central columns held together a tile mural of Sheikh Mujibur Rahman, depicting him making a fiery speech with his right fist raised. The other set, granite-slabbed but unassuming, belonged to India.

In between the two sets of pillars lay a large, tree-fringed open area on which ran a strip of white paint: Radcliffe Line. On either side of the boundary line was a long but orderly queue of people waiting to cross over to the other side. Most of these people belonged to the urban middle-class, bhodroloks and bhodromohilas, who could have well been queuing up to board a flight. Of course, the queues included the visibly less-fortunate too: how can any picture from the subcontinent be complete without the poor figuring somewhere in the frame.

As they waited—many of them with small children—for formalities to be completed, porters pestered them. Porters who wore either red shirts or greens shirts were Indians. The Bangladeshi ones, on the other hand, wore shirts that were vertically split across the buttons into red and green: the red side had green sleeves, while the green side had red sleeves.

If you overlooked the shirts, the porters all looked the same: Bengalis. The same could be said about the travellers who had queued up: none had 'Indian' or 'Bangladeshi' written on his or her face. They were all Bengalis, divided by the white strip. Here I noticed, for the first time, a female sentry of Border Guard Bangladesh, or BGB. The last time I had noticed a female sentry on the opposite side was at Hussainiwala: she had worn a Pakistan Rangers cap on top of her hijab.

Even as the immigration process went on, Indian trucks continued to groan their way into Bangladesh, right under the gaze of Sheikh Mujibur Rahman. Simultaneously, Bangladeshi trucks were also rolling into India—but from another gate about 200 metres away, not visible from here. This border crossing accounted for nearly 60 per cent of the four billion-dollar trade between India and Bangladesh, and is therefore the biggest land port in the subcontinent.

As I watched the buzz from behind the white strip, with the BSF officer standing behind me, a man in BGB uniform held my wrist and pulled me across the Radcliffe Line, through the queues, into Bangladesh.

'Come, take a closer look,' said the man, who seemed to be the senior-most of the BGB sentries on duty there.

I took pictures of the mural and then, standing against it, posed with the BGB man as another Bangladeshi sentry took pictures.

'Follow me,' said the BGB man, as he led me into the gate to the rear of the two columns that held the mural. By crossing the Radcliffe Line, I had merely set foot upon Bangladeshi soil, but by crossing the gate, I had formally entered Bangladesh.

On the rear side, too, was a tile mural: portraits of

Rabindranath Tagore and Kazi Nazrul Islam, with a line each from their immortal poems and their signatures placed below their images. These lines were intended for those exiting Bangladesh. The gist of Tagore's line: 'If we meet again, walk straight into my heart.' And Nazrul's: 'I sing of equality, there is nothing nobler than humanity.'

These lines—when a 'Please visit again' sign should have sufficed—testified to Bangladeshi hospitality and the richness of Bengali culture.

The BGB man escorted me back to the Radcliffe Line and requested the BSF officer to let him serve me some tea. The BSF officer, politely but expectedly, turned down his request. I gratefully shook the BGB man's hand and—technically speaking—stepped back into India.

Back in the guest house, over lunch, the BSF officer told me a bit about himself. He hailed from Haryana and was fighting insurgents in Kashmir until a few months ago when he got posted to Petrapole. He was a trained Black Cat commando: he had had a stint with the National Security Guard or NSG, during which he protected several VIPs.

'Your Amma is a great lady,' he said, referring to Jayalalithaa, the Tamil Nadu chief minister. 'She really cared for us. There were many who didn't, who treated us shabbily. Oh yes, how can I forget Farooq Abdullah—what a lion-hearted man! He always made sure we ate before he did.'

There were two clocks in the dining hall. One showed Indian time and the other Bangladeshi time. India is half an hour behind, but the clock seemed to move faster than usual as we discussed his experiences with some of the country's top politicians—who was colourful, who was uncouth, who was elegant, who was kind... The officer did not give out too many details, but I got the picture.

On the face of it, Black Cats may belong to a prestigious commando force, inspiring awe and fear, the real-life avatars of screen heroes who can, single-handedly, take on ten baddies and make them bite dust. But most of the time, they end up enhancing the prestige of the politician they throw a ring around.

After lunch the officer took me for a drive around the border. The man, who until the other day was fighting militants in Kashmir, now knew this part of Bengal like the back of his hand. Talk of adaptation.

'Have you picked up any Bengali yet?' I asked him.

'Very little,' he replied stoically. 'I am trying to learn.'

We drove along a stretch of the border that was fenced. The asphalted path we drove on—with the fence running to our right—was absolutely empty, not even an animal in sight. All we came across were bundles of jute stalk placed by the road. From time to time, I heard cries of 'Jai Hind, sir!' The cries emanated from observation posts—nothing but crudely-erected asbestos sheds—dotting the strip of land to our left. Some of the observation posts were held by pairs of women constables. The BSF officer nodded in response with a dignified 'Jai Hind!'

If only the sun was a little gentler this would have been what you call a perfect day. Every colour visible to the eyes was well-defined: the sky a clear blue, the clouds luxuriant white, the bundles of jute stalk golden, the road ahead grey, the barbed fence black, the farmland beyond the fence light green, and the trees beyond the farmland deep green.

But where were the people?

It was two-thirty: was it the heat, or was it time for their afternoon nap? Bengalis dread the first, look forward to the second. And no place could be more Bengali than this: here the Radcliffe Line saw the confluence of the two Bengals, west and east. A thought crossed my mind: what if the BSF in West Bengal was made exclusively of Bengalis?

We drove on that road until we reached a border outpost, whose signboard said we were in the village of Jayantipur. The officer turned the jeep around and we retraced our path, once again being greeted with cries of Jai Hind, coming from the same set of sentries.

Soon we entered another village, Kalyani, where we stopped at a riverside hamlet called Haldarpara. The river was Ichhamati, which was bereft, at the moment, of any activity. Across it lay Bangladesh. A young woman emerged from one of the river-facing houses to feed a dog her leftover lunch.

Her name was Meera Haldar, and she had been living in this house ever since she got married, seventeen years ago.

'Who all do you live with?' I asked her.

'My father-in-law, mother-in-law, my husband, my two children, my brother-in-law, his wife, and their two children.'

'How old are your children?'

'The elder one is in high school, the younger one is eight.'

'And what do they want to do when they grow up?'

'The elder one says he wants to join the police, but his father says he must join the army.'

By now another woman, younger than this one, had emerged from the house to see what was going on. She was the sister-in-law, Mampi Haldar.

'Your father-in-law always lived here?' I asked the older woman.

'He was born there,' she said pointing across the river, 'in house no. 10.'

'Is he home?'

'No, all the men are out.'

'What does he do?'

'All of them work in the farms—he, my husband, my brother-in-law. They also fish.'

'They work in their own farms or other people's farms?'

'Other people's, we don't own farms.'

'My husband does, he bought a piece of land recently,' Mampi, the younger sister-in-law, interrupted.

'How does it feel to be living here?' I asked them. 'On one side is the river, and across the river is Bangladesh, don't you find your movement restricted?'

'I never felt that way,' the elder of the women replied. 'Why, we do travel. When I say we, I mean myself, my husband, and our children. Darjeeling, Digha, Gangtok—we have been to all these places. Why don't you come in and have tea, since you have come all the way?'

The younger woman repeated the request, '*Ashun na, cha kheye jaan*.'

I looked at the BSF officer for his approval.

'You can go in if you want to,' he said. 'I shall wait for you in the jeep.'

I didn't like the idea of keeping him waiting. I told the women, 'Some other time.'

At 4.45, after I had rested for a bit in the air-conditioned bedroom at the guest house, the officer and I drove again to the border crossing for the flag-lowering ceremony.

The ceremony here was only two years old and—since Bangladesh was a friendly country—devoid of the jingoism one witnessed at the Wagah border. No roaring crowds here; only Kumar Sanu's voice blasting over the speakers:

*Kitna haseen chehra, kitni pyaari aankhen*
*kitni pyaari aankhen hai, aankhon se chhalakta pyaar*
*kudrat ne banaya hoga, fursat se tujhe mere yaar...*

Two rows of chairs had been placed on the Bangladeshi side, nearly all the chairs occupied by women. A small crowd of men stood around the chairs. On the Indian side was a tin-roofed gallery that could hold about a hundred people. In front of the gallery was placed a sofa and a table laden with a flower vase and bottles of drinking water: the guest of honour was to be seated here.

In all there wouldn't have been more than two hundred people gathered, both sides included, to witness the flag-lowering. This was however a border crossing that, in terms of trade and transit of people, was far, far busier than the Wagah-Attari border. Jingoism, naturally, is a bigger crowd-puller.

The music stopped. As I eyed the gallery, wondering where to seat myself, the officer, to my great horror, motioned me to sit on the sofa. How could a writer who had merely come to take a look, that too while clad in a V-neck T-shirt and chappals, be the chief guest at an event that involved men in their ceremonial uniforms? I felt as if I had won the Booker for a novel which even I knew was terrible.

So overcome was I by embarrassment that I could barely register what was going on. All I managed to notice was that the drill here involved far more handshakes between the sentries of the two countries as compared with the single, brusque handshake between the platoon commanders at the Wagah border. Also that, just like it happens at Hussainiwala, the sentries lowered their respective flags by standing on the soil of the opposite country.

I breathed easy as the flags were folded and carried away. The evening—and my role as the guest of honour—had come to an end.

# 18

The map of West Bengal is thought to resemble a chicken, even though I find it looking more like a crudely-drawn swan because of the long neck. Right at the centre of that neck sits Malda, sandwiched between Bihar and Bangladesh.

Had Malda been severed from India during Partition, West Bengal would have been cut off from its head, made of Darjeeling and surrounding districts. It almost was.

Both Malda and neighbouring Murshidabad, which sits directly below Malda on the swan's neck, were Muslim-majority districts and it was considered a foregone conclusion that Sir Cyril Radcliffe would place them both in East Bengal.

Accordingly, Pakistani flags flew in these districts right from the moment Pakistan became independent, on 14 August 1947, until August 17, when Radcliffe's boundaries were made public. Perhaps for reasons of geographic contiguity, Sir Cyril had kept both these districts with India, while handing Hindu-majority Khulna and Buddhist-dominated Chittagong Hill Tracts to East Bengal.

What a complicated surgery Cyril Radcliffe had had to perform to create two nations out of one in a span of five weeks. A few lines from W.H. Auden's 1966 poem *Partition*, in which he imagines, perhaps quite accurately, the circumstances under which Radcliffe carried out the thankless assignment:

> Shut up in a lonely mansion, with police night and day
> Patrolling the gardens to keep assassins away,
> He got down to work, to the task of settling the fate
> Of millions. The maps at his disposal were out of date
> And the Census Returns almost certainly incorrect,
> But there was no time to check them, no time to inspect
> Contested areas. The weather was frightfully hot...

Radcliffe was merely the executioner. The murders for which the British finally decided to sentence India to Partition had taken place exactly a year before: the Great Calcutta Killings. That, to my mind, is the greatest irony about Partition: when Jinnah called upon his supporters to observe 16 August 1946 as Direct Action Day, the hot-blooded Punjabis had remained surprisingly peaceful; it were the Bengalis who butchered each other in the name of religion, thus setting the ball rolling for Partition.

Calcutta—today Kolkata—appeared incapable of such savagery as I headed for Howrah Station to catch the Shatabdi Express to Malda, making my way through the very streets where butchered bodies had lay strewn sixty-nine years ago, driving past the crumbling warehouses and defunct offices that must have worn a fresh coat of paint back then.

The traffic came to a halt every few metres, and I wondered if I could make it to the station in time. Only fifteen minutes were left for the train to leave when the driver got onto the Howrah Bridge—and only two minutes to go when I boarded.

The railway station at Malda, contrary to what I had imagined—and I don't know why I had so imagined—turned out to be clean and organized. Here I had my first idlis in weeks, from a railway cafeteria. On the platform, a large notice board displayed an assortment of mugshots along with a question for the commuters: 'Has any of these travelled with you recently?' These people, the notice board cautioned, were in the business of offering drug-laced eatables to unsuspecting passengers and making away with their belongings.

Outside the station too, there was none of the clutter that usually defines an Indian railway station: no gangs of taxi or autorickshaw drivers waiting to pounce on emerging passengers. I walked out of the compound in the pleasant autumn evening and climbed onto a cycle-rickshaw and asked to be taken to the hotel.

What had fascinated me most about the map of Malda was the presence of a large market called English Bazaar, sometimes written as Ingrej Bazaar, which I found hugging the border with Bangladesh. I had found the name very charming—I could visualize the sahibs and memsahibs shopping there in the evenings—and tried imagining what it must be like shopping there today, with the call of its vendors reaching Bangladesh.

'How far is English Bazaar from the hotel?' I asked the rickshaw-puller.

'This whole place is English Bazaar, *babu*,' he said.

'What do you mean?'

'English Bazar is the old name for Malda Town, *babu*,' he explained. 'Then there is old Malda, called Malda Sadar, which lies to the west, across the Mahananda River.'

The map now made sense, thanks to the rickshaw-puller. The hotel sat right on the highway: NH34, as the rickshaw-puller told me. In my head, it represented the neck of the swan.

'Is it true that Malda celebrates Independence Day on August 17 and not August 15?' I asked the receptionist as I wrote down my name and address on the register.

'Not anymore,' he replied. 'That used to be the case many years ago.'

The following morning I set out for Mahadipur, the nearest border crossing with Bangladesh, about 25 kilometres southeast of the town. The driver, a middle-aged man called Raju, looked as shabby as his Ambassador, but he had a smile that made him instantly likeable.

We drove south on NH34, in the direction of Calcutta, and after 10 kilometres of a bumpy ride—my notebook kept sliding into the crevice between the seat and the backrest of the battered car—we branched off onto the highway leading to Bangladesh. The point where the road split, the driver said, is called Sustiani Mod, where caravans once halted so that weary travellers could rest their backs before continuing with their journey. *Susti*, a Hindi word, stands for relaxing or lazing.

From here on the road was smooth, and we now zipped past fields, mango orchards, and also a petrol pump with a lone attendant. Malda is the mango capital of India. 'People here also rear cattle and produce cheese,' the driver said. 'The cheese goes to all corners of Bengal.'

We stopped at a village called Ramkeli, famous because Sri Chaitanya Mahaprabhu, the great religious reformer of Bengal, had stopped here on his way to Vrindavan, some 500 years ago. His footprints are preserved in a small shrine that was locked; the lock was opened by an elderly woman who took care of an adjacent Krishna temple. The footprints, when I saw them, were sprinkled with fresh flowers and coins.

We were in the city of Gour, the capital of ancient Bengal. Nothing remains of that city, of course, except about a dozen monuments from the time when the Turks ruled Bengal: they stand amid mango orchards and mud-house villages of present-day Malda like oases of architectural splendour.

They all predate the Taj Mahal by 100 to 200 years but stand nearly intact, surrounded by manicured lawns, with hardly a soul—neither a caretaker nor a visitor—to be spotted around these buildings, even though they are under the protection of the Archaeological Survey of India, or ASI. I could have hammered a brick out of the wall of a historical mosque without anyone noticing.

I did find a caretaker, though, at the 1526-built Baradwari Mosque, a few hundred metres from the shrine containing Sri Chaitanya's footprints. He gave me a long lecture on the architecture of that era—how Hindu and Islamic styles were fused—and also about the neglect of government employees in West Bengal.

'I joined the ASI in 1987 as a labourer,' he said, 'and I still remain a labourer. My boss tells me, "Why does it hurt your sentiment if I call you a labourer? You *are* one." Now tell me, will I be motivated to work?'

He went on: 'My duty at this place is from eight in the morning to four in the afternoon. After four o'clock, there is nobody to look after this place. People come here at nights to drink, to have sex. Who is there to stop them? I could have shown you the empty bottles and the used condoms, but I must go for lunch now.'

He got onto his bicycle and said, 'You must write a big article on how we labourers are treated.' He was gone, leaving the entire medieval-era mosque to me.

I stepped out of the compound and asked Raju, the driver, to take a picture while I stood under a mango tree.

'If you come here in April,' he said, 'you will find all the trees laden with ripe mangoes.'

'Don't the birds eat them away?'

'How much can the birds eat!' he laughed. 'There are millions and millions of mangoes, you will find them strewn on the ground. Even the cows refuse to eat them after a while. There is a variety of mango called fazli, each weighs about 750 gm. You can't work or drive after eating it because it makes you drowsy.'

I have plucked raw mangoes from a balcony, but never a ripe one. I told the driver I would consider returning in April—if not the coming April then another April. The city of Gour was worth returning to. Nowhere else had I seen historical structures sprout from a setting so idyllic.

Take the Firoz Minar, for example. Standing on a manicured mound, it rises twenty-six metres into the sky—a dwarf when compared with the Qutub Minar but still holding on its own, ringed by mango orchards and overlooking a green, serene pond. You share the Qutub Minar, at any given point, with at least a hundred other tourists, but out here, the only humans happened to be the driver and me. You could feel the human presence, of course: the manicured lawns, the ASI signboard, the tended orchards, the plaque erected by the pond—but where were those people?

Firoz Minar, the ASI signboard said, was 'probably constructed' by Saifuddin Firoz, an Abyssinian who became the Sultan of Bengal in 1486 by killing Barbak Shah, who, as I was to find out later, was also an Abyssinian and the founder of the Habshi Dynasty. Habshi was derived from Habbash, the Arabic word for Abyssinia (now Ethiopia), and later adopted in the subcontinent as the generic term for Africans.

So Bengal was ruled by Africans at some point—a vital

piece of information I had stumbled upon in a mango orchard tucked away in an idyllic corner of Malda.

After brief stops at some of the other monuments, we finally headed for the border crossing, and drove past a queue of about a hundred trucks to reach the BSF check-post.

The check-post turned out to be located on the remains of an arched gateway—called the Kotwali Darwaza—built during the reign of Allauddin Khilji or even before. The ASI signboard said it could have been erected sometime between 1235 and 1315 and had served as the southern entrance to the city of Gour. Today it served as an entrance to India—or Bangladesh—depending on which side of the border you came from.

The arch is long gone, but the two gigantic walls that supported it still stand. Each wall is thirty feet tall and seventeen feet wide, and one of them is open to public: it can be climbed only after you have deposited an identity proof at the BSF check-post.

The two BSF men stationed at the check-post looked hassled and I hesitated approaching them. They had too much to deal with: truck drivers fighting for their turn to take their cargoes into Bangladesh, papers produced by each driver to be scrutinised, a group of villagers pleading with them to be allowed to cross over 'for a few minutes' to meet relatives waiting on the other side, keeping an eye on who—or what—is coming in from the other side.

Finally I walked up to them and introduced myself. The

senior of the two sentries hailed from Uttarakhand and the other, who looked menacing because of his height and the cane he wielded, from Rajasthan: one man from the hills and another from the desert, dealing with Bengalis in Malda.

I told them about the places I had visited and also that I found it unfortunate that the BSF, in spite of being the first line of defence, was not as glorified as the army. Tea materialized a moment later, in plastic cups, carried to us by a female constable.

'The kind of locations we serve in,' the senior sentry said, 'a civilian won't be able to spend even a few hours there, leave alone an entire night.'

Even as he spoke to me he kept checking the papers of the truck drivers: every five minutes a truck entered Bangladesh. Nearly 300 of them cross this border every day, carrying vegetables, ginger, chilli and peanuts, apart from stone chips and boulder stones. Imports mostly comprise jute.

The group of villagers approached him once again. 'Our relatives are standing right there,' pleaded one of them, pointing to some people gathered at a distance across the historical gateway, 'we will meet them and come back in no time.'

The officer tried to wave them away, saying, 'Apply for passports if you are so eager to meet your relatives. I won't stop you if you have passports.'

'How can we suddenly produce passports, sir? Please, sir, the meeting is important.'

'But how can I let you cross the border without papers?'

'Just let us cross the gate, sir. We won't venture anywhere else. We will be right under your eyes.'

'No, get yourselves passports first.'

The group, sulking now, moved away and stood under a tree to contemplate their next move. Probably they would plead again, and again, before the sentry relented, on humanitarian grounds.

I handed my ID card to him and climbed the stairs leading to the top of the moss-coated wall of the Kotwali Darwaza. I stood facing Bangladesh, watching Indian trucks disappear into, as well as emerge from, the canopy of green on that side. It was a day of healthy trade. A thought struck me:

Once upon a time, about 700 years ago, the wall had served as the gateway to the city of Gour. Today, it serves as the gateway to India. Who knows, 700 years later, the wall, if it still remains, may serve as the gateway to an entirely different country. History tells us cartographers have never had a leisurely moment from the time human beings organized themselves into nations. The time we live in today is nothing but a speck of sand in the clock of history.

# 19

The day was breaking when I stepped out of the suffocating and depressing confines of my hotel room in Malda to hail a cycle-rickshaw for the railway station. The train to Murshidabad was leaving in about thirty minutes. I not only had to buy a ticket but also find myself a seat in one of the unreserved coaches.

Once upon a time, Murshidabad used to be a riverside caravanserai by the name of Makhsudabad. Behind its renaming was a man called Quli Khan, who was born in a Brahmin family in south India but was raised as a Muslim who went on to impress Aurangzeb with his bookkeeping skills.

The Mughal emperor made him the de facto governor of Bengal, whose boundaries at the time also included Bihar and Orissa. Later, pleased by his service, Aurangzeb bestowed him with the title of Murshid. In 1704, when Murshid Quli Khan shifted his base from Jahangir Nagar (now Dhaka) to Makshudabad, he renamed the settlement Murshidabad.

After Aurangzeb died, the Mughal Empire rapidly fell into decline and Murshid Quli Khan declared himself the Nawab of Bengal. He was succeeded by his son-in-law Shuja-ud-Din, who in turn was succeeded by his son Sarfaraz Khan, who had barely ascended the throne when he was deposed by his seventy-year-old general Alivardi Khan.

Since Alivardi Khan did not have a male heir, he named his grandson, Siraj-ud-Daulah, his successor. Siraj was twenty-three when he took over the reins of Bengal but he lived for only one more year. In June 1757, his defeat at the hands of the East India Company at Plassey and subsequently his death at the hands of his own people proved to be a turning point in history: the British, mere traders till now, were set to become rulers. It was Murshidabad that witnessed their transformation.

There is no railway station by the name of Murshidabad, which is today better known as a large district with its administrative headquarters located in the town of Berhampore. To get to Berhampore, you must alight at either of these stations: Berhampore Court or Khagraghat Road. The train I was about to board made a halt at the latter.

After buying the ticket, as I walked along the train to get to the unreserved coaches, I noticed the chart pasted on the AC coach and found that it had empty seats. I asked the conductor for an upgrade. He seemed to be in no mood for paperwork early in the morning and allotted me a seat after he had discreetly slipped the hundred-rupee note I gave him into his pocket.

I hardly sat in my place though. I spent most of the

three-hour journey standing by the open door, watching the unfamiliar landscape as the train made its way down the swan's throat.

Standing by the door has its rewards. As the train came upon the barrage across the Ganga at Farakka, I found the river looking more like an ocean, frightfully wide and voluminous, gushing in the direction of Bangladesh, the border barely 15 kilmometres to the east, the waters sparkling in the morning sun. I pulled out my phone and began taking pictures fervently, not sure how long the ocean-like river would remain in view. I need not have hurried: the train took forever to cross the Ganga at Farakka.

'Make sure the conductor doesn't catch you taking pictures,' a man standing next to me cautioned.

'Why so?' I asked.

'You are not supposed to take pictures of the barrage.'

It is at Farakka that the Ganga splits into two. The broader channel goes into Bangladesh and acquires a new name: Padma. The narrower turns south and flows under the name of Bhagirathi for some distance before becoming Hooghly as it nears Calcutta.

The idea behind building the barrage—the construction began in 1961 and ended in 1975—was to divert some of the water from the Bangladesh-bound river to the Calcutta-bound river to increase the latter's flow and therefore reduce sediment-deposition at the Calcutta harbour.

When I had looked at the map, I had found the Bangladesh-bound Ganga turning southwards upon touching the border and flowing *on* the Radcliffe Line for a short distance before finally curving into that country. The curving, according to the map, happened at the village of Jalangi, in Murshidabad.

Jalangi, therefore, was one of the places I wanted to visit. The other places I had in mind were Lalbagh, where Siraj-ud-Daulah's palace once stood; Khushbagh, where Siraj lay buried; Plassey, where Siraj lost to Robert Clive; and Panchthupi, my ancestral village. There apparently exists a well-known documentary called *Panchthupi: A Village in West Bengal*, made in 1956 by Harisadhan Dasgupta for Burmah Shell. I had seen neither the documentary nor the village.

I asked the man standing next to me whether he knew of good hotels in Murshidabad. He named a few and even briefed me on how to get there. Then he asked me, 'Where are you from?'

'Chennai.'

'But you seem to be a Bengali.'

'I am a Bengali. But I work in Chennai.'

'So where in Bengal are you from?'

'Murshidabad.'

'Then why are you enquiring about hotels?'

'My ancestral house is in Murshidabad, but I have never been there. I grew up in Kanpur. This will be my first visit.'

'Who lives in the ancestral house then?'

'One of my cousins, whom I have never met.'

It then occurred to me that I was, in a sense, a son of the soil I was going to set foot on.

Outside the Khagraghat Road station, I found two modes of transport available for Berhampore. One was the motorized bullock-cart: a wooden plank foisted on a pair of wheels and attached to a bike; passengers were expected to sit cross-legged on the plank. The other was the battery-operated cart, which has become synonymous with public transport in small-town India.

I had no desire to sit on the wooden plank, and the battery-run trishaws were hard to find. As soon a trishaw would arrive at the station it would get packed in no time. I wanted to travel all by myself. It was with some difficulty that I found a trishaw for myself by offering the driver to not only pay for all the seats but also a little extra.

On the way leading out of the station I noticed a couple of eateries whose signboards identified them as 'Hindu hotel'. I guessed they were relics from pre-Partition days, when Hindu eateries in Muslim-majority areas thought it necessary to distinguish themselves from Muslim eateries which probably served beef. Indian society, as I have mentioned before, was quite neatly partitioned into Hindu and Muslim long before Partition took place.

On reaching Berhampore I found many more 'Hindu' hotels. I also founds pandals erected at various places by the road, and in each pandal was erected the idol of what looked like Kartik, one of the sons of Goddess Durga. Perhaps today was Kartik Puja.

'Where should I drop you?' the trishaw driver asked me.

I gave him the name of one of the hotels that had been recommended to me.

'Why that hotel?' he sounded surprised. 'That won't be up to your standard.'

I suspected he had a deal with another hotel, so I insisted that he take me to the one I named.

'What is my problem,' he shrugged. 'You can have a look for yourself.'

The driver was right. The hotel that had been recommended to me by the man in the train—'five-star quality', he had said—looked just a notch above a cheap lodge. I surrendered to the driver and asked him to take me to the best hotel he knew.

An hour later at the hotel, a bandana-wearing owner of a travel company sat facing me in my room. He turned my idea of Murshidabad upside down. I had imagined that everything worth seeing in Murshidabad could be covered in a day. But from the hotel, Jalangi lay 50 kilometres away; Khushbagh, where Siraj-ud-Daulah and his family members lay buried, some 20 kilometres away; Lalbagh, the seat of the nawabs, about 15 kilometres away; Plassey 40 kilometres away—all in different directions. And Panchthupi, my ancestral village, lay 50 kilometres away—in yet another direction.

I decided to drop Panchthupi from my plan.

'Why, why would you want to do that?' the man with the bandana asked me. 'You are a son of Panchthupi.'

'I don't think I will be up to it. I shall come back. As of now, I am tired of being on the road.'

'So my suggestion would be, today you finish Khushbhagh and Jalangi. Tomorrow you do Lalbagh and Plassey. What say? But why are you going to Plassey?'

'I would like to see the spot where the battle was fought.'

'Nothing remains of that place—absolutely nothing. Houses have come up there.'

'Really? Then I must ask those people how it feels to be living on a famous battlefield.'

'But the road is not very good.'

'It cannot be worse than the road to Karimganj. My tailbone still hurts. You must have heard of Karimganj.'

'That place in Assam? What took you to Assam?'

The driver that the bandana-wearing man assigned to me turned out to be the exact opposite of his garrulous employer. He was a wiry young man, wearing Amitabh Bachchan-style hair and faded bellbottoms, and was so unusually quiet that I wished I had forceps to extract words out of his mouth.

As we crossed a pandal near the hotel—Lord Kartik was being entertained with Vengaboys' *To Brazil!*, blaring top volume from the loudspeakers—I asked the driver if today happened to be Kartik Puja.

'No, Vishwakarma Puja,' he mumbled.

Vishwakarma: the god of workmanship. So far the images I had seen of him depicted him with a flowing white beard, but here in Berhampore he resembled the young, moustachioed Kartik one saw at Durga Puja pandals. Perhaps Bengalis worshipped the younger version of Vishwakarma.

What's in a face, anyway? It's the devotion that counts.

Since the artist has no specimens to follow, he tries to create the most perfect face as possible—since god is perfect—and in doing so makes the gods interchangeable. If he paints a third eye on Vishnu, then Vishnu becomes Shiva. Just as Durga, if her face is painted black, becomes Kali. Hand the veena to Lakshmi and she becomes Saraswati. And so forth. Perhaps Ganesha is the only god, among the many, whom the idol-makers cannot palm off to a buyer as any other god.

We crossed many more pandals, speakers blasting dance numbers in each of them, as we made our way out of Berhampore to the highway leading to Khushbagh, the Garden of Happiness.

We drove through a largely monotonous terrain, a road flanked by farmlands that could have belonged to Uttar Pradesh or Madhya Pradesh. There was nothing Bengali about what I saw.

Wait, there *was* actually something very Bengali that sprung up every now and then: the mud houses of the villagers. Each house was roofed in the fashion of the Bengal temples. It did not matter whether the roofs were made of straw or asbestos sheet: they were all shaped to resemble an upturned country boat, which is how the roofs of Bengal-style temples look. Such replication was unique to Murshidabad and spoke volumes about Bengali artistry.

In hindsight, I should have stopped by one of those mud houses to ask the owner why exactly he had roofed his dwelling like a temple. But I was more eager to finish my visit to Khushbagh as quickly as possible so that I could reach Jalangi, the riverside border village, well before sunset.

Khushbagh lay, quite literally, in the middle of nowhere: nothing around for miles except a brick kiln and a small railway station by the name of Lalbagh Court Road. It was a garden—and still remains a well-maintained garden—built by Alivardi Khan, Siraj's maternal grandfather, who ruled Bengal for sixteen years.

Alivardi Khan had buried his mother there and in all probability had willed that he should be buried there too. But he probably would not have imagined that the Garden of Happiness would turn into a Garden of Graves shortly after his death. His beloved grandson was to join him there barely fifteen months later. Over the years, other members of the family also went on to be interred there. They all lie buried at the centre of the garden, in a square, flat-roofed chamber.

There were other graves too scattered across the garden, including that of the fakir who had revealed Siraj's location to the enemies of the nawab after he had escaped from Murshidabad following his defeat at Plassey. Buried next to Siraj is his wife Lutf-un-nisa, who escaped to Dhaka immediately after her husband's death and returned to Khushbagh to tend his grave and rose bushes.

Siraj-ud-Daulah's grave alone had a headstone, the inscription was in Urdu:

Nawab Siraj-al-Daulah<br>
Khan Bahadur Haibat Jung<br>
Tarikh Wafat San 1757 Masih

It said the Brave Leader, who was a Terror in War, died in the Christian year 1757. The headstone was unlikely to have been installed during the burial, but then when? It was difficult to tell. Even the ASI sweeper, who identifies the graves for visitors in return for some money, did not know.

Pointing to the grave, he said: 'I may be an illiterate man, but I can tell you something that no book will tell you: no one knows what exactly is buried here. Some people say Siraj was cut into four pieces and that one piece was buried here. Some say only one of his fingers is buried here. No one knows the truth—no one will ever know the truth.'

The same could be said about all the thirty-four graves in the manicured garden, perhaps with the exception of Alivardi Khan's, which was right at the centre of the chamber and looked stately. Who lay in which grave: that was knowledge handed down orally, generation to generation, and over the years the knowledge has become a secret, known only to a few people—including the sweeper.

The man was shouting in Bengali over the phone. He was berating the person on the other end for not delivering a consignment on time. Now, nothing unusual about a man in Bengal shouting in Bengali, only that this man was a Sikh, and at this moment a very angry Sikh.

But his anger melted like butter when he came to ask me, in Bengali, what I would like to eat. He ran a dhaba on the highway, not very far from Khusbhbagh, and the bandana-wearing man who had planned my itinerary had strongly recommended that I have lunch here.

'What's your specialty?' I asked the Sikh.

'Tarka-ruti,' he said, referring to the Bengali-style dal tadka served with rotis.

'I will have that.'

After lunch I set out for Jalangi, on the eastern tip of Murshidabad. I stared out of the window as we alternated through fields and settlements, the road very often lined by upright bundles of jute stalk. When you see hourglass-shaped bundles of jute stalk left to stand by the road, you know you are in countryside Bengal.

I braced myself to see the Ganga at its mightiest self, gushing into Bangladesh with great force. I imagined the possible sights that would greet me at Jalangi, and each time I ended up imagining the sea, because images from Farakka were fresh in my mind.

The Ganga at Jalangi, however, resembled a pond, still and lifeless. The opposite bank was so elevated that I could see nothing across the river except a growth of kans grass—kash phool in Bengali—and the top portions of numerous hourglass bundles of jute stalk sticking into the sky.

This side of the river, however, was lively at dusk. Elderly men sat on cement benches and on circular platforms built around large trees. Lovers and groups of boys were there too, just hanging around. This seemed to be the place where the villagers gathered in the evenings. Here too, by the river, stood numerous hourglass-shaped bunches of jute stalk. Several country boats were also anchored, and so was one speedboat.

I introduced myself to two elderly men seated on a

bench. They immediately shifted to one side to make space for me. I asked them if the land across the river belonged to Bangladesh. They said the land that was visible to me, where the kash phool grew and the jute-stalk bundles stood, was very much a part of India. Bangladeshi territory, they said, began a few hundred metres ahead of those bundles.

I then asked them how a river, which had resembled the ocean at Farakka, barely 100 kilometres upstream, could look like a pond now. The two men, both in their early seventies, laughed and explained to me why. That is when I realized that old maps do not tell you about the new courses of the rivers—and rivers are forever changing their courses. I had referred to an old printed map before coming to Jalangi.

Once upon a time, the village of Jalangi extended a few hundred metres to the east and sat right where the mighty Ganga curved into Bangladesh as the Padma. But one day in 1994, the river shifted slightly west and swallowed a chunk of Jalangi. What the river swept away included a jute mill, a Food Corporation of India godown, the panchayat office, the local police station, a school and its playground, several shops, countless orchards, farmlands.

'It all happened so quickly,' recalled one of the men, Idris Mondal, a farmer who owned twelve bighas of land in the portion that got washed away. 'It was the time of Muharram, and there was a fair going on in the village. I left the fair and rushed here because I was told that my land was going too. In forty minutes Jalangi, as I knew it, was gone—in just forty minutes.'

The villagers readjusted their lives around the new course of the Padma, many rebuilding their lives from scratch. On the morning of 12 January 1998, they woke up to another terrible tragedy. A bus carrying schoolchildren plunged into the river—barely a few metres away from where I now sat with the two men.

The children, belonging to Murshidabad, were headed for a picnic in the neighbouring Nadia district, and the driver had missed a curve due to heavy fog and driven into the river. Some sixty bodies were recovered.

A few months after the accident, the river decided to move eastward—just as dramatically as it had decided to move westward four years before. As it shifted away from Jalangi, it left behind a narrow branch on whose banks we sat now. And right across it had re-emerged the land of Idris Mondal, who went back to cultivating paddy, wheat and jute on that patch—only that he now used a boat to get there.

But Mondal is more prosperous than before. Apparently, when a river, especially a Himalayan river like the Ganga, drifts away from a piece of land it had submerged, it leaves the land far more fertile. Such land is called chhar land—the land left behind.

'So the washing away of the land actually turned out to be a blessing in disguise,' joked Mondal's companion, a genial elderly man who gave his name as Mohidul Islam, 'Nature *ee dobachhe*, nature *ee tulchhe*'—It is nature that sinks us, it is nature that lifts us up.

'Are you also a farmer?' I asked Islam.

'No, I am a teacher. I give tuitions.'

'What do you teach?'

'I teach Bengali literature, English literature. The boys here are very scared of the English language. I try to help them overcome their fears.'

'And do the two of you meet here every evening?'

'Not every evening, but almost every evening. There are some other people as well in our group. We gather here for adda.'

Unlike Mondal, who wore a vest and a lungi, Islam was clad in a freshly-starched white kurta and pyjama. Mondal was unlikely to have ever read a book, whereas Islam had probably never felt the earth with his bare hands. Yet the two sons of Jalangi, now in their twilight years, made quite a pair.

'Have you—or your children—ever aspired for life in a big city?' I asked them.

Mondal was the first to respond. 'Whatever for?' he asked, 'We love our village and have no ambition of going to the city. We are villagers, we shall remain villagers.'

Islam said: 'If the villages prosper, the country will prosper. And let me tell you, farmers are better off than people who go from villages to big cities to make a living.'

Their replies reminded me of the apocryphal conversation between a city dweller visiting a village and a villager lazing under a tree.

City Dweller: 'Why don't you work instead of wasting your time?'

Villager: 'What happens if I work?'

City Dweller: 'You will earn money.'

Villager: 'What happens if I earn money?'

City Dweller: 'You can get rich.'

Villager: 'What happens if I get rich?'

City Dweller: 'You can enjoy life, you can relax.'

Villager: 'What do you think I am doing right now?'

'So today how far is the Padma from here?' I asked the two men as I got up to leave.

'Oh, that has drifted away some 10 or 15 kilometres into Bangladesh,' Mondal replied.

'And the river that you see here,' Islam said, 'has become a horseshoe lake. It is 36 feet deep.'

'What is a horseshoe lake?' I asked.

'Wait, not horseshoe lake, there is another term,' Islam shut his eyes and tapped his forehead, 'sorry, what I meant was an oxbow lake.'

Oxbow lake, when I later looked up the term, stood for a U-shaped body of water that forms when a wide meander from the main stem of a river is cut off, creating a free-standing body of water. So the teacher had taught me something new.

I could now see two BSF sentries, sitting on chairs under a tree, guarding the oxbow lake. I hadn't noticed their presence until now. For a moment I was tempted to walk up to them, but the thought of introducing myself to them and convincing them that I meant no harm to the nation made me decide against it.

'The BSF was not so strict here before,' Mondal said, 'they became strict after the attacks on America.' He was referring to 9/11.

'Until those attacks,' he said, 'Bangladeshis would freely come to Jalangi to buy things for their daily needs—groceries, medicines, clothes, fertilisers. Things are much cheaper here than in Bangladesh. But now they don't come anymore. Whether that's a good thing or a bad thing, I don't know.'

Berhampore was lively, still celebrating Vishwakarma Puja, when we got back to the town. I bought two large, ripe wood apples from a roadside vendor. At the hotel, I handed them to the room boy and told him, 'Scoop out the pulp and mash it nicely with a dash of mustard oil and salt. Also add slices of green chilli. Got it?'

'Got it, sir,' the boy replied.

# 20

Greed and ambition of its own people have often proved to be the undoing of many an Indian kingdom. Bengal was one of them.

Siraj-ud-Daulah was acting in the interests of Bengal when he, finding the East India Company carrying out fortifications at Fort William in Calcutta, captured the fort and held close to 150 Europeans captive in its guardroom. Unfortunately for him, many of the captives suffocated to death overnight.

The East India Company despatched Robert Clive from Madras to recover Calcutta from the nawab and avenge the deaths. Clive arrived with an army of 1,000 Europeans and 2,000 south Indian sepoys and regained the fort in no time.

But he did not stop at that. He went on to capture the French fort at Chandannagar and from there marched to Plassey, to meet Siraj-ud-Daulah's army of 50,000 for a battle whose outcome had already been decided in his favour.

Clive had entered a secret understanding with a small group of Indians that included Jagat Seth, a powerful banker from Murshidabad, and Mir Jafar, the nawab's general. Seth's role was to provide Clive with a loan to finance the military offensive and the bribe paid to Jafar and other officers of the nawab's army. It was agreed that once Siraj-ud-Daulah was overthrown, Seth would be granted trading privileges and Jafar would be made the new nawab.

The Battle of Plassey played out to Clive's script. Siraj-ud-Daulah—sent home by his scheming generals in the midst of the battle with the assurance that they would take care of the enemy—had to flee Murshidabad in disguise. He was captured a few days later and was murdered, it is believed, at the palace of Mir Jafar.

I now stood outside that palace, under a blazing sun. The palace is long gone, only the archway remains. It is today known as the Namak Haram Deorhi, or Traitor's Gate. The archway propped up a grille gate that was left ajar. I noticed a signage on the pillar: 'Entry prohibited (Private).'

As I stood there and stared, I saw a goat enter the gate. The animal was followed, shortly afterwards, by an elderly woman who seemed to be a local villager. I thought of following her but I saw nothing immediately beyond the archway: only an empty patch of land. I asked the driver to take pictures as I posed against the gate.

I was at the heart of Murshidabad—the erstwhile riverside caravanserai that had been turned into the capital of Bengal by Murshid Quli Khan. Today this capital city of the nawabs is better known as Lalbagh. It is replete with old graves and old buildings—and new hotels. I spotted numerous flags of the Trinamool Congress and Bharatiya Janata Party, as well as a bust of Indira Gandhi. Many of the once-stately buildings now looked gaudy because of the advertisements painted, in bright colours, on them: Sunrise Pure Mustard Oil, Rajlakshmi Hotel.

One of the graves, where lay buried one of the daughters of Murshid Quli Khan, had a macabre story behind it. Once the daughter had fallen gravely ill and was advised by a hakim to eat the liver of one infant every day. She did as advised—secretly. By the time her husband, who was the nawab at the time, found out what she had been up to, 199 infants had already been put to death on her orders. Enraged, he buried her alive under the stairs leading to a mosque built by her—the idea being that the devout would, symbolically, walk over her grave. The story was told to me by a guide for a fee of fifty rupees.

Could the story be true? I wasn't sure. History—real, imagined as well as exaggerated, all three served together like a tossed salad—lent Lalbagh, the tourist destination, a halo that was visible even under a blazing sun.

To get here we had driven along the Ganga—known in Murshidabad as the Bhagirathi—for some distance, driving past the Hazarduari Palace, the opulent European-style mansion built in 1837 by a latter-day nawab near the site of the original fort of Murshidabad. Fortunately today happened to be a Friday, when the Hazarduari Palace is closed to the public. I had not known this while setting out from the hotel, but the fact that it was closed today saved me from wasting my time gaping at imported architecture.

To me, the Namak Haram Deorhi was the most important edifice of Murshidabad. The murder of Siraj-ud-Daulah, after all, had spread out the red carpet for the East India Company to rule India. In a sense, he was the first freedom fighter of India—if the fight for freedom meant challenging British dominance. Rani Lakshmibai of Jhansi arrived on the scene a good hundred years later.

After lunch at a 'Hindu hotel' back in Berhampore, we set out for Plassey—or Palashi, in Bengali—located in the neighbouring Nadia district.

I braced myself for a bumpy ride because the owner of the car—the bandana-wearing man—had warned me that the road was bad. He had also told me that the battlefield, where countless mango orchards stood back in 1757, had now turned into an urban jungle: so how to spot the settlements that had come up on the exact site of the battle?

Meanwhile, my admiration for the driver had grown. He more than made up for his reticence with his driving skills and knowledge of routes. All the journeys with him, so far, had been smooth—very smooth.

Even the journey to Plassey was turning out to be smooth. The road was potholed all right, but it wasn't a collection of potholes pretending to be a road. Moreover this was, after all, rural Bengal: it was unfair to expect an expressway laid out here.

We passed a few madarsas, one of them housed in a building imposing enough to look like a public school—a reminder that Murshidabad was a Muslim-majority district. We also passed growths of kash phool—a reminder that Durga Puja was round the corner.

After about an hour on the road, the driver announced: 'We are in Plassey now.'

'I want to go to the spot where the Battle of Plassey was fought, can you take me there?'

He didn't reply. He merely drove on. After a few minutes, he turned right from the highway into a narrow tree-lined road that terminated at a walled obelisk. An elliptical plate embedded on the obelisk read: 'Battlefield of Plassey, June 23$^{rd}$, 1757.'

Just outside the boundary wall stood a gold-coloured bust of Siraj-ud-Daulah. He gazed innocently at the narrow road. The bust, the plaque said, was installed in, as recently as, 2007. Another plaque said the obelisk had been renovated in 1998.

The memorial, which stood amidst a vast expanse of cultivated land, seemed to be the spot where the men of Plassey converged every evening to catch up with one another. They sat on concrete benches dotting the narrow road. Every small town in India has a nerve centre where the men gather at dusk: riverside, market square, clock tower, memorial. Women are almost never seen in such public places, where only men are entitled to unwind. Women, at dusk, are in their kitchens.

None of the men I spoke to was able to tell me when exactly the obelisk was erected. But they did tell me something: that once upon a time, each face of the four-faced column bore a plate, each made of pure brass and carrying the same inscription, 'Battlefield of Plassey, June 23rd, 1757'. Also that the obelisk itself was encircled by a concrete perimeter, implanted on which was a grille fence. Oh yes, there was a cannon too.

This piece of information indicated that the memorial was most likely to have been built during the days of the British. They had every reason to erect an obelisk whereas the Indians had none. The bust of Siraj-ud-Daulah had been placed there as an afterthought, that too in 2007—sixty years after Independence and 250 years after the decisive battle.

Over the decades, the men told me, thieves plucked out every single item made of brass and iron. Subsequently the government uprooted the concrete perimeter and split it into segments and installed them as benches along the tree-lined path. It was on these benches that local men now sat to catch up with one another.

I spent a few minutes at the obelisk—the walled compound was littered with plastic cups—and then walked past the memorial into the fields behind it, looking for another plaque which—I had read—stood at the precise spot where Mir Madan, the chief of the nawab's artillery, was felled by the enemy during the battle.

I walked on a muddy path right into the fields that looked bright and prosperous enough to belong to Punjab rather than Bengal. I spotted sugarcane plantations standing tall amidst rice fields: I later learned, from the men sitting on the benches, that sugarcane was produced at Plassey to feed the 1936-built sugar mill located barely a few hundred metres from the obelisk.

I must have walked about half a kilometre, sighting not

a plaque or soul, when I found a lone man on a motorcycle driving in my direction. He stopped upon seeing me.

'You don't seem to belong to this place, do you?' he asked me.

I introduced myself. He too introduced himself: his name was Hamid Sheikh and he worked for the Central Reserve Police Force and was currently posted in Delhi. He had come home on leave. His ancestors, he said, had been living in the village for nearly a century.

'I don't remember ever seeing a plaque around here,' he said, 'Even if there was one, thieves would have made away with it long ago. Come, I will drop you back to the memorial.'

He dropped me right under the bust of Siraj-ud-Daulah and, gazing at Siraj's face with disgust, said: '*Saala*! *Ek number ka ayyaash, ek number ka randibaaz*.' What he meant was that Siraj was a great seeker of pleasure and a great womaniser.

His comment made me examine the bust closely. The sculptor, tasked with creating the nawab of Bengal out of his imagination, had given Siraj a Bengali face: soft and chubby, someone who could pass off even as Kartik, the son of Goddess Durga.

Back on the highway, I found the sun, a clearly-defined orange circle now, hanging low over the horizon. I pulled out my phone to take pictures but found its storage full. I swiftly proceeded to delete a few pictures, but the process cost me precious moments. By the time I was able to point the camera at the horizon, the sun had disappeared, leaving behind an orange halo. Smoke rose from kitchens. Brown cows had their heads buried in mangers. Other cows were walking home. Birds hurried back to their nests. It was the magical cow-dust hour, which continues to cast its spell in the vast swathes of India that still remain undisturbed by the cosmetic changes.

In between me and the orange halo lay spread out the large expanse of agricultural land where modern India's future had been written—with guns—in the summer of 1757.

Destiny seemed to have handpicked Clive to decide the future of India. Six years before he won the Battle of Plassey, Clive, who began his career with the East India Company as a lowly clerk, had defeated the French during the Siege of Arcot. His victory at Arcot—a town in present-day Tamil Nadu—may not have paved the way for the British Raj back then, but it did put an end to France's colonial ambitions in the subcontinent.

Had Clive lost in Arcot, I would probably be composing these lines in French, sipping wine and not blended Scotch.

Upon returning to Clive's erstwhile capital—Calcutta—I set out for Park Street one evening. Even though I had been in and out of the city of late, I had hardly indulged myself—by indulgence I mean going to Park Street, strolling on its sidewalks, spending time at Oxford Bookstore, having dinner at Peter Cat or Mocambo.

That evening, from Oxford Bookstore, I picked up *India*

*Wins Freedom* ('The Complete Version') by Maulana Abul Kalam Azad, one of the leading figures of the freedom movement and India's first education minister, a post he held till his death in 1958.

The Maulana had dictated the book to his secretary, Humayun Kabir, but had directed that certain portions—mainly containing reflections of a personal nature, which could hurt his contemporaries—be left out for a period of thirty years.

The restored version was published in 1988, but not before a courtroom drama that had ended in the favour of the publishers. I was in school at the time, and I vividly remember the controversy over its publication making headlines for several weeks. Now, nearly three decades later, I held a copy in my hands: the subject was closer to my heart than ever before.

That night I stayed up—not unusual for me—and by six in the morning I had finished reading all its 250 pages. My first reaction was to feel ashamed that, all these years, I had known nothing about Maulana Abul Kalam Azad—except that there was a man by that name who happened to be a freedom fighter and India's first education minister. That's all we were taught at school.

To my astonishment, I found that the Maulana was not only a scholar but also a clairvoyant: he had predicted, though not in so many words, the creation of Bangladesh long before that country even came into being:

> Mr Jinnah and his followers did not seem to realise that geography was against them. Indian Muslims were

> distributed in a way which made it impossible to form a separate State in a consolidated area. The Muslim majority areas were in the north-west and north-east. These two regions have no point of physical contact. People in these two areas are completely different from one another in every respect except religion. It is one of the greatest frauds on the people to suggest that religious affinity can unite areas which are geographically, economically, linguistically and culturally different. It is true that Islam sought to establish a society that transcends racial, linguistic, economic and political frontiers. History has however proved that after the first few decades or at the most after the first century, Islam was not able to unite all the Muslim countries on the basis of Islam alone.

The Maulana dedicated the book to 'Jawaharlal Nehru, friend and comrade.' He clearly did not share the same warmth with Sardar Patel, who is described in the book as 'the founder of Indian partition'. It was refreshing to have read this book now, and not before I set out on my journey along the Radcliffe Line. I had arrived in Amritsar on a drizzly morning towards the middle of August, and now this was late September: during this period I travelled and I read.

I read pretty much everything about Partition that came my way, not with the seriousness of a scholar but with the curiosity of a traveller reading up about a place he is going to visit. The reading lifted the curtain on my ignorance, the travelling widened my horizon; and now I found my thoughts on Partition resonating with those of the Maulana. He said:

> If Partition evoked such feelings of anger and sorrow in the hearts of all Indians, why did the Indian people accept it? Why was there not greater opposition to it? Why was there such a hurry in taking a decision which almost everybody regarded as wrong? If the right solution of the Indian problem could not be found by 15 August, why take a wrong decision and then sorrow over it? I had again and again said that it was better to wait till a correct solution was found. I had done my best but my friends and colleagues unfortunately did not support me. The only explanation I can find for their strange blindness to facts is that anger or despair had clouded their vision. Perhaps also the fixation of a date—15 August—acted like a charm and hypnotised them into accepting whatever Lord Mountbatten said.

I put the book away and was about to get some sleep when the cook served me tea. I carried the tea to the terrace. My mind felt as clear as the autumn sky. A thought came forth.

We all read history until high school, but rarely ever get to pursue our curiosities after that because other subjects take precedence over a soft subject like history. As a result, most of the time, our knowledge of history, no matter how old we get, remains that of a fifteen-year-old. When you are fifteen, you view history as black and white—the good people and the bad people, the victors and the vanquished, the oppressor and the oppressed—and never as grey. History is grey. Gandhi and Nehru and Patel, for example, were not perfect men, but they appear so in Indian textbooks. Jinnah, on the other hand, had his virtues, which are always overlooked.

A majority of Indians picture the fight for freedom taking place on a sheet of calendar. On one side the evil British, on the other side an assortment of Indians: Gandhi, Nehru, Patel, Subhas Bose, Bhagat Singh, Chandrashekhar Azad, Rani of Jhansi and so forth. The Indians fought and fought until the British, pushed back a little each day, reached the square denoting 15 August 1947, when they couldn't withstand the Indian onslaught any longer and quit India.

In reality things worked out differently. When the British, after the end of the Second World War, decided to leave India, they had no fixed date in mind, but they were clear that they would not stay beyond June 1948. It was Lord Mountbatten who, for reasons best known to him, set 15 August 1947 as the date for transfer of power. He made the announcement at a press conference on 4 June 1947, thus giving India just seventy days to reorganize itself into two independent nations. Thereafter events, including Partition, hurriedly adjusted themselves around that date.

Seven decades on, the subject of Partition is like a well that was once filled with blood. The blood has long dried up, but the well remains, like a gaping hole on the chest of the Indian subcontinent. Those who used to stop by it and kneel against its wall to shed a tear or two have passed on. Their children and grandchildren have moved on: the well no longer falls in their path.

But there are people who still come all the way to peep into it: researchers, filmmakers, writers. I too peeped into it. What I found was endless paddy fields, glistening green under the afternoon sun. It was impossible to tell which of the fields belonged to India and which to Pakistan or Bangladesh. The line separating them, after all, is imaginary.

# Acknowledgements

Some of the journeys described in the book were originally documented, in somewhat different and much shorter form, in pieces written for *The Hindu* and its web-only platform, thREAD. I would like to extend my sincerest thanks to Dr. Malini Parthasarathy, who was the editor of *The Hindu* when I travelled and wrote those pieces. I am immensely grateful to Q. Rumman Dastgir, Sudeep Chowdhuri, Sharanyaa Chandrashekaran and Ashutosh Chatterji: they read every word of the manuscript and offered constructive feedback. I would also like to express my gratitude to those officers of the Border Security Force who went out of their way to help me but who did not wish to be named: if you find them named in the text, those are not their real names. Finally, a big Thank You to Sanghamitra Biswas, my editor at Westland, who, like a conscientious sentry, body-searched the manuscript for flaws and errors before sending it off to the press; and Gautam Padmanabhan, the CEO of Westland, who has always ensured that my works had a home even before the first word was written.

